Harvard Historical Monographs ❖ *LV*

PUBLISHED UNDER THE DIRECTION
OF THE DEPARTMENT OF HISTORY
FROM THE INCOME OF
THE ROBERT LOUIS STROOCK FUND

TOCQUEVILLE
AND ENGLAND

by Seymour Drescher

❖

Harvard University Press

Cambridge, Massachusetts

1964

for Ruth

Preface

"SO MANY of my sentiments and ideas are English, that England has become intellectually my second country." Thus wrote Alexis de Tocqueville to one of his oldest and closest English friends in the last decade of his life, reiterating that thought which he had expressed at the moment when his *De la démocratie en Amérique* catapulted him into fame.

The main purpose of this work will be to study the ramifications of this statement and to see Tocqueville's ideas about England and the English in the context of his life and thought. A general renewal of interest in Tocqueville has been attested to by a large number of books, articles, and the publication of a more accurate and complete edition of his *Oeuvres complètes* under the direction of J.-P. Mayer and a French national commission. No attempt, however, has yet been made to show the development of his views on English history and society or to link them to his public career and to the French historical situation.

The following pages will illustrate the continuous influence of English institutions and society upon his intellectual development as well as the importance of England as a basis for his standard of the good society. These two aspects of Tocqueville's thought, the analytical and the normative, are generally difficult to separate, and, as regards his views on England, their intimate tie is undeniable. Tocqueville reveals in relation to England a combination of patriotism and cosmopolitanism which affirmed that an intense involvement with the fate of one's country required the intellectual and physical distance provided by another society.

A special word must be said concerning the extensive use of the thought of Gustave de Beaumont throughout the work. Although Professor G. W. Pierson has rightly insisted on the inseparability of Tocqueville's and Beaumont's ideas with regard to their American voyage and the common origin of many concepts in the *Démocratie,* the unity of their subsequent careers and ideas has so far received almost no scholarly attention. J.-P. Mayer has performed an invaluable service in bringing new documents to light concerning Tocqueville's experience in England. Beaumont, however, receives only brief mention in the annotation of Tocqueville's travel diaries in the new *Oeuvres complètes.*

Tocqueville added to their common fund of ideas a wealth of insight which justly claims greater scholarly attention, but it was Beaumont who, after their journey to England and Ireland in 1835, attempted an extended analysis of the British constitution, while Tocqueville's thoughts remained in splintered and undigested notes. Beaumont's notes for the journey are more extensive than those of Tocqueville and, as there are large time gaps in the latter's observations, Beaumont shows the changes in their thought during the voyage with more continuity. In addition, he recorded invaluable conversations with Tocqueville and others which are otherwise unavailable. At other times it is possible to observe Beaumont directly expounding an idea given him by his friend, or Tocqueville's transformation of an exposition by Beaumont of a particular institution to a broader framework. Thus, as an incidental but necessary outgrowth of the demands of the study, the significance of an important intellectual relation will be clarified.

Finally, this book is an investigation of the transmission of the political and social experience of one country to another through the agency of a creative and aroused intellect. It traces not only the intellectual development of one of the foremost publicists, historians, and political philosophers of the nineteenth century but exhibits one of the means by which the continuity of the Anglo-French liberal tradition was preserved and extended during the nineteenth century.

S. D.

Acknowledgments

FOR facilitating the progress of this study a note of appreciation is due to a number of individuals and institutions. I wish to thank M. André Jardin and Mr. J.-P. Mayer of the Commission nationale pour l'édition des oeuvres d'Alexis de Tocqueville, and M. René Rémond and the Fulbright Commission in France for their assistance, both official and personal, in 1957–58.

Efficient and helpful service was rendered by the staffs of the University of Wisconsin Memorial Library; the Newberry Library in Chicago; the Widener and Houghton libraries of Harvard University; the Bibliothèque nationale and the Archives nationales in Paris; the Public Records Office in London; and especially, Miss Marjorie Gray Wynne of Yale University Library.

Professor George Wilson Pierson's organization of the Tocqueville and Beaumont Collection and his personal aid throughout this investigation were invaluable. I am equally indebted to Professors Henry B. Hill, William L. Sachse, Raymond Aron and H. Stuart Hughes for their comments on the manuscript at various stages. My deepest gratitude is reserved for Professor George L. Mosse, whose understanding and encouragement have extended far beyond the confines of this study.

Contents

Tocqueville and England

I ❖ L'Homme politique et liberal

THE LIFE of Alexis de Tocqueville (1805–1859) coincided with the failure of constitutional government in France in the first half of the nineteenth century. Born under the autocratic rule of the first Bonaparte, he was destined to die under the second. His whole career as publicist, legislator, and scholar was an unrelenting attempt to free his country from the endless round of revolution and despotism. Against the instability of nineteenth-century France, torn by class war and ideological conflict, Tocqueville pitted the consistency of his career and thought.

Tocqueville was always exceedingly proud of the political faith which won him acclaim in mid-century England and turned him into a voluntary semiexile in his own land. Late in his career, he remarked to a friend that his perception of social facts had sometimes changed, but that his basic beliefs had not, and he was especially gratified when some of his reviewers noted the moral continuity between his two major works, *De la démocratie en Amérique* of 1835 and 1840, and *L'Ancien Régime et la Révolution,* published in 1856. Soon after the appearance of the latter work he wrote: "The unity of my life and thought is the most important thing which I need to maintain before the public eye; the man is as involved in that as the writer." [1]

Although Tocqueville insisted emphatically upon the unity of the man and the thinker, it is Tocqueville the thinker who is usually

---

[1] Tocqueville to J. J. Ampère, August 1856, J. J. and A. M. Ampère, *Correspondance et souvenirs* (Paris, 1875), II, 308; see also Tocqueville to Mme. Swetchine, Feb. 11, 1857, Sophie Swetchine, *Lettres inédites* (Paris, 1866), 481.

brought to the forefront, while the actor, for the most part, is dismissed and forgotten. There is good reason for this attitude: it is his books that have continued to influence men. But there is also another factor in the separation of the two—another reason why he is viewed as having belonged "by character" to the race of thinkers, not of actors.[2] His lack of success as a politician has tempted scholars to look upon his political ambitions as a shortcoming—time wasted by the political philosopher yearning to play the statesman. It has even led some to the conclusion that in spite of Tocqueville's activities in the political arena, his real affinity was with "philosophical asceticism and spiritual solitude."[3]

Presenting Tocqueville in this way overlooks his total dedication to playing a concrete political role in the resolution of his country's future. It results in a tendency to underplay one of the central facets of Tocqueville's personality. Whatever the success or failure of his purely political activities, he regarded participation in politics as one of the highest goals of human fulfillment. By character he was an *homme politique.* The question, then, is not whether Tocqueville belonged to the race of thinkers or actors. Wherever his talents lay, he conceived of his entire life as a quest not only to find the basis of a free society but to convince men, by whatever means were available, to participate as politically aware and interested citizens. He rejected the separation of acts and ideas. On his reception at the Académie française in 1842 he declared: "There is nothing more clearly established in the divine laws concerning human society than the necessary relation which ties great intellectual movements to great political movements."[4]

[2] George Wilson Pierson, *Tocqueville and Beaumont in America* (New York, 1938), 777. See also Richard Herr, *Tocqueville and the Old Regime* (Princeton, 1962), 73, 76; Maxime Leroy, "Alexis de Tocqueville," *Politica,* I (August 1935), 397; and Harold Laski, "Alexis de Tocqueville and Democracy," in *The Social and Political Ideas of Some Representative Thinkers of the Victorian Age,* ed. F. J. C. Hearnshaw (London, 1933), 102.

[3] Albert Salomon, "Alexis de Tocqueville: Moralist and Sociologist," *Social Research,* II (1935), 429.

[4] *Oeuvres* (B), IX, *"Discours de réception à l'Académie française* (21 avril 1842)," 5-6. For a complete listing of the *Oeuvres complètes,* see the *Abbreviations,* below.

Political activity was not a fanciful indulgence between the writing of the *Démocratie* and the *Ancien Régime*. It formed the basis of his investigations, formulated the questions, and judged the facts. His deep-rooted need to participate in public affairs never left him for an instant. In the wake of the astounding success of his *Démocratie* in 1835, he wrote to one of his closest friends, "As I advance in life I see it more from the point of view which I used to fancy belonged to the enthusiasm of early youth; as a thing of very mediocre worth, valuable only in so far as one can employ it in doing one's duty, in serving men, and in taking one's fit place among them . . . Would that providence would give me an opportunity to do good and great things, whatever perils might be attached to it." [5]

In pursuing his ambition he had to struggle desperately with lifelong physical frailty and illness: "I own that in one respect my future is clouded; I cannot reckon on the first condition of success, which is life." His weak though mellow voice, his terrible anxiety before every speech, his utter exhaustion afterward, his bouts with self-doubt, his hatred of backstage intrigue and coteries, all conspired against his personal advancement, at least until 1848. Only the deepest commitment could have led him to endure these burdens without any immediate hope of gaining a triumph in the political arena equal to the acclaim with which the world of letters welcomed his intellectual efforts.

Soon after he entered the Chamber of Deputies in 1839, he turned away from major studies not connected with his public ambitions, and certainly hoped to crown his parliamentary career as a minister. His nine years in the Chamber of Deputies of the July Monarchy were passed in helpless frustration. He failed to become a real leader in the Chamber. All of his major programs or recommendations were defeated or stymied. His statements on political activity during this period are especially valuable since they indicate his disgust with the workings of a particular political system, not the lessening of his faith in the exalted place of genuine political life. One of his earliest speeches in the Chamber of Deputies epitomized his position during the whole of the reign of Louis Philippe: "If I believed that . . . a compact, homogeneous majority could arise, having doctrines, and, if you will, even, common passions . . . I could not ask more . . . even if I were to be condemned to fight this majority for my whole life and never to become, in turn, a member of a legislative majority." [6]

The Second Republic, though it gave him a brief taste of power as Minister of Foreign Affairs (June–October 1849), ended even more disastrously for him than the previous regime. He was fully convinced, however, that his public activity and especially his short term of ministerial power had given him experience in affairs and a confidence in himself which recognition of his theoretical talents had never done, and despite his personal failures, Tocqueville remained convinced that the tribune was the proper "field of battle" on which the destinies of societies were disputed and decided.[7] The approach of Louis Napoleon's *coup d'état* of December 2, 1851, produced in Tocqueville a terrible sense of moral isolation from his acquiescent countrymen. Years before he had lightly asked his English friend and translator, Henry Reeve, what their ancestors could possibly have discussed in the absence of politics. Now he could only lament: "What can we talk of in this time and country if not politics, and what subject is as sad as that? In truth, I haven't the courage to undertake such a task." [8] The pain that came from his political helplessness pervaded all his thought, and he found a meaninglessness in words themselves when they could not lead to action.

Even the real pleasure which his study of the French Revolution afforded him after the *coup*, did not change his more deeply rooted

[6] *Le Moniteur universel*, Feb. 7, 1840, 263.
[7] Odilon Barrot, *Mémoires posthumes* (Paris, 1874–1876), III, 482. See also Tocqueville, *Souvenirs d'Alexis de Tocqueville*, ed. Luc Monnier (Paris, 1942), 214–215, and Edward T. Gargan, *Alexis de Tocqueville: The Critical Years, 1848–1851* (Washington, D.C., 1955), 176–179.
[8] Tocqueville to Reeve, Nov. 27, 1851, *Oeuvres* (M): *Corr. angl.*, I.

allegiance to political activity. Despite the acclamations he received for his penetrating study of the old regime, he wrote to Reeve that should circumstances change, "Whatever savor I find in the life I am leading at this moment I would leave it, not unreluctantly, but without hesitation. For you know that I am and will be to the end of my life a warrior *of the good old cause.*" [9]

Tocqueville's esteem for public life did not end at the door of the legislature. Almost everything he read was seen through the eyes of the citizen. He could not put down a volume of Lamartine's poetry or a treatise on logic by John Stuart Mill without evaluating the work in terms of the political values which might be inferred from it. He declined to read novels with unhappy endings. Vivid emotions were to be experienced in real life and above all in political life, where "your own excitement is justified by the magnitude of the questions at issue, and is doubled and redoubled by the sympathy of your supporters. Having enjoyed that, I am ashamed of being excited by the visionary sorrows of heroes and heroines." [10] Although he was forced by his own experience to admit that the art of writing, as opposed to that of debate, could produce habits of mind unfavorable to the quick movement of public discussion, this was a fault which he exaggerated out of his very concern with every word he uttered. Nothing, according to Beaumont, could induce him to appear in deshabille before the public or even his friends.[11] More was involved than concern for style or reputation, for in a sense

[9] Letter of Feb. 11, 1857, *Corr. angl.,* I. See also Houghton Library, Tocqueville to Jared Sparks, Dec. 11, 1852.

[10] Conversation with Nassau William Senior, April 26, 1858, *Correspondence and Conversations of Alexis de Tocqueville with Nassau William Senior from 1834 to 1859,* ed. M. C. M. Simpson (London, 1872), II, 206–207. Hereafter cited as *Correspondence and Conversations.* See also J.-J. Ampère, "Alexis de Tocqueville," in *Mélanges d'histoire littéraire* (Paris, 1867), II, 310–311.

[11] Nassau W. Senior, *Conversations with Distinguished Persons during the Second Empire, from 1860 to 1863* (London, 1880), I, 190. Only a man fascinated by, if not at first the master of, the art of parliamentary debate could have concentrated with such delight on the most insignificant part of the 18th Brumaire, Napoleon's incoherent speech before the Five Hundred; see *Oeuvres* (M): *Ancien Régime,* II, 312–313.

Tocqueville felt himself vitally dependent upon interaction with others. Conversation was his greatest pleasure. "I confess my weakness," he confided to a friend, "I have always dreaded isolation; and to be happy, even calm, I have always needed to experience about me a certain interaction and to count on the sympathy of a certain number of my fellow men. To me, above all, could that saying be applied, 'It is not good to be alone.'" [12]

Tocqueville's passion for political activity was projected into his evaluation of the different countries through which he journeyed. Like a delicate instrument, he was carefully attuned to sensing the presence or absence of political activity in a newly visited city or town, and he made it no secret that this made the difference in his final judgment of its state of civilization.

He declared in the *Démocratie,* "On passing from a free country into another which is not free, one is struck by a very extraordinary sight. In the former all is activity and movement; in the latter all seems calm and immobile." [13] It was this ceaseless activity and its potential that won Tocqueville over to the possibilities of a free democratic government as he observed it in the United States. By contrast, his first day in Algeria, in May 1841, found him characteristically generalizing on the Moslem architecture and its link with the needs and manners of the Arabs. He observed the walls that surrounded every house and remarked on this striking revelation of life turned inward, and the absence of all political activity under a "tyrannous and shadowy government which forces its subjects to hide from the world and tightly encloses all passions in the interior world of the family." [14]

The important point here is not the sociological validity of Tocqueville's inferences from a few hours' study of Moslem architecture, but the customs that he immediately sought to ferret out—those connected with the existence of public life or its absence. The detection

---

[12] Tocqueville to Mme. Swetchine, Jan. 7, 1856, *Oeuvres* (B), VI. See also Lady Elizabeth Eastlake, *Mrs. Grote: A Sketch,* 2nd ed. (London, 1880), 116–117.

[13] *Oeuvres* (M): *Démocratie,* I, 252.

[14] *Oeuvres* (M): *Voyages Angleterre,* 191–192.

of a lack of public life invariably caused Tocqueville to move from sociology to condemnation. The emotional reaction varied from a sense of calm superiority with regard to Algerian society to varying degrees of sorrow and dismay when he turned to the state of his own nation. Thus one of his most enduring goals is easily formulated: to save France from gradual loss of civic spirit. It was for this that he undertook his journeys, wrote his works on democracy and the French Revolution, and sought with increased desperation for that new science of politics needed for a new world.

His claim to be unattached to any party did not imply, then, that he had no cause, since he repeatedly affirmed his loyalty to liberty, the primary requisite for political activity. Civic spirit appeared to Tocqueville inseparable from the exercise of political rights, and liberty, politically understood, was the precondition of all other social and economic benefits. Tocqueville also gave liberty a wider meaning than its strictly political sense, sometimes referring to it as a universally attainable ingredient of the human personality, at other times treating it as an instinct restricted to the possession of a happy few. In the *Ancien Régime,* he simply concluded: "It [liberty] is the pleasure of being able to speak, breathe, and act without restraint, under the rule of God and the laws alone. Whoever seeks from freedom anything but itself is made to serve . . . Do not ask me to analyze this sublime sentiment; it must be felt. It enters of itself, into the great hearts of those God has prepared to receive it; it fills them; it enraptures them. We cannot give understanding to those mediocre souls who have never felt it." [15]

This is eulogy or incantation, not definition, but from the nature of the eulogy it is obvious that Tocqueville could never treat any of its elements singly, since in spite of his youthful avowal that absolute, demonstrable truth did not exist, liberty for him came close to possessing the attributes of an absolute. Liberty remained an indefinable though tangible phenomenon for Tocqueville. It was not a hesitating conception of liberty which prevented all decisions. In 1830, to the disgust of his family and many of his friends loyal to

[15] *Oeuvres* (M): *Ancien Régime,* I, 217.

the Bourbon claims, he took the oath to Louis Philippe and the Revolution. He was adamantly sure he had done right. He sincerely regretted the July uprising, he explained to his legitimist friend Louis de Kergorlay, but could see no chance of a restoration against the wishes of the majority of the nation; "Nor do I think that it would be able or willing to establish amongst us certain liberal principles to which I attach as much importance as to the Restoration itself." [16]

His conception of liberty, though never precisely defined, always included the idea of a particular relation between the individual and the social order, beyond any purely constitutional arrangement. The destruction of intermediary corporate institutions which had formerly interposed themselves between the state and the individual had already been described by French liberals during the Restoration. Pierre Paul Royer-Collard had observed that the breakdown of these institutions had led to an immense growth in governmental power, leaving men naked before the state: "From a society reduced to dust emerged centralization." [17]

Tocqueville found centralization to be a universal rather than just a French tendency and linked the gradual emptying of the public realm to a new relationship between the members of society. As bureaucratic domination increased, the independent channels of communication between men disappeared. The effect of this process was to confine the individual within a progressively narrower range of activities and to the ultimate abandonment of all political interests. This was the basis for his use of the term "individualism" to describe a new occurrence in Western civilization. It was a "mature and calm feeling, which disposes each member of the community to sever himself from the mass of his fellows and to draw apart with his family and friends, so that after he has formed a little circle of his own he willingly leaves society to itself." [18] For Tocqueville, identi-

---

[16] Letter of Dec. 26, 1836, *Oeuvres* (B), V.
[17] Cited in R. P. Marcel, *Essai politique sur Alexis de Tocqueville avec un grand nombre de documents inédits* (Paris, 1910), 153.
[18] *Oeuvres* (M): *Démocratie*, II, 105.

fication with any private group exclusively was as fatal to public life as the complete isolation of individual persons from each other. His approach to these trends in Western civilization was to result in an effort to substitute new communal bodies for the defunct aristocratic ones.

There is an ambiguity in Tocqueville's conception of individualism which must be noted. Tocqueville often spoke of the decline of individuality as an inevitable tendency of democratic society whether it enjoyed political liberty or not. This type of individuality, characterized by the plurality of human types, and productive of great divergencies in customs on the social level and creativity on the artistic, was, Tocqueville feared, the inevitable casualty of a growing equality of conditions. The slum and the castle might provide greater room for human diversity, but men would no longer tolerate the extremes of economic and social deprivation and extravagance to provide a picturesque background for the great deeds of great individuals. The imaginative impulse would have to seek out other sources of social and artistic contrast.

On the political plane, however, Tocqueville's condemnation of an individualism of withdrawal was clear. Men could not be permitted to forget that declarations of human equality and autonomy had to be joined to a feeling of responsibility for public affairs and a desire to participate in them. The indifference of man to man at the moment when they were becoming socially indistinguishable would, in the end, confine the individual "entirely within the solitude of his own heart." [19]

Tocqueville's conception of the relation between the free individual and the state thus went beyond that of liberal thinkers who thought only in terms of guarantees of the autonomous individual

---

[19] *Démocratie,* II, 106. During the composition of the second part of the *Démocratie,* Tocqueville began to cross out *égoïsme* and substitute *individualisme* (see Yale Mss(T) C.V.a: copy of notes for the *Démocratie* of 1840, paquet 8, p. 29). Tocqueville was not the originator of the concept of individualism, which was first widely propagated by the Saint-Simonians; see Koenraad W. Swart, " 'Individualism' in the Mid-Nineteenth Century (1826–1860)," *Journal of the History of Ideas,* XXIII (January–March 1962), 77–86.

against the state. The conception of liberalism elaborated by some Restoration liberals stressed a sphere of individual activity which necessarily remained outside all social control. The individual's true liberty lay less in the principle of popular sovereignty or participation in government than in the legal limitation of the sovereign power. The realm of private activity was thus the part of human life which necessarily remained most independent. Tocqueville was as concerned with political participation and the functions of citizens as with the guarantees of the individual against the state.[20]

He was equally far, however, from sharing the Messianic expectations of a Michelet or a Lamennais from the entrance of the masses into politics. As the electorate expanded, the decision-making process seemed to him to become potentially cruder and more capricious, and the individual's role less significant. (Tocqueville kept aloof from the agitation to extend the franchise during the July Monarchy, and reserved some of the bitterest sarcasm in his *Souvenirs* to describe the dismay of the revolutionaries of 1848 when the people, whom they summoned to the polls, rejected them at the first opportunity.) An alternative lay in the creation of small basic units of government supplemented by a multiplicity of voluntary cultural and civic associations. From this pluralistic network might emerge a clearly defined political process which would not only shelter dissident voices but allow them to unite easily in collective dissent. It offered the individual the possibility of an effective alternative to the choice of being either the echo or the solitary critic of the will of the majority.

It is important to note that Tocqueville's ultimate standards for both judgment of and action against the state were placed in a realm beyond it, a realm of absolute religious and moral truths. But he was hesitant to invoke these ultimate principles when individual rights might be better protected by a continually alert citizenry. He

---

[20] His notes for the *Démocratie* stated succinctly: "Europeans believe that in order to reach liberty, power must be diminished in the hands of him who possesses it, and they thus reach a state of disorder" (Yale Mss(T) C.V.b: copy of notes for the *Démocratie* of 1835, paq. 13, p. 15. Tocqueville's emphasis).

counted most on the self-restraint of a politically mature populace
not to invoke the principle of public utility excessively. And this
maturity was to be fostered less by building impenetrable walls
around the individual and his private sphere of activity than by
drawing him into public life.

Generally speaking, a society was both civilized and free for
Tocqueville to the degree that it could replace silent obedience,
superstitious loyalties, and compliance from fear by organized public
discourse, rationally justifiable allegiance, and voluntary consent. If
violence remained the ultimate means of action in all political or
social relationships, that government was best which sanctioned the
greatest number of nonviolent channels of action both to decrease
physical and moral violence and to increase the sum of human
activity. A society with a minimum of activity was more debasing
than one racked by conflict, whether civil, religious, or social.
Although Tocqueville's conception of the proper limits of political
life was often that of a class-conscious property owner, he identified
himself at the outset with that part of the political spectrum which
in Restoration France seemed to promise an extension of political
life. In later, more bitter years he looked back with nostalgia to the
"*grand parti libéral* [of 1830], to which I had the glory of belong-
ing." [21]

Tocqueville reacted sharply, however, to the antireligious strain
in French liberal thought. It was chiefly in terms of the relation
between liberty and religion that Tocqueville parted company with
many of his contemporaries and justified his calling himself a "liberal
of a new kind." Tocqueville engaged himself to prove the mutual
dependence of liberty and faith on each other, but throughout his
life and from the nature of his problem he viewed religion from a
political point of view and considered only the relation of religion

---

[21] *Moniteur,* April 20, 1843, 850. He clearly stated his position to his electorate
of Valognes: "I am a liberal and nothing more. I was one before 1830; I am still
one" (Tocqueville, "A MM. les électeurs de l'arrondissement de Valognes," 24 June
1842, in *Chambre des députés. Elections 1840–1842,* I, Bibliothèque nationale, cat.
no. Le⁵⁴ 1527.

to political freedom in his work, not the value of any dogmatic belief in and for itself: "I am neither a philosopher nor a theologian, but a statesman who believes in the necessity of beliefs and who passionately desires to conserve what is left of them in his country, and, if possible, to foster them." [22]

Among other things religion provided a highly integrated and widely dispersed moral system for a society. Like the Victorian sexual code it was "a form which powerful minds, whether for good or evil, break through, but which serves as a barrier for the weak and ordinary." [23] Tocqueville was not disposed to emphasize any supernatural separation between religious and other institutions which influenced social values. He thought of local government as the place where rights and duties might be endlessly multiplied "in order to attract man by its benefits as a religion does by its observances." [24]

To treat religious beliefs and practices in terms of the psychological attitude and patterns of activity which they fostered was to allow terrestrial requirements to set the limits of mystical or ascetic aspiration. While preparing a chapter for the *Démocratie* on religion as an antidote to materialism Tocqueville noted: "In order that the subject were exhausted and my philosophical position clearly stated, it would be necessary to be able to add a small chapter, in which, turning from the fanatic spiritualists, I would show that, in the interest of the soul itself, the body must prosper. I would *rehabilitate the flesh,* as the Saint-Simonians say. I would look for that middle way between Saint Jerome and Heliogabalus which will always be the main road of the human species." [25]

Even the faith into which he was born was not evaluated in an essentially different way. Tocqueville inevitably spoke in terms of

---

[22] Quoted in J.-P. Mayer, "Tocqueville as a Political Sociologist," *Political Studies,* I (1953), 133. See also Tocqueville to Eugène Stoffels, July 24, 1836, *Oeuvres* (B), V.

[23] Tocqueville to Kergorlay, Feb. 1, 1837, *Oeuvres* (B), V.

[24] Yale Mss(T) C.V.b: copy of notes for the *Démocratie* of 1835, paq. 13, p. 17.

[25] Yale Mss(T) C.V.g: rough drafts for the *Démocratie* of 1840, paq. 9, cahier 1, p. 183.

his political and sociological orientation, since his allegiance to Catholicism remained obscure to the last days of his life. Apart from peripheral participation in the social Catholic movement, he held himself aloof from the various political circles of French Catholicism, including Liberal Catholicism. He might affirm that the gospel had introduced an element of charity into the realm of morality and politics, something entirely different from the body of philosophical ideas which had preceded it, but he found the great weakness of both early Christianity and contemporary French Catholicism in their neglect of the duties of men toward each other as citizens—"in a word, the public virtues." [26]

At no time was the political man very far from the sociologist and historian. In his study of the old regime Tocqueville worked with social and economic groups as the only feasible subjects of study: "I speak of classes—they alone must occupy history." [27] Yet his every page is a condemnation of everything which in men's consciousness prevented them from thinking beyond their class. Sixteen years before the publication of the *Ancien Régime* he had declared in the Chamber of Deputies: "I don't like to use this word 'class' . . . I don't

[26] Tocqueville to Arthur de Gobineau, Sept. 5, 1843, *Oeuvres* (M): *Corr. Gobineau*. Tocqueville's religious convictions have long been a matter of dispute. Born a Catholic, his early faith was severely shaken by the accidental discovery of certain eighteenth-century philosophic works in his father's library. To his devoted family priest, the abbé Lesueur, he wrote at nineteen: "I believe, but I cannot practice." In the *Démocratie* of 1835 (I, 309) he wrote, "The religion that I profess brought me into particularly close contact with the Catholic clergy in America," but a few years later he confessed to Gobineau, "I am not a believer (*je ne suis pas croyant*), which I am far from boasting about, but unbeliever that I am, I have never been able to suppress a profound emotion within myself when reading the Gospel" (letter of Oct. 2, 1843, *Oeuvres* (M): *Corr. Gobineau*). The long, heated debate over his later religious position is now a century old. See C. F. R. Montalembert to Ernest Renan, Aug. 9, 1859, Ernest Renan, *Correspondance, 1846–1871* (Paris, 1926), 381. See also Doris S. Goldstein, "Church and Society: A Study of the Religious Outlook of Alexis de Tocqueville," unpub. diss., Bryn Mawr College, 1955, and her "The Religious Beliefs of Alexis de Tocqueville," *French Historical Studies,* I (December 1960), 379–393, as well as John Lukacs' "Comment on Tocqueville Article," *ibid.,* II (Spring 1961), 123–125.

[27] *Oeuvres* (M): *Ancien Régime,* I, 179.

like to speak of the middle class, of the upper class, of the lower class . . . I prefer to speak of the general interests of France." [28] If he spoke of the actions of classes against each other in the past it was in the hope of uniting his contemporaries.

Tocqueville's feeling that he was above party, while it was not Olympian where liberty was involved, made him all the more sure of his impartiality when he came to investigate the emergence of egalitarian societies in the Western world. Born into an era of transition between the disappearance of an aristocratic society and the birth of a democratic one, he felt free from those political illusions which attracted most of his contemporaries toward one type of society or the other.[29] On certain important points Tocqueville's

---

[28] *Moniteur,* Feb. 7, 1840, 263.

[29] Apart from his observations on American society itself, antecedents existed in France for many of Tocqueville's general ideas about democracy. (See, for example, Chateaubriand's "Avenir du monde," an extract from the *Mémoires d'outre-tombe,* first published by Sainte-Beuve in the *Revue des deux mondes* of April 15, 1834.) His search for a liberal settlement to the democratic revolution was blended with historical perspectives deriving from nonliberal doctrines. Like Maistre, Bonald, and Chateaubriand on the Right, and the Saint-Simonians on the Left, he considered the French Revolution to be only a symptom of a centuries-old crisis in Western civilization. To an extent he adopted their view that a once organic medieval society had dissolved in a process marked by continuous social decomposition, as well as by the disintegration of a once unified religious, moral, and intellectual outlook. Viewing the political instability of France as part of a total crisis, Tocqueville's analytic interests moved naturally into studies of patterns of attitudes and behavior far outside the general purview of liberal political concerns. The philosophies of history which regarded the triumphs of liberalism as an interlude between more organic epochs never succeeded in dominating his vision of the present or the future, but they brought him to emphasize the fragility of these triumphs from the outset. He rejected all solutions to the crisis, however, which aimed at abolishing the liberal constitutional framework, as well as social conflict and intellectual anarchy, by means of exclusive intellectual or religious hierarchies ruling in the name of God, labor or science. Fearing that "the unity, the ubiquity, the omnipotence of the social power (*pouvoir social*), the uniformity of its rules, constitute the outstanding features which characterize all recent political systems," he had little tolerance for thinkers who counted political controversy as the primary symptom of a sick society (*Oeuvres* (M): *Démocratie,* II, 299).

By the time he completed the *Démocratie,* Tocqueville had come to fear the future immobility of the human mind much more than the "intellectual anarchy which we are witnessing," and of the political realm he noted, "the hydra of anarchy is the sacramental word of all enemies of liberty" (Yale Mss(T) C.V.c: copy of notes for

upper class origins decisively influenced his thought, but scholars who attempt to deal with him as an essential aristocrat, hoping merely to salvage certain elements of the old order from the democratic onslaught, have perhaps misstated the problem. Conflicting documents show Tocqueville leaning at some times toward aristocracy and at others toward democracy. There is the statement in the *Démocratie* on the providential nature of the egalitarian revolution as a divine ordinance to be accepted by man: "We may naturally believe that it is not the singular prosperity of the few, but the greater well-being of all that is most pleasing in the sight of the Creator and Preserver of men ... A state of equality is perhaps less elevated, but it is more just: and its justice constitutes its greatness and its beauty." [30]

Tocqueville here attempted to attain the perspective of true impartiality toward what was, after all, only a form of society relative to its time and place.

A less exalted view is apparent when the above statement is compared with a discarded note entitled "Mon Instinct, Mes Opinions": "I have an intellectual taste for democratic institutions, but I am an aristocrat by instinct, that is I fear and scorn the mob (*la foule*)."

"I passionately love liberty, legality, the respect for the law, but not democracy; that is the deepest of my feelings." [31]

The primacy of liberty is here beyond doubt. His ambiguous position toward democracy is easily explained if it is realized that Tocqueville's meaning of the term varied. When he merely identified democracy with the leveling tendency of the modern world he could be analytic and neutral toward it. [32] When, however, it

---

the *Démocratie* of 1840, paq. 5, cahier 1, p. 16, Feb. 7, 1837). See also *Oeuvres* (M): *Démocratie*, II, 263–266, 295.

[30] *Oeuvres* (M): *Démocratie*, II, 337–338.

[31] Antoine Redier, *Comme disait Monsieur de Tocqueville* . . . (Paris, 1925), 48.

[32] A note for the *Démocratie* entitled "Final Chapter, Chief and primary idea," stated: "For it is only *Démocratie* [Tocqueville appended a note: "By this word I mean self-government"] which can diminish and make bearable the inevitable evils of a democratic social condition" (Yale Mss(T) C.V.k: copy of notes for the *Démocratie* of 1840, paq. 7, cahier 2, p. 53, Sept. 5, 1837). Although the word

was linked with an expansion of public spirit and civic rights he returned to that note of impassioned eloquence which impinges on all his works. This is strikingly demonstrated by a passage which was to appear in his continuation of his study on the French Revolution. It is from the last fully written and contiguous chapter and brought his study down to the meeting of the National Assembly in 1789. "I do not believe," he declared, "that at any moment in history, in any part of the world, a similar number of men so sincerely impassioned for the public good, so entirely forgetful of their interests, so absorbed in the contemplation of a great design, so resolved to risk all that men hold most precious in life, have made an effort to raise themselves above the petty passions of the heart." [33] For an instant he chose to ignore the revolutionary deluge which was about to thrust the classes of France into an undreamt of state of antagonism. For one instant at least France felt that "the first virtues are the public virtues." As in the *Démocratie* the extent to which a society or an institution fostered political life was its greatest justification.

Tocqueville's prophetic insights into the leveling tendencies in Western civilization, and his analysis of the processes of atomization, political disintegration, and mass culture, are the aspects of his thought which have primarily concerned the contemporary political philosopher and sociologist. It is only by viewing Tocqueville in his political role in the broadest sense that his relation to England can be understood.[34] He had an extraordinary understanding of men

---

démocratie has usually been translated in this work as "democracy," the reader should be aware of the multiplicity of meanings which Tocqueville assigned to it. In his notes there is evidence that he was fully aware of the ambiguities of the term but wished to keep it as comprehensive as possible. Generally it can be used interchangeably with "equality of conditions"—political, civil, social, or economic. Sometimes it indicates merely the absence of permanent class barriers or distinctions, and sometimes egalitarian attitudes—the belief that all men are or ought to be equal in rights, dignity, intelligence, or power. See also Pierson, *Tocqueville and Beaumont,* 158n, and Jack Lively, *The Social and Political Thought of Alexis de Tocqueville* (Oxford, 1962), 49–51.

[33] *Oeuvres* (M): *Ancien Régime,* II, 133–134; see also II, 167; I, 208.

[34] English contemporaries were struck by the essentially political nature of Tocqueville's outlook. See Henry Sidgwick, "Alexis de Tocqueville," in *Miscellaneous Essays*

struggling to shape their human environment so as to maintain themselves as free moral and political agents while they decided their collective fate. In this he was the heir of a tradition which held that the man who could not or would not share in the benefits of political association was either a beast or a god. Tocqueville was also bound to the political and intellectual alternatives of the nineteenth century. In his concrete recommendations for the salvation of the civic spirit he remained well within the confines of his generation, if not his nation. England, as much as any single nation, became a source of elusive institutional solutions to the modern condition in general and to France's in particular. It is also in direct connection with his decision to enter politics that Tocqueville first grappled with the enigma of the English polity.

---

and Addresses (London, 1904); Henry Reeve, "Alexis de Tocqueville," in *Royal and Republican France* (London, 1872); W. R. Greg, "M. de Tocqueville," in *Literary and Social Judgements,* 4th ed. (London, 1877); and especially [R. Monckton Milnes], "Alexis de Tocqueville," *Quarterly Review,* CX (October 1861), 517–544. A Spanish scholar has recently added, "Few thinkers are known so exclusively political" (Luis Diez del Corral, "Tocqueville et la pensée politique des Doctrinaires," in *Alexis de Tocqueville: Livre du centenaire, 1859–1959* (Paris, 1960), 63. Hereafter cited as *Livre du centenaire.* An important recent study, Jack Lively's *The Social and Political Thought of Alexis de Tocqueville,* concludes: "Whatever depth and insight his analysis of democracy may have springs directly from the extent of his political commitment" (p. 252).

II ✥ The Point of Departure

ON OCTOBER 5, 1828, the youthful Alexis de Tocqueville began composing a long letter-essay on English history.[1] Writing from the family chateau on the coast of Normandy, he was surrounded by the past. Nearby lay Barfleur, where some of his ambitious Norman ancestors had departed for England with William the Conqueror. The chateau itself was evidence of generations of importance among the local gentry, parts of it dating from the reign of Louis XII. In 1828 there was still no regular road up to it and Alexis could recall his grandmother's coming and going in a litter. Almost twenty years later an English visitor was so startled by the remoteness of the place, surrounded by a tranquil cider- and sour-milk-drinking peasantry who went regularly to mass and took the sacraments (except for one villager who got drunk and read Voltaire), that he imagined himself back in the old regime. But the dovecote of the chateau also stood as a reminder to an age buried in violence. Above the entrance to its lifeless skeleton was the stain left by the missing family escutcheon, torn from its place by the Revolution—a symbol of the violent separation of the nobility from the fabric of French life. This ancient chateau was soon to be Tocqueville's inheritance, and the private realm in which he would compose his works. From here too he was to enter politics, to become president of the *conseil général* of the department of La

[1] In Tocqueville, *Journeys to England and Ireland,* ed. J.-P. Mayer, transl. George Lawrence and K. P. Mayer (London, 1958), 21–41. Hereafter cited as *Journeys to England.* See also James Pope-Hennessy, *Monckton Milnes: The Years of Promise, 1809–1851* (London, 1949), 240.

Manche and to serve as a representative in the parliaments of two regimes.

Tocqueville's letter lingered only momentarily over ancient memories. At twenty-three this third son of a family of the petty nobility which had suffered deeply from the Revolution and had reached a pinnacle of good fortune under the returned Bourbons was slowly moving away from his traditions and into the liberal camp.[2] As France's first experiment with constitutional monarchy veered toward disaster under the impetus of Charles X, Tocqueville, like many others, was looking for a point of reference. Political thinkers like Benjamin Constant and François Guizot carefully studied British institutions in preparation for future eventualities. Charles de Rémusat, Duvergier de Hauranne, and the Duc de Broglie, future parliamentary associates of Tocqueville, sought, in traveling across the Channel, facts and examples in support of their ideas. There was a flurry of comment upon the revolutions of 1640 and 1688, and on the possibility of their recurrence in France.[3] It was almost a prerequisite, then, for a young and ambitious Frenchman to attempt to gain some perspective on this much discussed people, their constitution, and their development, especially if he felt more than a little distaste for the uncritical Anglomania that was rampant in liberal circles. Tocqueville was attempting to unravel the complexities of English history and to summarize his conclusions coherently in the essay written from the family manor.

Aside from one or two central ideas, the "Reflections on English History" was a rambling and not very brilliant effort. Its author was

[2] For a more complete account of Tocqueville's background, see Redier, *Comme disait Monseiur de Tocqueville,* chap. i, "Les Traditions"; Pierson, *Tocqueville and Beaumont,* chap. ii, "The Education of an Aristocrat"; and Reeve, "Alexis de Tocqueville," in *Royal and Republican France.* Tocqueville was born in Paris on July 29, 1805. He completed his nonprofessional education at Metz. In 1824 he began his legal studies and in 1827 was appointed to the magistracy at Versailles.

[3] See Margery E. Elkington, *Les Relations de société entre l'Angleterre et la France sous la Restauration (1814–1830)* (Paris, 1929), 121ff, and Ethel Jones, *Les Voyageurs français en Angleterre de 1815 à 1830* (Paris, 1930), chap. v. Tocqueville himself once planned to visit those "rascally English who are made out to be so strong and flourishing" (Tocqueville to Louis de Kergorlay, Amiens, 1824, *Oeuvres* (B), V).

still young enough to be roused to an "unreflecting instinct of hate" when he mentioned the Hundred Years' War, and was "prouder to be born on this side of the Channel than . . . to claim that the blood of the Plantagenets or Tudors ran in my veins,"[4] because the haughty English had once meekly submitted to the Tudor yoke. Yet it was the beginning of a lifetime of more serious reflections. Even in this early effort some foreshadowing of the mature thinker was already in evidence. Tocqueville avoided a simple reiteration of events (which he drew from John Lingard's *History of England from the First Invasion by the Romans*) in favor of general reflections on the development of social classes. His greatest interest lay in tracing the rise of the commons in England, which at this juncture was parallel with the third estate in France. He even referred to the "third estate's" having overthrown the English nobility in 1640. The rise of the masses thus appeared to him to be the most significant fact in English history, a fact which united England to the general movement of Western civilization. Although impressed by the unique resiliency of the English ruling class, the young aristocrat observed that the whole course of both French and English history moved toward the abolition of privileged classes. He summarized this development with the moral reflection that "after all, rational equality is the only state natural to man since nations get there from such various starting points following such different roads . . . That's the natural way for the world to go."[5]

Deeply involved in the constitutional and political struggle that raged about him with increasing intensity, Tocqueville late in 1828 was already attempting to come to terms with the great impulse toward equality which had culminated with the French Revolution and now seemed under way once more. The conflict between his family loyalty to the Bourbons and his sympathy for the liberals evoked the observation on Richard II that "perhaps peoples would realize what it costs to sacrifice the principle of legitimacy, and doubtless their rulers too would learn that one cannot make sport

---

[4] *Journeys to England*, 33, 39.
[5] *Journeys to England*, 28.

of the rights of nations unpunished." [6] Although Tocqueville saw a historical consonance between the two nations up to the English revolution of 1640, he implicitly refused to draw the parallels of his fellow liberals between 1688[7] and the French present. His rejection went beyond a fear for the doomed French king. Tocqueville, like most of his liberal contemporaries, regarded the 1640 revolution as a temporary triumph of the commoners after which the aristocracy had resumed its sway.

The English revolution of 1640 had not been final because of the peculiarity of the English situation, where, in a three-cornered struggle, the "feudal nobility," by fighting to a great extent on the side of the commons, was able to maintain its privileged position. It was obvious that Tocqueville not only considered the commons as a true analogy to the third estate but that he also was under the impression that the contemporary English aristocracy was the direct heir of the old feudal nobility which had once covered western Europe. It was already obvious to him that in his own nation the natural and rational equality of mankind had already reached a point where an effort to resurrect the old privileges was neither desirable nor possible. Such an attempt, as Tocqueville rightly predicted, meant either despotism or revolution, a defeat for him and his principles in either case.

Just as significant as his reflections on English history was the person to whom it was addressed, Gustave de Beaumont. With a warmer personality than Tocqueville, Beaumont was always regarded as the more lighthearted and impressionable of the two. Partially because his own study of American society was presented in the form of an effusive romantic novel, *Marie, ou l'esclavage aux Etats-Unis* (1835), he was often regarded by his fellow politicians more as *littérateur* than statesman. Beaumont acknowledged that his too vehement display of sentiment hurt his political reputation. The two young Frenchmen met at Versailles, where they had

---

[6] *Journeys to England,* 36.
[7] Pierson, *Tocqueville and Beaumont,* 22n, cites other letters by Tocqueville, to Beaumont and others, against the 1688 parallel.

both secured positions in the magistracy, and were quickly united by a community of sentiments which extended from personal attraction to ideas and schemes for the future. "The same studies, the same plans, the same places unite us, and can do so all our lives," wrote Tocqueville.[8]

As early as their departure for America in 1831 their interaction had become so thorough that George Wilson Pierson could not consider the development of their ideas except as a unit: "Though they had known each other only three years they already knew that they agreed absolutely on fundamentals, and were fast finding how effectively they could work together . . . Consequently, when they talked over their ideas and developed their thoughts in their daily tête-à-têtes, they would time and again reach identical conclusions, if, indeed, they had not found themselves in perfect agreement from the start. So characteristic was this process with them that it is often impossible to ascertain which one of them originated a given idea." [9]

This pattern was to be repeated in their comparisons of the English and Irish aristocracies, and in their mutual division of literary and political subjects. The whole course of their careers until Tocqueville's death in 1859 was one of intense and continuous collaboration—political, intellectual, and literary. Though the means by which they presented their ideas varied, they frequently even used the same extended metaphor to describe a political or ideological situation.

A brief glance at their political careers suffices to reveal the same striking parallelism in the realm of action. Except for some minor tactical divergences they usually acted as a unit, often cooperated in a division of parliamentary projects, and spoke in identical terms on large issues to reinforce their position. Their contemporaries clearly recognized this overlap of personal friendship into the

---

[8] Tocqueville to Beaumont, May 8, 1830, *Oeuvres* (B), VI. See Appendix, below. For a short summary of Beaumont's character and career, see George Wilson Pierson, "Gustave de Beaumont: Liberal," in *Franco-American Review*, I (1936–37), 307–316.

[9] *Tocqueville and Beaumont*, 47.

political field. Odilon Barrot, describing Tocqueville and Beaumont as members of the Constitutional Commission of 1848, stated simply that he had to refer to them with the conjunction since they possessed a "perfect communion of sentiments and convictions." [10]

From the first, Tocqueville confidently wrote to Beaumont, "Il n'y a pas à dire, c'est l'homme politique qu'il faut faire en nous." [11] Hence it was natural that the two should enter together into a series of studies designed to prepare them for their careers.

While the Bourbon regime slowly disintegrated under the inept Polignac ministry, Beaumont and Tocqueville made further progress in developing a framework for the study of history and politics. They attended Guizot's course on the history of France at the Sorbonne. Here they found their views on the progress of history confirmed and elaborated. Guizot insisted, as had Tocqueville in his letter, upon the unity of European civilization as a starting point, with France as its most typical specimen. Guizot's interpretation of history, the slow rise of the middle class and its inevitable triumph, made a deep impression upon Tocqueville as the conflict outside the Sorbonne neared its climax.

When, after his July ordinances had backfired into revolution, Charles X fled into exile, the event had greater significance for Tocqueville than a change of monarchs or even a constitutional victory for the liberal party. He felt he was observing the irresistible current of history in its final act in France. As Louis Philippe made his way through Paris wearing the tricolor, Tocqueville saw the seal of the revolution and its message of equality irreversibly triumphant in France.

Most of the liberals rejoiced in their "French 1688" and in their successful imitation of English history. Tocqueville found rather that 1789 had now been fulfilled, not 1688, and the triumph of the middle class bore within it the dangerous seeds of new disorders. The lower classes showed signs of dissatisfaction. France, rather than imitating England, was now in advance of her. The Revolu-

---

[10] *Mémoires posthumes,* II, 329.
[11] Letter of Oct. 29, 1829, *Oeuvres* (B), VI, and Yale Mss(T) A.III.

tion of 1830 seemed to confirm his conviction that England could not be looked to as a model.

His personal position under the new regime soon became untenable. In spite of an oath of loyalty which cost him the rebuke of his legitimist friends and family, he was suspect by the new regime for these very family connections. Under the combined pressure of a desire to escape from a delicate personal situation and his dwindling hopes of playing an important political role in the near future, the trip to America was conceived. Tocqueville and Beaumont succeeded in having themselves appointed official commissioners to investigate the penitentiary system in the United States. Their mission would also enable them to study the successful republic across the Atlantic, with possible benefit to both their country and their careers. It was also of decisive importance that Tocqueville went to England only after his American experience.

Tocqueville and Beaumont arrived in New York in May 1831 already imbued with the idea that history had effectively sealed the victory of the democratic movement in the world. Nine months of intensive travel and the recorded conversations with a host of the most prominent men in America were to provide them with evidence that a society could retain effective political liberty in a democratic social order.

America's equality and its novelty made a deep impression from the very first days of the journey. Almost immediately they concluded that universal equality was at once the principal social fact of American life and the ideal that gave it coherence, and the country in Europe conceived of as being closest in this to America was France. "Democracy," wrote Tocqueville to a friend, "is either in full progress in some states or in its fullest possible development in others . . . We are ourselves going, my dear friend, toward an equality [*démocratie*] without limits." [12]

The English background and its part in the formation of the new republic and its people had scarcely occurred to Tocqueville when he and Beaumont began their journey to the frontier in the

[12] Tocqueville to Kergorlay, "Calwell, 45 miles de New York," *Oeuvres* (B), V, 315.

summer of 1831. It was only on the western frontier of American civilization, and in French Canada, that they realized that the country did have a history and its people inherited habits. And these habits seemed so durable as to pose for them the problem of racial inheritance as a factor in the formation of national character.

At Saginaw, on the Michigan frontier, they suddenly came into contact with the descendants of the early French settlers in America. Tocqueville was astounded by the fact that this scattered remnant retained its distinctiveness almost a century after the British victory in the New World. He concluded at this point that the philosophers who stressed the unity of mankind, and accounted for differences in nations on the basis of their institutions were wrong: "Nations, like individuals, reveal features which belong to themselves . . . Laws, customs, religions change, empires and wealth displace each other . . . Among all these diverse changes you always recognize the same people. Something inflexible appears in the midst of human flexibility." [13] This observation, noted almost in passing in Tocqueville's notes at Saginaw, was soon to present a real methodological problem to him. Thus far, it appeared, a new social condition had established itself in a new world—quite unlike anything which had preceded it. Now, here, where Englishman and Frenchman met, he had to deal with the problem of national character. If it were truly basically inflexible, then Tocqueville and Beaumont would have to alter their sociological emphasis considerably, and (by implications which were unfolded fully only twenty-five years later) the political efficacy of certain institutional changes would be severely limited.

At this moment on the edge of the civilized world, however, Tocqueville simply made some tentative observations on the striking differences in the descendants of the two peoples. "The men who inhabit this small cultivated plain belong to two races who have existed on the American soil and obeyed the same laws for almost a century. Yet they have nothing in common. They are as English and French as those who are seen on the banks of the

[13] *Oeuvres* (M): *Voyages Etats-Unis,* 377–378.

Seine and the Thames." He contrasted the uncalculating, impulsive Frenchman who roved through the woods, making no attempt to change or civilize his surroundings, with a typical descendant of the English race: "cold, tenacious, a pitiless arguer," not wandering through the wilderness but binding himself to the soil and tearing it from savagery.[14] Bit by bit this relentless and calculating pioneer made the land conform to himself and the orderliness of his customs.

A permanent characteristic of Tocqueville's mental habits was revealed for a second time since the start of the American voyage. He always attempted to convert specific observations into the broadest generalities that the facts at hand could be made to bear. Thus very frequently his conclusions would fluctuate drastically as he was confronted by a new situation. Some of his richest insights and grossest oversimplifications flowed from the same psychological source.

The problem of national character was infinitely magnified when Tocqueville and Beaumont, a month after their Saginaw expedition, found themselves for two weeks in the midst of what they almost believed to be a remnant of the old regime in the heart of Canada. As Tocqueville wrote to his former tutor Abbé Lesueur: "I am astonished that this country is so unknown in France . . . today there are in the single province of Lower Canada 600,000 descendants of the French . . . They are as French as you and I." [15]

The first reaction of the two young Frenchmen to this discovery was an outburst of the intense patriotism that Tocqueville had revealed in his essay on English history. Almost in the teeth of all evidence they hunted for signs that Canada was on the verge of a revolution which would re-establish an independent French nation on the American continent. And until nearly the end of their brief visit, they refused to be converted to the opinion of most enlightened public men that initial independence would only mean eventual absorption in the republic to the south. Tocqueville and Beaumont, however, did not allow their vision to become complete-

---

[14] *Voyages Etats-Unis,* 378–379.
[15] Letter of Sept. 7, 1831, *Oeuvres* (B), VII.

ly occluded by their desire to see the decision of 1763 undone, and Tocqueville's later conclusions on Canada when they entered his carefully worded works bore no trace of their initial martial ardor.

Tocqueville found himself, as he believed, in that portion of the New World which most resembled the Old. On the one hand appeared an almost idyllic people, sprung from his own roots, and identical to his own Norman peasants, trait for trait. "Like us they are lively, alert, joking, passionate, great talkers and difficult to lead when their passions are aroused." [16] In their midst and all about them, also native born, were the English, "as phlegmatic and logical as on the Thames, controlling the commercial and political life of the country." In short, in matters of personality traits Tocqueville believed he would find the English and Americans strikingly similar. Henceforth, when Tocqueville spoke of the global expansion of the races of Europe the Americans were linked to the English.

Under the powerful effects of these cultural contrasts Tocqueville moved closer to an acceptance of inborn racial characteristics than he was ever to do again. He was astounded that an entire nation could, in isolation from any cultural elite, have preserved its identity after a century under foreign laws. How important, after all, was his searching for a delicate pattern of institutional and social relationships? "Would not one be truly tempted to believe that the national character of a people depends more on the blood from which it comes than the political institutions or the nature of the country?" [17] A few weeks later, in Boston (September 1831), Tocqueville still weighed the factor of derivation from a northern race as first among a group of circumstances (including religion, business habits, equality of birth, and rational education) accounting for the purity of American morals. But in the listing it was only one consideration among five. The democracy of New England slowly shifted his perspective back to the novelty

[16] Tocqueville to Abbé Lesueur, Sept. 7, 1831.
[17] Tocqueville to Abbé Lesueur, Sept. 7, 1831.

of American society, and as the two travelers moved south moral considerations drew him into a complete rejection of racial determinism. Perhaps the most effective block against the acceptance of a racial theory was the reaction of Tocqueville and Beaumont to the condition of the Negro in America. No sustained believer in moral and political improvement could concur with the arguments for Negro slavery based on fixed, inherited inferiority. Beaumont later explained to one of his English friends that this had been crucial in his rejection of a racial explanation for the social condition of peoples.[18] The innate racial superiority of Englishmen for political activity was obviously not a very satisfying answer intellectually, nor gratifying to him as a Frenchman.

Toward the end of the journey to America, Tocqueville slowly dropped physical heredity down the scale of important factors in the formation of national character. As the impact of the Canadian experience faded, Tocqueville once more turned to his initial premise, that America had been essentially new ground for a new people. Even in Canada he noted that feudal privileges had been abolished, and he finally concluded in the *Démocratie* that the environment for all three great colonizing peoples had been at least potentially democratizing, and separated the New World from the Old and especially the English from the Americans.

Moreover, the Canadian experience, beginning with a patriotic search for revolutionaries, ended with an intense interest in comparative colonial institutions, and in the public spirit of the eighteenth-century American colonies. Why, Tocqueville inquired, had England succeeded in establishing flourishing colonies all over the world while France had failed?

In his estimation, the example of the New World had proved that if individual energy and the art of self-government were useful to established societies, they were infinitely more so for isolated colonies. The contrast between the English and French methods

[18] George C. Lewis, *Letters of the Right Honorable Sir George Cornewall Lewis, Bart., to Various Friends,* ed. by Sir George F. Lewis (London, 1870), 48–50.

of government appeared to have the clarity and finality of a scientific experiment. In French Canada he found centralized administration, lack of confidence in local government, and bureaucratic regimentation. Despite enormous sacrifices of men, money, and time the new society had remained stationary, gaining neither strength nor riches, and finally succumbing to the foreigner.

Tocqueville, employing his style of contrasting images once more, summed up the English colonial experiment, started not by the government but by people fleeing its yoke: "Once they set foot on American soil, it could be said that they became strangers to England, so little did the latter seem to take care to govern them. From the very first they have had their political assemblies and tribunals; they elect most of their magistrates, organize their militia, provide for their needs, make their police regulations and laws . . . and these establishments thus abandoned to themselves, which cost neither money, nor worry, nor effort to the mother country . . . become centers of wealth and enlightenment." [19] And as the crowning achievement, under the new but lighter domination of the English, the French Canadians, despite their racial background and cultural inheritance, had multiplied tenfold. It is no wonder that French and English Canada were to reappear in his *Ancien Régime* as perfect contrasts in political spirit. It was from French Canada, then, that Tocqueville first formulated a theory of the basis of English success in colonization, without ever having visited the predominantly English portions of Canada or any other English colony. By the time of the Canadian rebellion of 1837, Tocqueville had become convinced that the interest of the French Canadians lay in continued association with the English. When requested to give his view of the uprising to the Privy Council, he expressed the opinion that the English government was the French Canadians' best bulwark against Anglo-American domination. Through the influence of his Canadian notes and the *Démocratie* on Sir Charles

[19] *Oeuvres* (M): *Ecrits politiques,* I, 39–40 (from a discarded portion of Tocqueville's essay on penal colonies, written in 1832; see note 21).

Dilke he was also to have a hand in the formulation of nineteenth-century imperial ideology.[20]

Tocqueville was also led by his colonial comparison to focus more closely on the institutions of self-government in the United States, and especially on New England, which he regarded as the heart of American society. He discovered the ultimate source of American civic spirit in her democratic local self-governing bodies, which kept the ordinary citizen closely and continually embroiled in politics. With the aid of lengthy analyses sent from France by friends and relatives, he became inclined to view the administrative centralization of France, both in its practical effects and bureaucratic attitudes, as exercising a deadly influence on local initiative. Although he placed great emphasis upon the initial isolation of early American settlements as the prime cause of the hypertrophy of local self-sufficiency, he thenceforth would seek for the key to the political attitudes of every country in local government and public administration. This pattern of investigation was to be decisive in his visits to England.

It was also in connection with the analysis of American self-government that Tocqueville and Beaumont hit upon a primary organizational concept for their later works—the idea of the *point de départ,* or point of departure. Methodologically, an inductive discovery of the basic tendencies or fundamental social fact of the present led to a historical search for the original act or circumstances from which the present could be seen to have unfolded. As early as their joint work on the penitentiary system this principle of analysis was fully elaborated.[21] The second chapter of Tocqueville's *Démocratie* was to bear the title "On the Point of Departure

[20] See Edgar McInnis, "A Letter from Alexis de Tocqueville on the Canadian Rebellion of 1837," *Canadian Historical Review*, XIX (1938), 394–397, and Sir Charles Wentworth Dilke, *Problems of Greater Britain* (London, 1890), 29–30, 487, 492–494.

[21] Beaumont and Tocqueville, *Du système pénitentiaire aux Etats-Unis et de son application en France* . . . (Paris, 1833). See especially the appendix on penal colonies, written by Tocqueville. Beaumont wrote the text and Tocqueville the notes and appendices.

and Its Importance for the Future of the Anglo-Americans," and the identical idea was reiterated in his first paper before the Academy of Moral and Political Sciences in 1837.

At the same time, the fundamental principle on which a government or a society rested might also have embedded within its point of departure the germ of its degeneration. Thus Tocqueville was to declare that human institutions were in their very nature so imperfect that to destroy them "it almost always suffices to draw from their principle all the consequences." [22] Tocqueville and Beaumont were to assume the validity of this principle from their first works to their last, although a different view of the present often altered their starting point. From the *Démocratie* to the *Ancien Régime,* unless Tocqueville could discover a social context with objectively discernible characteristics from which all subsequent developments could be logically explained, he did not feel that he had successfully encompassed the problem. This was especially the case in the formation of his ideas on England.

As Tocqueville and Beaumont moved back and forth across America, an emphasis on a sharply defined beginning from which all political, social, and ideological aspects of its development could be seen to flow took hold in their thought. In his notes on English colonial policy Tocqueville had underlined the increasing divergence between the Old World and the New, since under the British system of maximum local initiative the Americans became "strangers to England." This conviction was strengthened by Americans on whom he relied for information. Jared Sparks, for instance, in some observations on Massachusetts town government drawn up at Tocqueville's request, declared that "As far as the rights and forms of government were concerned, the new settlers when they landed, were in a state of nature." [23] Here if anywhere was America's point of departure from the mother country. Eng-

---

[22] *Oeuvres* (M): *Ancien Régime,* II, 347. He later fought the analogy between declining Rome in its revolutionary era and France after 1789 by emphasizing a difference in the point of departure of the two civilizations (*ibid.,* 320).

[23] Herbert B. Adams, *Jared Sparks and Alexis de Tocqueville* (Baltimore, 1898), 17.

land slowly came to be imagined as the embodiment of *aristocratie,*
a term even less precise in original formulation than the term
démocratie. Aristocratie vaguely comprised what in Continental
terms was the *ancien régime,* and, with regard to England, referred
to the "aristocratic" constitution, which Tocqueville believed to
have essentially remained in the form it took in 1688.

America, meanwhile, seemed more and more divorced from this
aristocratic ancestor as the journey wore on. In October 1831 he
referred to America in a conversation as a democracy without
limits, and by the end of the year he believed himself to be witnessing an absolutely new society in the western cities, reinforcing the
impression he had received when first arriving in New York.

Tocqueville and Beaumont imperceptibly found themselves looking upon the English heritage as a fixed and static quantity, parts
of which were discarded as they came into conflict with each new
wave of equality. They began to conceive of the Americans as
Englishmen who were progressively abandoning English institutions or changing their spirit out of all context with the original.
After seeing the explosively growing young city of Cincinnati,
Tocqueville concluded, "The Americans in coming over brought
with them what was most democratic in Europe. They arrived
having left on the other side of the Atlantic most of the national
prejudices in which they had been raised. They became a new
nation, developed habits, new customs, something of a national
character. Today a new emigration is beginning, producing the
same effects. The new emigrants bring to their adopted country a
democratic principle even less encumbered by ties, still fewer inherited customs, and minds even freer from precedent." [24]

In his study of American legal habits and methods, Tocqueville
most clearly perceived the encroachment of democracy against the
strongest bonds of the English inheritance. In Tocqueville's opinion customary law and the superstitious respect for precedent had
been a most powerful auxiliary of aristocratic English institutions.
Their transference to the American legal mind hindered what he

[24] *Oeuvres* (M): *Voyages Etats-Unis,* 282–283.

found elsewhere to be universal traits of egalitarian societies: the mania for generalizing and the irresistible power of the numerical majority. But there were signs that even the inertia of the law could not resist the social environment forever. The strongholds of precedent were discarded like excess baggage on America's westward march. "A defective English law," noted Tocqueville, "and there are many, is brought to America by the first immigrants. They modify it, appropriate it more or less to their social state, but still have a superstitious respect for it; they cannot do away with it altogether. The second [westward] movement takes place . . . This time the law is modified in such a way as to lose the mark of its origin." A third wave forgets the law, and the long legal heritage of the Anglo-Saxons further diminishes. "One can't help being astonished," Tocqueville concluded in this connection, "at the influence, for good or evil, of the point of departure on the destiny of peoples." [25]

The English law, as in the passage above, was often regarded as defective either because of its illogical form or its aristocratic bias. For example, the two Frenchmen felt that by the use of the bail in criminal proceedings, the rights of the poor were unfairly infringed upon in the United States. It was an obvious hang-over from the English inheritance.[26] On the other hand, Tocqueville considered the jury as a political institution almost hostile by nature to an aristocratic society. It was the most direct application of the principle of the sovereignty of the people, providing the greatest opportunity for public service by the ordinary citizen. But was it not an English institution? "I am sure," he mused, "that in England juries are not chosen, as in America, from all classes." [27] Tocqueville's generalizing tendencies reached their natural conclusion in

[25] *Voyages Etats-Unis*, 283. James Kent's *Commentaries on American Law* appears to have reinforced Tocqueville's ideas on this point (*ibid.*, "Notes sur Kent," 254).

[26] Beaumont and Tocqueville, *Système pénitentiaire*, 316, and *Oeuvres* (M): *Démocratie*, I, 43–44.

[27] *Oeuvres* (M): *Voyages Etats-Unis*, 201. See also Yale Mss(T) C.V.h: copy of notes for the *Démocratie* of 1835, paq. 3, cahier 1, pp. 31–32, "Notes relatives au jury anglais et américain."

the *Démocratie,* three years after the journey. There, whenever he found an "aristocratic" law in America, he classed it as a remnant from England.

His "point of departure" resulted in a steady pressure to dissociate all American developments from their English background. If "one of the most salient features of American institutions [was] to form a perfectly logical chain," [28] English origin was the cause of anomalies within the system. The very term "Anglo-American," which Tocqueville used extensively in the first part of the *Démocratie,* was a differentiating rather than a unifying term, setting the Americans as far apart from the English as from the French or Spanish. America was so blatantly democratic, so stridently progressive, that it could scarcely be anything but the antithesis of England. "It is thus," wrote Tocqueville late in the American journey, "that the English character could only be aristocratic. What makes me believe it is the immense difference which exists between the English and their American descendants." [29] He had yet to set foot in England.

Probably it was in order to verify inductively his conclusions that Tocqueville decided, before leaving America, that a visit to England was necessary. There may have also lingered the influence of the liberals of the Restoration, who had found so much in England they deemed useful for France. In any event, he and Beaumont planned to return to Europe by way of England. The impatience of the French government for their immediate return, however, forced them to depart directly for France in February 1832, and they missed the opportunity of seeing the climax of the agitation for the Reform Bill of 1832. Only in the following year was Tocqueville able to arrange his first trip across the Channel.

[28] *Voyages Etats-Unis,* 203.
[29] *Voyages Etats-Unis,* 191, Dec. 26, 1831.

III ❖ The English Aristocracy and the Democratic Revolution

WHEN TOCQUEVILLE prepared to visit England for the first time in August 1833, it was almost inevitable that he would have some very fixed ideas about its social structure and historical situation. Engrossed as he was in reviewing his American experience, an investigation of five weeks' duration would naturally reflect both the methods and ideas worked out in America. He was certain to bring his *idée mère* of the world democratic revolution across the Channel, along with his conviction that England represented the specific aristocratic condition from which the United States had long since emerged.

There was another reason why Tocqueville chose to take a firsthand look at England when he did. England now seemed to be about to succumb to the turbulent "spirit of the age," and to join America and France in the democratic column. The July Revolution, which many of Tocqueville's countrymen had acclaimed as bringing France its 1688, seemed, in its turn, to have contributed to the demise of unreformed England. This interpretation of the sequence of events was popular on both sides of the Channel.[1] Tocqueville must have felt confirmed in his previous

---

[1] Even today, scholars differ over the influence of the July Revolution on English reform. See especially Elie Halévy, *A History of the English People in the Nineteenth Century, vol. III: The Triumph of Reform, 1830–1841* (London, 1950), 3–8, and Norman Gash, "English Reform and French Revolution in the Election of 1830," in *Essays Presented to Sir Lewis Namier,* ed. Richard Pares and A. J. P. Taylor (London, 1956).

rejection of English society as a model for France. No one could yet predict with certainty how far or fast England might go in transforming itself. Tocqueville himself reckoned on dramatic changes in the very near future and was anxious to observe the unique specimen before it was too late. "One hears," he wrote just before his departure, "that they are positively taking to revolution and it is necessary to hurry to see things as they are. So, I hasten to England as to the last showing of a fine play."[2] He was intent on viewing an aristocracy under mortal attack.

The analyst of democracy reasonably expected to find the embodiment of the aristocratic complement to America in the England of 1833, before further legislative action should permanently have changed her social state. The majority of French travelers who preceded Tocqueville to England agreed on the basically aristocratic nature of the constitution. Charles Cottu, one of the major sources of Tocqueville's knowledge of the English legal and administrative system, had based his entire work on the assumption that the English aristocracy was the true governing power in England.[3]

As soon as he set foot in England Tocqueville found himself not only face to face with aristocracy but submerged by it. On the road to London, the all-important first glimpse at a new land made its usual lasting impact on him. The parks, the splendid country houses replete with handsome livery and horses, were the beginning of a series of dazzling impressions. His reception in the capital only intensified the initial effect. In America, he and Beaumont had been approached by dignitaries in every city they visited, anxious to aid the prison commissioners from France. Now he wrote to Beaumont from London: "It would be difficult

[2] Tocqueville to the Comtesse de Pisieux, July 5, 1833 (Yale Mss(T) C.XI.c), also cited in George Wilson Pierson, "Le 'Second Voyage' de Tocqueville en Amérique," in *Livre du centenaire*, 71.

[3] See Cottu, *De l'administration de la justice criminelle en Angleterre et de l'esprit du gouvernement anglais* (Paris, 1820), 165–166.

to describe the impressions I've felt since I set foot in this immense metropolis. I feel in perpetual confusion and deeply aware of my insignificance. We were great figures in America. We are not much in Paris. But you must go below zero and use what mathematicians call minus quantities to calculate what I am here . . . I wander all over London like a gnat in a haystack." [4] Tocqueville attempted to explain his initial impression partly through the vastness of London, but found himself already generalizing to Beaumont from the usual bent of his thought and the image he had formed of England in America. The aristocratic nature of society, he confided, was perhaps the cause of his own reaction. He found the aristocratic principle even more exalted than he could have imagined. The advantages afforded to persons of high birth and great wealth placed them "a million feet above others." Tocqueville restrained himself in the letter from trying to sum up the entire English character on the basis of his first impression, but he already wrote with assurance of the "aristocratic spirit," which descended through all classes, and found his estimation of the American point of departure as a new and separate society confirmed. Nothing struck him more than the difference between the two societies. "Nowhere," he observed, "do I find our America."

Tocqueville's introduction to the English political system further crystallized his image. His first recorded observation was of the House of Lords engaged in a dull debate on the Slavery Bill. In spite of the fact that Tocqueville was unmoved by the rhetorical ability of the Duke of Wellington, he was careful to record the unconscious superiority which emanated from the peers. They were "ranged around a large table at the far end of the House or nonchalantly reclining on cushioned benches." In their frockcoats and boots, most were as casual in their attire as their attitude. Only Lord Brougham in his immense powdered wig and some bishops

---

[4] Letter of Aug. 13, 1833, *Oeuvres* (B), VI. The unpublished portion of this letter, in Yale Mss(T) C.I.a, shows that Tocqueville intended to concentrate on the aristocracy and "the degree of liberty which it enjoys."

in full dress reminded one of the majesty of the House. Yet over everything hung a relaxed air of breeding, of good taste, in short— "a certain *parfum d'aristocratie.*" [5]

In the following weeks he was able to see some of England outside the sprawling capital, but his itinerary was not such as to decrease his initial conclusions about the basis of English society and the English character. Tocqueville appeared to be captivated by traces of that *parfum* which he had detected in the House of Lords. At Oxford, he was far more concerned with the connection between the university and the aristocratic social system than with the educational system. He was pleased by the appropriately gothic architecture but took a dim view of the tremendous land endowment serving to keep a small group of oligarchs and functionless Fellows in comfort. On the whole, the institution impressed him as a replica of an abbey of the old regime, an abuse tolerable only in an aristocratic society.

This picture of gothic feudalism in decay appears to have struck a rare romantic chord in Tocqueville, or at least awakened some ambition of youth. He traveled northward to see the castle at Warwick and rode one night amid the ruins of Kenilworth. In a vibrant letter he shared the experience with his English-born bride-to-be, Mary (Marie) Mottley. Though she seems rarely to have affected his political and social views, their marriage in October 1835 was to provide an imponderable personal link between Tocqueville and England. He evoked for her the moon-bathed castle, which he peopled with characters from Sir Walter Scott. "Was I not in the realm of the dead? There I sat on a stone and fell into a kind of trance, while it seemed that my soul was drawn toward the past with indescribable force." [6] After this "feudal in-

---

[5] *Oeuvres* (M): *Voyages Angleterre,* 11. See also Tocqueville, *Journeys to England,* 42. The citations for the English journeys will be drawn from the translation unless close attention to the original text is warranted.

[6] *Oeuvres* (B), VII. Tocqueville wrote from Warwick, Aug. 26, 1833; Miss Mottley was in France. Born in Stonehouse, Devonshire, she was reared in France and met Alexis de Tocqueville at Versailles in 1828. The marriage was childless. Mme. de Tocqueville survived her husband and died in 1864.

toxication" it was difficult to return to the realization that the day of the knight was gone.

In spite of the fact that these reveries were confined to the recesses of his mind and personal letters, they could not help but reinforce the total impression of England as the land of the well-born. Tocqueville was convinced that on this island bastion of aristocracy he was finding the point of departure of all European history and viewing habits and modes of thought peculiar to a passing age. His eyes were riveted on the aristocracy of England.

He completed his journey with a trip to Longford Castle in Wiltshire. This last, however, was inhabited by a living representative of the aristocracy, who fully personified that combination of birth and great fortune which Tocqueville first perceived in London. Lord Radnor, an eminent Whig, was able to offer him the opportunity of viewing at first hand the operations of local government under the firm direction of an English aristocrat. Tocqueville attended a sitting of petty sessions at which Radnor presided and was able to question his host on the functions and limits of his office as justice of the peace.

Altogether, from the conversations, notes, and observations which Tocqueville had accumulated during his short trip to England, it would appear that he was more than ever convinced of the aristocratic essence of English institutions and of their all-pervasive influence on her customs. Tocqueville had decided early in his American voyage that no political framework could be equally favorable to the development of all the classes of society. It was not possible in a strong society to combine the polar tendencies of aristocracy and democracy.[7] England was not the "mixed" constitution which so many eighteenth-century observers had been anxious to discover in the divisions of her legislature into King, Lords, and Commons, or in the balance of monarchy, aristocracy, and democracy. She had always been an essentially aristocratic state with, at most, minor democratic elements.

[7] See *Oeuvres* (M): *Démocratie*, I, 262, and Yale Mss(T) B.II.b, p. 12.

Tocqueville sought the institutional and moral pillars of this aristocratic edifice—those which had made it so formidable a structure, while its continental counterparts had crumbled. Two years before, during his journey through the United States, John Livingston had drawn his attention to the fact that pre-Revolutionary America had possessed rich proprietors who had lived like "English gentry," resembling them in traditions, ideas and manners. Livingston had told of the sudden disappearance of this class when primogeniture was abolished in the wake of the American Revolution.[8] Tocqueville perceived a parallel division of landed property in France, brought to a climax by the French Revolution. He believed that both in America and France, the effect of the law was to make real property pass rapidly from hand to hand, the number of great properties diminishing and the number of middling properties remaining the same. Thus the Jeffersonian ideal of small, independent property holders seemed to be a necessary effect of the democratic revolution. There was nothing, Tocqueville insisted, more favorable to the functioning of democracy than the division of the land into small, independent properties. The small proprietor was not only dependent upon association with others for effective action, but retained perfect liberty in his own small sphere, and his own mental tranquillity was assured and spread to the society about him.

In France especially, Tocqueville regarded property law and practice as the most conspicuous sign of the breakup of the old regime, "overthrowing the walls of our dwellings and removing the landmarks of our fields."[9] The correlation of land-inheritance law and democracy was a fact of universal significance, and "the law of inheritance was the last step to equality." Tocqueville could not see why more influence had not been attributed to this law and he devoted almost an entire chapter in the *Démocratie* to

---

[8] See *Oeuvres* (M): *Voyages Etats-Unis*, 59, and *Journeys to England*, app. 5, "On Bribery at Elections," June 22, 1835, 220–221.

[9] *Oeuvres* (M): *Démocratie*, I, 49. "Give me," he wrote during his trip to America, "thirty years of equal division of inheritance and freedom of the press and I will bring you to a Republic" (Yale Mss(T) B.II.b, p. 10).

tracing its influence in the United States and France. In England, of course, the great estates had created and preserved the aristocracy, "for not by privileges alone, nor by birth, but by landed property handed down from generation to generation is an aristocracy constituted. A nation might exhibit immense fortunes and extreme wretchedness; but unless those fortunes are territorial, there is no true aristocracy, but simply classes of rich and poor." [10] This was to be the basic element of Tocqueville's early definition of aristocracy, as well as his conception of its historical basis.

In England, contrary to his former experience, the concentration of property in a few hands was not only a fact, but a fact accepted with equanimity by the middle as well as the upper classes, the economists as well as the lawyers. The landowners made the laws, applied the laws, and punished infractions of the laws. The almost sacred character of the land and land inheritance was stressed by Beaumont in his *L'Irlande* a few years later. Beaumont clearly indicated that land, not the proprietor, was the object of the law's protection. "The law heeds neither peer, nor commoner; it protects not the owner, but the estate, conspiring to perpetuate it undiminished." [11]

Tocqueville later confirmed this pervasiveness of the spirit of entail in laws involving the sale of land with clear title. The obscurity and clumsiness of the law made it absolutely necessary to hire a lawyer for each sale of property, since ownership was complicated and vague. This naturally resulted in the purchase of property only in large blocks and by the rich alone. The poor were thus effectively excluded from buying property. Under the combined influence of law and custom, all classes appeared to accept the restrictions on the soil as something sacred and the unity of estates as a moral principle.

Tocqueville agreed with his French and English contemporaries

[10] *Démocratie*, I, 29. For Tocqueville's most detailed description of the origins of the aristocracy see his "Mémoire sur le paupérisme," *Mémoires de la Société académique de Cherbourg* (Cherbourg, 1835), 307ff.

[11] Beaumont, *L'Irlande sociale, politique et religieuse*, 3rd ed. (Paris, 1839), II, 205.

in seeing the power of the aristocracy as fortified by great accumulations of landed wealth, but he did not try to trace the true strength
of the aristocracy through its influence on parliamentary elections
or in the constitutional relations of Lords to Commons. He sought
rather to assess the exercise of power in local government and
administration and to gauge the strength of the British aristocracy
in the same areas where he had found the source of American civic
strength.

Tocqueville had no means of approaching the English administrative process systematically in 1833. His English contemporaries
could not supply him with a full and accurate contemporary treatise
on local government in Britain. It was only much later in the nineteenth century that such an analysis was attempted. He was therefore forced to fall back on sources as meager as Blackstone and the
verbal and written summaries supplied by English acquaintances.[12]
Lord Radnor was his major source of information on the numerous
powers of the aristocracy in their unpaid offices as justices of the
peace.

These magistrates, Radnor explained, were nominated by the
king, but drawn always from the local aristocracy, and were prac-
tically unchecked by any administrative superior. Their decisions
were subject to judicial review, but the central government had
"nothing to do with provincial matters, nor even their supervision."
Tocqueville noted the ill-defined nature of their competence and
especially the lack of distinction between administrative and
judicial decisions. To his fellow Frenchmen he could only define
an office without analogy on the Continent as a sort of middle

---

[12] Sidney and Beatrice Webb, *The Parish and the County* (London, 1906), 279n,
found no convenient treatise on English county government available to them. The
difficulties of getting precise information in the 1830's are illustrated by Beaumont's
account of his visit to the Home Office in 1837. The office had only two clerks.
When Beaumont asked the head clerk how many "magistrates" there were in
England he could give no figure but felt sure there were "thousands." Beaumont
then asked when the Home Office got reports from them. "When something extraordinary happens," was the reply (Yale Mss(B) C.X.5: "Centralisation," May 24,
1837, in Beaumont's notes for *L'Irlande;* hereafter cited as *L'Irlande,* notes).

term between the magistrate and the man of the world, between the administrator and judge. Tocqueville could not help admiring this mixture, which he imagined made the magistrate unconsciously carry a certain spirit of judicial forms and the publicity of open court into his functions, and which put certain legal limits to arbitrary action. The justice by background was usually an enlightened and wealthy citizen, not even necessarily trained in law. Drawn, or rather co-opted, from an exclusive and homogeneous social stratum of landed proprietors, unchecked by an electoral process, serving as unpaid magistrates, and financially immune from ministerial pressure, the justice of the peace seemed to be the aristocrat par excellence.

That Tocqueville in 1833 considered the justices of the peace the only important administrative authorities in the country only deepened his conviction that they were the institutional focus of the power of the landed aristocracy in England. The magistrates of the English countryside dominated his notes as rural England predominated in his itinerary. As far as he could see, "Most localities do not have corporate municipal bodies, or at least the municipal body only manages very few things. It is the justices of the peace who administrate." [13]

Tocqueville had in fact stumbled into the twilight of the golden age of the justice of the peace in England. He was never fully aware of the historical background but was certain of their entrenched position. Lord Radnor did not inform him that the truly golden age was already over and that one function after another had been removed or was being threatened. Tocqueville was not to discover until his second visit the extent of the movement, which, beginning with the Licensing Act of 1828 and culminating in the new Poor Law Amendment Act of 1834 and the Prisons Act of 1835, resulted in the curtailment or abolition of the justices' powers of licensing public houses, of inspecting cotton factories and prisons, and of supervising poor relief, the most important branch of parish ex-

---

[13] *Oeuvres* (M): *Voyages Angleterre,* 21.

penditure. He was likewise unaware of the limitations of judicial publicity in the sphere of administration conducted "out of sessions." [14]

Nevertheless, Radnor's information was not totally misleading. If some functions were being whittled away there was no immediate threat to the office itself, and Tocqueville's host, alarmed by so many weaknesses in the English body politic, had no fear of a popular movement in that quarter. Tocqueville correctly noted that the justices were assaulted "indirectly and on certain points of detail, but there is no great current of opinion against them." Indeed, when the tide of reform ebbed temporarily in 1837 no fundamental change had occurred in the office, and two decades later Rudolf von Gneist, the first systematic analyst of English local government, still considered England "a country ruled from top to bottom by her gentry." [15]

The conviction that the true source of English power was the network of landed magistrates gave an important turn to Tocqueville's investigation in 1833. It meant that his political and social analysis was focused on one power nexus. Land and local administration seemed to support each other and in turn the entire foundation of the social structure. But Tocqueville found another source of strength in the English aristocracy, one in which he saw the source of its endurance. For the Continental aristocracies too, if they followed the universal prescription, must have been built upon large landed territories. And their fate, as Tocqueville was well aware, had been very different. Almost casually he began an inquiry that was to become one of the major preoccupations of his investigation of the causes of the French Revolution. He noted the participation of the English aristocracy in public affairs and its

[14] See *Oeuvres* (M): *Démocratie,* I, 74; Sir W. Ivor Jennings, *Principles of Local Government Law,* 4th ed. (London, 1960), 30ff; and Sidney and Beatrice Webb, *Statutory Authorities for Special Purposes* (London, 1922), 393ff.

[15] Elie Halévy, "Before 1835," in *A Century of Municipal Progress: The Last Hundred Years,* ed. Harold J. Laski and others (London, 1935), 35. See also Webb, *Parish and County,* 557–558.

frequent defense of liberty. But its truly distinctive feature was accessibility—the ease with which the upper class had opened and continued to open its ranks. That men of all social ranks could reach positions of power was, he felt, less true than most believed. But with great wealth anyone could hope to enter the ranks of the aristocracy, giving its privileges the allure of the faintly possible. Hence the English aristocracy had so far survived with property and power where all others succumbed either to kings or commoners.

The English aristocracy, in addition to openness, also possessed the immense advantage of vagueness. A rigid body fixed by birth, as in France, laid itself open to hatred. In England its limits were unknown and its prejudices were diffused in diminishing proportions through the ranks of the entire nation. One could see where the aristocracy began but not where it ended. In this lack of definition Tocqueville found another trait of the English character which aided the aristocracy—an inability or lack of desire to form general ideas. This he regarded almost as a parallel to the uncoordinated individuality of local government and the self-contained, large landed estates. He thus began a line of reasoning that was to lead him to tie the dispersion of political, social, and economic power in an aristocracy directly to its intellectual life: "Would it not be part of the aristocratic temperament to isolate oneself and, as each enjoys a fine estate, to be *more* afraid of being disturbed in one's own domain, *than* wishful to extend it over others?" [16]

Cottu, one of Tocqueville's sources, had described the penetration of this lack of class definition into the language itself: "*Gentleman* in England is applied to every well-educated man whatever his birth, while in France *gentilhomme* applies only to a noble by birth." [17] The historical divergence of this word, originally identical in England and France, seemed to Tocqueville more illuminating than

---

[16] *Journeys to England*, 81, May 26, 1835.
[17] *La Justice criminelle*, 7. This distinction was a commonplace among contemporary travelers.

many long arguments. It was to reappear in a somewhat elaborated form more than two decades later in his study of France before the Revolution.

When he abandoned feudal intoxication at Kenilworth, however, he was sure that even the English gentleman would shortly go the way of the feudal knight. The important question was how he would exit. Were the habits of aristocracy so deeply ingrained that only a violent upheaval could destroy them, or would reforms effect the change at a continuously accelerating rate? He had landed in Weymouth eager to detect the tempo of the last act, "convinced that the country was on the point of being precipitated into the misfortune of a great revolution." [18]

Some of his early notes clearly bear the impress of this conviction. As in Canada, he started looking about for the leaders of the expected revolution. At a public meeting in support of the Poles in Exeter Hall he was sure he had found them. The meeting, unimpressive at first, was presided over by a lord and was largely dominated by parliamentary speakers, "all uttering commonplaces," until a member of the "Political [National?] Union of the Working Classes" named Duffey castigated those members of Parliament who limited themselves to private charity instead of public action.[19] Although the speech did not stray from its subject, and *The Times* report appeared unimpressed by any revolutionary undertones, Tocqueville, totally unused to an English public meeting, was carried away by his words. "In him," he recorded, "I saw the precursor of those revolutionaries who are destined, in a short time, to change the face of England." The newly arrived visitor saw a portent in the raucous meeting directed by peers of the realm. He dramatically imagined them to be symbolically besieged at the front of the hall and forced to flatter the prejudices and passions of democracy in order to purchase its praise. English society, old and new, seemed to face each other, ready for battle.

A by-election in London gave him another shocking introduction

---

[18] *Oeuvres* (M): *Voyages Angleterre*, 36.
[19] *Journeys to England*, 45–47, Aug. 19, 1833.

to a basic ingredient of the English political system. It seemed no more than a disgusting farce. The faces of the predominantly lower-class crowd "were stamped with those signs of degradation only to be found in the people of big towns." [20] The shouting, whistling, and cheering prevented him from following the vote, and the style of the victory speech, after the results were announced, seemed as "vulgar as the assembly who heard it." Tocqueville was further amazed by the speech of the beaten candidate, who braved the insults of the crowd to reaffirm his principles. The plight of the beleaguered Tory, hurling his principles at the jeering victors, reminded Tocqueville of the "savages of North America who amuse themselves by insulting their enemies while they are being burnt." The metaphor was appropriate to the beholder's imagination.

Nevertheless, the disorder and abusive shouts of those who participated in the "saturnalia of English liberty" appeared an actual deterrent to revolution. These riotous gatherings, by giving the middle classes a horror of democracy in these hideous manifestations, might contribute to the maintenance of the aristocracy. In his experience of revolutions, Tocqueville had never seen the lower classes, of themselves, make a revolution, and he concluded that in general a lasting revolution could not come from their ranks alone.

However, he was as convinced as ever that England was undergoing a revolution in the sense of a substitution of one fundamental social principle for another. Here Tocqueville's emphasis that there could be no "mixed" constitution was crucial. Democracy and aristocracy were viewed as distinct conditions with mutually incompatible tendencies, one of which had to predominate in any society save one dominated by anarchical disorder. In spite of its reserves of defense, Tocqueville felt the aristocracy to be on the defensive, "since the aristocratic principle, which was the vital

---

[20] *Journeys to England,* 44. It is interesting how the electoral process unconsciously reminded him of one aspect of America, for the very words which Tocqueville used to describe it were from the lips of one of his American interlocutors (see *Oeuvres* (M): *Voyages Etats-Unis,* 118).

principle of its constitution, is deteriorating every day and it is probable that in a given time the democratic principle will replace it." [21]

In speaking of a "democratic principle" Tocqueville was vaguely indicating what he regarded as the prime and providential fact of modern history, a world movement of ideas and institutions which no fortress could finally resist. The *Démocratie,* which was to appear in 1835, was to commence the study of the principle of equality in America with an introduction outlining its rise in France over a period of seven centuries. Its author believed that wherever he looked in the Western world he could see an identical progress. Everywhere aristocracy was bowing to "the general movement common to humanity the world over in our time. The century is primarily democratic. Democracy is like the incoming sea . . . The immediate future of Europe is democratic." [22] The English aristocracy was thus only a powerful and worthy class futilely battling the will of providence in history.

As Tocqueville himself realized, this postulating of a vague and generalized force to explain historical development was dangerous. It conferred on these forces an extrasocietal power, independent of all human actions and institutions. Against this disembodied force stood the still solid foundations of the aristocracy in law, institutions, and customs, foundations which he had himself confirmed in the course of the trip. In one case, the concentration of landed property, the aristocracy seemed actually to have taken the offensive and to be flying in the face of his providential fact. In order to bridge this gap he had recourse first to the external ideological stimuli which might play an increasing role in English politics. The greatest of these was, of course, the "French spirit."

England, like France, had experienced a period of revolution, but the English revolution had not attained the fundamentally egalitarian character which had predominated in the other. The masses had not participated to the same extent, nor had the civil law undergone a

[21] *Oeuvres* (M): *Voyages Angleterre,* 36.
[22] *Oeuvres* (M): *Voyages Angleterre,* 37.

radical transformation. It was the French Revolution, with its new definition of liberty and equality based on the rights of man, which was arousing the English masses.

Tocqueville did not attempt to identify the political carriers of this "spirit" in England nor to indicate how it would concretely affect the social situation. The "French spirit" was thus not much more useful than the "democratic tide" in estimating the direction of English reform. The difficulty was that he was trying too hard to locate some psychological basis for one specific type of reform. He spoke of "vague desires for growth and power," of "restlessness," but not of programs, organizations, or events, or where, in the present social condition of England, lay the seeds of its transformation.[23]

He had pointed to accessibility as a strength—henceforth it would no longer suffice. The aristocratic lottery was becoming harder to win and the swarm of applicants more numerous and enlightened. In those near-aristocratic classes, Tocqueville reasoned, there was an increasing realization that they could reach the positions of power by another way—by democratization of the constitution. This resulted in a kind of psychological acceleration in favor of reform. Every time a new group achieved the right to political participation and power it would increase the number who preferred the quicker rewards which democracy promised to the rarer and less accessible ones which aristocracy offered.

Another approach to the problem, in slightly modified form, was to be incorporated in the *Démocratie* two years later. Since almost all democratic movements had been directed by men of the upper classes, Tocqueville, in addition to citing the impatient ambitious groups from the lower ranks of society, noted that no aristocracy could employ all the talents and passions of all its members. Here, then, might be found the leaders of the masses, perhaps impoverished, and alienated from their class by the very land practices which upheld the aristocratic system of inequality. With sources of sinecures like those at Oxford threatened by reform, the younger sons

[23] *Oeuvres* (M): *Voyages Angleterre,* 37.

would be forced back to the land and the custom of unitary inheritance would have to be broken.[24]

Tocqueville was here led back to the legal shield of the aristocracy, the land-inheritance laws. Without its perceptible modification the aristocracy would retain its "cornerstone." The problem would have been simple if Tocqueville had found a system with entailed estates, no matter how well entrenched, under violent attack. But he was obviously disturbed not only by the increase in concentration but by the absence of any widespread movement against the system. This was an unavoidable fact. "It is not rare to hear an Englishman complain of the extension of aristocratic privileges and to speak with bitterness of those who exploit them; but tell him the only means of destroying the aristocracy, changing the inheritance law, and he will recoil at once. I have not yet met a single person who was not frightened by such an idea." [25] Common conceptions seemed to act against the division of the land even where the law did not require it, and few Englishmen divided their estates. The middle classes appeared to be as attached to the maintenance of large territorial possessions as the landed proprietors. The masses were distressingly unexcited by the land question.

To bring England into line with the universal pattern he had discovered in France and America it had to be shown why land concentration also resulted in an inevitable movement toward democracy and not aristocracy, its logical concomitant. Outward strength must reveal an inward flaw. Tocqueville found this flaw in the condition of the poor. "The state of the poor," he wrote, carrying over ideas formed in America, "is the deepest trouble of England." [26] Tocqueville observed that the logic of aristocracy itself demanded that the well-being of the poor be sacrificed for the privileges of the few. Even the English aristocracy, the most liberal that had ever existed, could not, however worthy and enlightened, avoid this

---

[24] Tocqueville, *Journeys to England*, 55, 61. See also *Oeuvres* (M): *Démocratie*, I, 276.

[25] *Oeuvres* (M): *Voyages Angleterre*, 41.

[26] *Journeys to England*, 72.

alternative: "In England the number of proprietors is tending to decrease instead of increase and the number of proletarians grows unceasingly." Such conditions, contended Tocqueville, ceaselessly augmented the taxes of the rich, who "cannot employ the poor as [they otherwise] would have been able to do . . . such a state of things cannot but indefinitely stimulate poverty." [27]

Unfortunately, his theory did not impress his English listeners. They were "still imbued with that doctrine, which is at least debatable, that great properties are necessary for the improvement of agriculture, and they seem still convinced that extreme inequality of wealth is in the natural order of things." [28] In the face of this blank psychological wall he could not detect the presence of any general revolutionary sentiments. It seemed English imaginations were far behind those of France in 1789.

Clearly, Tocqueville did not yet consider the aristocratic fabric to be really rent in spite of the furor over the Reform Bill. His American experience had perhaps caused him to direct his gaze away from the forces operating at the center of the political arena. In choosing the landed magistracy as the representative English institution, he concentrated on the authority whose constitution and even some of whose powers were relatively secure. In 1833 specific legislative issues like the reform of the poor law or municipal government, the secret ballot, or even the ebb and flow of party strength in Parliament interested him infinitely less than the strength of feeling against primogeniture. He did not discuss the background of the struggles over Catholic emancipation or the organizations which had played a role in the formulation and victory of the Reform Bill. His alphabetic notebook did not even include an entry on reform. It may be that Tocqueville was so unimpressed by the immediate results of the electoral reform that he was unwilling to grant that it had broken the power of the aristocracy at any vital point. Between the English political movement and her static land consciousness he found a gap which one could only expect to close

[27] *Journeys to England*, 72. See also *Oeuvres* (M): *Démocratie*, I, 245.
[28] *Journeys to England*, 72.

after the social attitudes themselves began to change. But there was one more result of the failure to assess what had been gained thus far by the Reform Bill. So sharply had he pointed his questions at the dividing line between aristocracy and democracy, and so earnestly had he sought for the potential division of two social forces along these lines, that he had almost overlooked the existence of the middle class.

Tocqueville kept his sights closely focused on the role of the landed aristocracy and attempted to trace the progress of the democratic impulse against it. His investigation was obviously intended to enable him to complete his work on America, and England was still most important to him in revealing the place from which the world had traveled. There were few references to France or to the applicability of English ideas and institutions to modern social problems. When Tocqueville spoke of France it was usually in terms of the incomprehensibility of certain English aristocratic institutions to the democratic French point of view. For the moment he valued England most for her social hierarchy, her inheritance laws, her justices of the peace, and her proud traditionalism. What Tocqueville did not realize in 1833, or well into his second trip to England, was that the lines were not as clearly drawn between aristocracy and democracy, as his analysis wished to make them. He applied them to England from definitions external to its situation. Tocqueville's pattern of analysis had become fixed in America and, as Pierson put it, his questioning at times resembled a nun's telling over her rosary, so automatically did one conclusion lead to another.

Thus the framework of his American conclusions dominated the first journey. The idea that the essence of a constitution was to be found in local government and administration had led him away from urban forces and the center of power to the administration of rural England. His emphasis on the importance of land law and distribution in relation to political power led him to both discovery and dilemma. He found, happily for his theory, that social inequality was connected with attitudes toward land, which was separated by law and custom from other forms of wealth. On the other hand, he had stumbled upon a very hard fact—a continuous movement toward increased inequality in landed holdings. Through all the internal ratiocination of his "last impressions" one thing was abundantly apparent. Tocqueville's image of the sweep of history, soon to emerge in the Introduction to the *Démocratie,* was struggling with the English situation. He was fascinated by the grandeur of the English upper classes and he was certain that England was in a state of peaceful revolution—substituting one regulative social principle for another. But in his conception of what a prerevolutionary situation should be like he was groping. He sought for definite, basically hostile divisions where there were none: in the ranks of the aristocracy and over the landed estates. A closer and more intensive study would reveal to him the fluidity and variety of political and social life in England.

Tocqueville, it appears, was on the whole satisfied with his initial image of the English aristocracy and of the point of departure he had discovered in America. When the first part of the *Démocratie* finally appeared early in 1835, England was the contemporary example of the aristocratic principle and all its workings.[29]

[29] See *Démocratie,* I, especially app. B, 451–452.

IV ❖ England 1835: The Aristocracy of Wealth

WHEN, in April 1835, Tocqueville began his second English journey, now accompanied by Beaumont, he had become the recognized critic and philosopher of the democratic revolution.[1] To ensure that this time he should not arrive unknown, Tocqueville had taken care that the *De la démocratie en Amérique,* just off the Paris press in January, was rapidly distributed to the leading English reviews and to the eminences of politics. The effect, as in France, was almost universal recognition of a landmark in political science.

An English translation was arranged at once. Henry Reeve began his lifelong friendship with Tocqueville by undertaking to render into English the lucid and simple style of what he judged "the most important treatise on the Science of States that has appeared since Montesquieu." [2] Reeve was to become one of Tocqueville's permanent links with both government circles and the English press. His close connections with Lords Greville, Lansdowne, and Claren-

---

[1] The dated notes of Tocqueville and Beaumont, along with their correspondence, indicate the following itinerary of their voyage in 1835: Starting from Paris on April 21 and traveling by way of Calais, they arrived in England on the evening of the 23rd and reached London the following day, where they stayed for two months. They left London for the North on June 24, stopping at Coventry on the 25th, going on to Birmingham the following day, to Manchester on the 30th, and to Liverpool on July 3. They visited Ireland together from July 6 to mid-August. After almost two weeks in Dublin they passed rapidly through Carlow, Waterford, Cork, Tuam, Galway, and Newport-Pratt, returning to Dublin at the beginning of August. Beaumont went to Scotland on August 13, and Tocqueville, whose money had run out, left Dublin for France on August 16, returning by way of Southampton to Cherbourg. Beaumont made a second journey in 1837.

[2] Reeve to Mrs. Reeve, Feb. 25, 1835, *Memoirs of the Life and Correspondence of Henry Reeve,* ed. John Knox Laughton (London, 1898), I, 42.

don were a valuable asset to Tocqueville in his political calling. As an influential correspondent of *The Times,* and, later as editor of the *Edinburgh Review,* Reeve was able to keep Tocqueville abreast of English public opinion and to maintain his friend's influence by lengthy reviews and republications of his works.

Tocqueville did not have to await a slow and begrudging judgment of a later generation to savor public acclaim. In 1835, he no longer sat among the anonymous onlookers in the gallery of the House of Lords, but was invited to participate in the work of Parliament itself. Giving evidence before a select committee of the House of Commons on bribery at elections, the new authority on democracy had his first opportunity to exert direct influence on the legislative process.[3] Thus it was England that witnessed his first appearance on the political stage. Within a few months Tocqueville's work on America became a sacred text. Radicals developed arguments from the *Démocratie* for the speedy extension of reform, and conservatives like Sir Robert Peel, after similar exegesis, arrived at very different conclusions.[4] It would not be long before one of England's first two school inspectors, H. S. Tremenheere, added Tocqueville's name to a list of philosophers from Aristotle to Burke whose works were to be anthologized for public education on the issue of democracy, and Professor William Smyth of Cambridge incorporated Tocqueville's concepts into his lectures on America.

Tocqueville no longer confined himself to wandering like a lonely shadow through the immensity of London and the abandoned castles of England. He and Beaumont had easy entry into the Whig strongholds at Lansdowne House and at Holland House, where in "a delightful gothic chateau" they dined and

[3] See Tocqueville, *Journeys to England,* 210–232, June 22, 1835. In 1833 Tocqueville and Beaumont's joint work had become part of English political controversy in a small way. See "Penetentiary System in America and France," *Monthly Review,* CXXX (April 1833), 507ff.

[4] See [John Stuart Mill], "Democracy in America," *Edinburgh Review,* LXXII (October 1840), 1, for a brief account of how the *Démocratie* made its way into Tory circles.

chatted with the Duke of Richmond, Lord Granville, and Lord Melbourne, the Prime Minister.[5] They discussed land reform with Lord Holland, centralization with the Earl of Minto, electoral manipulation with Henry Hallam (the famous constitutional historian), administrative reform with Thomas Frankland Lewis, chairman of the newly appointed Poor Law Commission, and with his already distinguished son George Cornewall Lewis. They were guests at the animated gatherings of John Murray, founder and guiding spirit of the Tory *Quarterly Review*. In the close-knit social and political circles of London, they also had an opportunity to consort with many of the prominent Radicals and Utilitarians of the day. They renewed Tocqueville's earlier contacts with Edward Bulwer-Lytton and John Bowring, and conversed with the most outspoken reformers in Parliament—Joseph Hume, John Roebuck, and George Grote. Grote's wife, Harriet, became one of Tocqueville's most devoted friends. Tocqueville and Beaumont also met with John Stuart Mill, who was as excited by the *Démocratie* as anyone in England.

The words of the leading lights of English society became part of the visitors' ever growing pile of observations and conversations, and the assorted marginal notes and "general ideas" revealed the impact. The pattern of questions, followed so vigorously and tightened so carefully since the voyage to America, began to expand. The first line of thought to be challenged and altered was the belief that democracy in England would move along the path of a social and economic revolution aimed at the great landed proprietors. The second was their conception of aristocracy itself.

On these themes the ideas of the first few weeks of the journey of 1835 were inseparably bound to those of 1833. Beaumont's notes bear striking witness to this. The early ones read like a recapitulation of Tocqueville's observations two years before. Just before the voyage Tocqueville had written: "I was traveling through Great Britain in 1833; others were struck by the prosperity of the

---

[5] Yale Mss(B) C.X.3: *L'Irlande,* notes.

country; I myself pondered the secret unrest which was visibly at work among the minds of the inhabitants. I thought that great misery must be hidden beneath that brilliant mask which Europe admires." [6] Beaumont thus arrived equally prepared to be struck by the pervasiveness of the aristocratic principle in England, and to ferret out the agents of the forthcoming democratic revolution. There were the inevitable "first impressions"; "immense merchant fleets in the ports, vast country estates with their air of wealth and abundance," and the exclamation "Quel luxe!" at the end of his account of visits to Chelsea and Greenwich. Simultaneously, he searched for the inevitable flaw. Describing the prosperous countryside on the road to London, Beaumont noted, "Magnificent exterior. Is it a deceitful prosperity?" [7] Everywhere he scanned the horizon for the terrifying proletarians, cast off the land and awaiting only a leader. The first cluster of Tocqueville's conversations also indicate the continued search for the development of a revolutionary "land consciousness" and the vanguard of democratic leadership in the aristocracy. They diligently annotated a new pamphlet, *Thoughts upon the Aristocracy of England,* by Isaac Tomkins (Lord Brougham), which demanded a reform of the succession laws.[8]

Once they began to discuss their ideas openly, however, the two travelers encountered powerful opposition from the English ranks. Almost immediately they had to face the accumulated wisdom of English political economy in the person of Nassau William Senior. Tocqueville was no longer the young man who had called unannounced at Senior's door in 1833. But an economist who was one of the most influential advisors of the Whig government and one of the authors of the most comprehensive poor-law reform in three centuries was not to be overwhelmed by revolutionary prognostications concerning the rural proletariat and the agricultural system of England.

---

[6] *Mémoire sur le paupérisme,* 332.
[7] Yale Mss(B) C.X.4: *L'Irlande,* notes.
[8] Yale Mss(B) C.X: *L'Irlande,* notes, contains the annotated copy.

Senior (1790–1864), a chancery barrister, was a charter member of the Political Economy Club, the first holder of the Drummond Professorship of Political Economy at Oxford, and "the outstanding as well as the fashionable economist of the time." His contacts with political and intellectual circles in London and Paris were prodigious, and after 1848 he was a constant visitor to France. The result was a series of diaries which captured two decades of conversations by leading French statesmen, including Tocqueville.[9] Since Tocqueville and Beaumont came to depend so heavily on Senior's economic writings, their debate with him over land distribution in England and their theory of democracy has significance beyond the immediate issue. It was a forecast of more disturbing economic developments, which came to plague their political analysis.

The debate already existed in embryo in 1833, in Tocqueville's remark about the English imagination being fettered by "the doctrine, at least debatable, that great properties are necessary for the improvement of agriculture." The *Démocratie* made Senior's reaction inevitable. Commenting on the process of land division in France and America, Tocqueville wrote that great landed estates once divided could never recover, since they ran counter to the general tendency toward equality and because the system of small proprietors was economically more productive. Typically, Tocqueville defended his argument on psychological rather than statistical grounds: "I do not mean to say that the small proprietor cultivates better, but he cultivates with more intensity and care, making up by his labor what he lacks by way of skill."[10]

This, together with the statement that the welfare of the poor

---

[9] Sidney and Beatrice Webb, *English Poor Law History, Part II: The Last Hundred Years* (London, 1929), I, 48–49n. Senior himself employed Tocqueville's speeches and writings in a number of articles and lectures. See Senior, *Industrial Efficiency and Social Economy*, ed. S. Leon Levy (New York, 1928), I, 340–341; and articles by Senior reprinted from the *Edinburgh Review* in his *Historical and Philosophical Essays* (London, 1865): "France, America and Britain" (April 1842), "Confederacy and Union" (January 1846), and "Lewis on Authority in Matters of Opinion" (April 1850).

[10] *Oeuvres* (M): *Démocratie*, I, 48n.

(*bien du pauvre*) in England had been sacrificed to that of the rich, led Senior to object to Tocqueville's statements in his very letter of congratulation on the *Démocratie*. He strongly denied that it was a question of sacrificing the "wealth of the poor" (note Senior's translation) to that of the rich. Questions of land cultivation, like every other kind of enterprise, were to be settled by determining relative economic efficiency. Intensity of feeling for the land could not alter the facts of comparative productivity as Senior saw them.

Neither Tocqueville nor Beaumont was prepared to challenge the economic arguments of Senior head on. From the first Tocqueville maintained that the *bien du pauvre* went beyond the question of wealth in its narrowest terms to matters of personal consideration, easy justice, and intellectual and aesthetic opportunity.[11] And they both insisted, with vehemence, on the special significance of land ownership. Beaumont rejected the treatment of agriculture as the simple equivalent of any capitalist industry. Tocqueville argued that since landholding played a greater role in the formation of political and social habits than other forms of ownership its political and moral effects were more important than economic considerations. More than a theory of economic productivity was at stake. The pattern of the democratic revolution seemed more jeopardized by Senior's arguments for the soundness and stability of English agriculture than when Tocqueville ascribed indifference to primogeniture as a simple lack of imagination.

In Senior's garden at Kensington, while another young foreign guest, Camillo Cavour, looked on with intense interest, the two vociferous Frenchmen shifted their ground without surrendering their conclusions. If they no longer sought to derive the democratic revolution in England from the economic contradictions of land accumulation itself, the momentum of the political and ideological revolution would do for English agriculture what it was not able

[11] See *Démocratie*, I, 245, 249; and Senior to Tocqueville, Feb. 17, 1835, and Tocqueville to Senior, Feb. 21, 1835, *Correspondence and Conversations*, vol. I. Senior was just completing a comparative study of poor relief in Europe and America.

to do itself. But a clash was inevitable. Beaumont was amazed
at how Senior persisted in the "utopian dream" that a small number of men could control the soil of England while the political
base of the country was rapidly expanding. How could common
sense fail to indicate that once the majority of a society could share
political power it would not begin to destroy the landed estates? [12]
Senior, for his part, could not see why land should be any more
liable to revolutionary expropriation than any other source of
wealth, especially since the returns on industrial capital were relatively greater.

Tocqueville conceded that the development of English agriculture seemed to defy the pattern laid down in the *Démocratie*.
Now, however, he saw, instead of a single uniform revolution ad-
vancing equally in every direction, two contrary and incompatible
movements: "A political democratic movement and a social aristocratic one; that is to say, on the one side a general and equal
redistribution of political rights amongst a continually increasing
number of individuals, and on the other a proportionately increasing concentration of wealth in the hands of a few. This anomaly
cannot last long without grave danger to the State." [13]

Whatever its economic efficiency, the existence of great estates
was a danger to the political stability of any democratic system, and
England was destined to reach that condition if her political reforms were to have any significance at all. From this angle the
productive advantages of large scale agriculture on the great
estates was irrelevant. Tocqueville was willing to concede a limited
autonomy to the economics of accumulation but insisted on the
folly of extending democracy within the political realm without
dividing the land.

One thing clearly emerged from the arguments with Senior,
ultimately more important than the viability of the system of land

---

[12] Yale Mss(B) C.X.5: *L'Irlande,* notes, "Aristocratie-pauvre."

[13] A. J. Whyte, *The Early Life and Letters of Cavour, 1810–1848* (London, 1925),
130, and Camillo Benso Cavour, *Dario inedito con note autobiografiche del conte
di Cavour* (Rome, 1888), 173, May 24, 1835.

ownership, accumulation and inheritance in England. It gave Tocqueville a more complex conception of the relation between land distribution and the total social structure. The dictum expounded in the *Démocratie*—that having once established the inheritance laws within a society "the machine moves under its own impetus and is automatically driven toward a given point" [14]— was completely abandoned. The very use of the concept of "two independent movements" in England brought him to question the centrality of the inheritance laws as the royal road to social analysis.

Within a year of the confrontation with Senior, he was discounting the importance of the revolution in land law, and even land distribution, during the French Revolution. He emphasized instead the continuous process of fragmentation which had developed in defiance of feudal law long before 1789. The failure of the law of primogeniture in the old regime now demonstrated that "there is something more powerful than the constant operation of laws in one direction; it is the constant operation of human passions in the contrary direction." [15] When this formula was applied to England it began to appear that the great estates would be the last rampart of the aristocracy, not its most vulnerable point.

The titles of Beaumont's travel notes changed imperceptibly from "Aristocracy–Decline" and "Aristocracy–Revolution" to "How the English Aristocracy Makes Itself Bearable" and "What Makes the Territorial Aristocracy and the Monopoly of Land Bearable in England."

Their first confrontation with English thinkers was forcing them to question the framework in which they had enclosed the English aristocracy. Senior, insisting that English estates were viewed as a capital investment as well as a source of power and prestige, turned their attention toward the social importance of wealth in a broader

---

[14] I, 47.

[15] *Oeuvres* (M): *Ancien Régime*, I, 43 ("Etat social et politique de la France avant et depuis 1789," published first in English in 1836). Tocqueville added, "I am led to believe that the influence of these laws is often exaggerated."

sense. They became aware of new social classes and new values.

These new observations forced Tocqueville and Beaumont to modify their views, not only on the link between the aristocracy and landed wealth, but also on the psychological framework of the English poor. Economic and political passions might not be directed, as had those of the French peasantry, toward landed inequality. As an English Radical informed Tocqueville, the taste for real estate was the taste of a rich man, one who had become wealthy through trade, since the returns from agriculture were relatively low. Similarly, anyone who wished to rise from the working classes went into commerce or industry. To buy land was an idea which would never enter the mind of an English peasant. For Tocqueville this was the end of any idea that agrarian unrest from landed inequality could be the deathblow to the system. "The habits and instincts of the English peasant," he concluded, "are therefore totally unlike our own. If he possesses more intelligence or capital than his neighbors, he turns his advantages to account in trade . . . With the English, land is a luxury . . . So while trade and manufactures attract laborers, the soil rejects them." [16] Beaumont, after raising the question everywhere, concluded that for most English statesmen the issue of "land hunger" did not exist— and he was no longer inclined to insist on it.

The real shift of focus came with a shift of environment. In London for all their activity, they remained within the world of English political and intellectual leadership. Wealth, in this context, meant the glitter and magnificence of an endless round of social activity. It was simply assumed and consumed, possessed or lacking. Their departure for Birmingham late in June brought them into a new world. The industrial revolution suddenly overwhelmed them. "It is an immense workshop," wrote Tocqueville after a few hours in the city, "a huge forge, a vast shop. One only sees busy people and faces brown with smoke. One hears only the

[16] Tocqueville to Count Louis Molé, May 19, 1835, *Oeuvres* (B), VI. See also Yale Mss(B) C.X.5: *L'Irlande,* notes, "Succession-égalité," conversation with Lord Holland, London, May 9, 1835.

sound of hammers and the whistle of steam escaping from boilers. One might be down a mine in the new world." Industrial and middle-class England seemed to unfold before them. Here was a new England, as much at the forefront of historical development as America. "We found as much good will here as in London," wrote Tocqueville, "but there is hardly any likeness between the two societies. These folk never have a minute to themselves. They work as if they must get rich by the evening and die the next day. They are generally very intelligent people but intelligent in the American way." [17]

"In the American way"—here Tocqueville found analogies to America in the steady unlimited pursuit of wealth, and in his mind the two countries were drawing closer together, not only institutionally but in manners and values. He found everyone working to make a fortune. There was no leisure class, since those who succeeded moved elsewhere. As the North was the workshop of England, so was America soon to be conceived as the further extension of the English middle class. "In spite of the ocean that intervenes I cannot consent to separate America from Europe," he would conclude in the second part of the *Démocratie* in 1840. "I consider the people of the United States as that portion of the English people who are commissioned to explore the forests of the New World, while the rest of the nation, enjoying more leisure and less harassed by the drudgery of life, may devote their energies to thought, and enlarge in all directions the empire of the mind." [18]

America economically became an extension of Birmingham, a unique society where the whole community was engaged in industry and commerce. American manners were now seen to be analogous to those of the English middle class. Beaumont thus described a manufacturer: "No elegance; good nature; polite; sometimes

[17] Tocqueville, *Journeys to England,* 94. Tocqueville and Beaumont had probably already received from John Stuart Mill his later published criticism of their rigorous separation of England and America; see [J. S. Mill], "State of Society in America," *London Review,* II (January 1836), 368–369.

[18] *Oeuvres* (M): *Démocratie,* II, 42. Also, *ibid.,* 160ff.

indiscreet; embarrassingly obliging; it's *absolutely America*. They are far from suspecting the comparison I make," he added, "for they have not stopped laughing at Americans." [19] The same observation was to appear in the *Démocratie* a few years later. To a great extent Tocqueville now saw a new significance in the great middle class which he was coming to regard as the future majority of mankind.

It was in the industrial North, too, that Tocqueville had the opportunity to glimpse those most removed from the wealth and leisure which had absorbed him in London. He began in Birmingham to take notes on the social, moral, and political condition of the working classes. Significantly, however, he obtained his information from manufacturers and professional men, not by direct conversation with any workers, a pattern which continued throughout his brief northern swing. He devoted much more space in his notes to local government and local political activity than to a full-scale study of economic conditions. He was apparently most impressed by the close political union in Birmingham between the workmen and industrialists, a carry-over from the agitation of 1832. Such unity was patently nonexistent in Manchester, the next city they visited.

On July 2, 1835, Tocqueville wrote the most powerful description of his journey, a description of Manchester illuminating the contrasts that the industrial revolution had wrought on the city:

On this watery land which nature and art have contributed to keep damp, are scattered palaces and hovels. Everything in the exterior appearance of the city attests [to] the individual powers of man; nothing to the directing power of society. At every turn human liberty shows its capricious creative force. There is no trace of the slow continuous action of government.

Thirty or forty factories rise on the tops of the hills . . . Their six stories tower up; their huge enclosures give notice from afar of the centralisation of industry. The wretched dwellings of the poor are scat-

[19] Yale Mss(B) C.X.3: *L'Irlande,* notes, "Hallem Manufacturier," n.d. For Tocqueville's use of this idea, see *Oeuvres* (M): *Démocratie,* II, 226.

tered haphazard around them. Round them stretches land uncultivated but without the charm of rustic nature, and still without the amenities of a town . . . The land is given over to industry's use . . . The roads . . . show, like the rest, every sign of hurried and unfinished work; the incidental activity of a population bent on gain, which seeks to amass gold so as to have everything else all at once, and, in the interval, mistrusts the niceties of life . . . Look up and all around this place you will see the huge palaces of industry. You will hear the noise of furnaces, the whistle of steam. These vast structures keep air and light out of the human habitations which they dominate; they envelop them in perpetual fog; here is the slave, there the master; there the wealth of some; here the poverty of most; there the organized effort of thousands produce, to the profit of one man, what society has not yet learned to give. Here the weakness of the individual seems more feeble and helpless even than in the middle of a wilderness; here the effects, there the causes.

Before him, as Tocqueville aptly put it, was a new Hades. "From this foul drain," he concluded, "the greatest stream of human industry flows out to fertilise the whole world. From this filthy sewer pure gold flows. Here humanity attains its most complete development and its most brutish; here civilisation works its miracles, and civilised man is turned back into a savage . . ." [20]

Tocqueville's description of Manchester has been regarded as a precursor of Engels' systematic survey of English slums in *The Condition of the Working Class in England in 1844.* This it is not. Engels brought his reader to Manchester only after having moved him through every industrial town in England. Slowly and methodically the reader is carried into the heart of hell after a long pedestrian skirting of the purgatories, and the narrative moves through Manchester at a walking pace. Not a street remains unnoticed, not an alley overlooked, not a hovel unaccounted for. We are escorted back and forth through the twisting city streets by a man who has lived here, upon whom these streets have made the deepest impression of any sight in England, the fruit of almost two years' minute study. Manchester was the heart and focus of

[20] Tocqueville, *Journeys to England,* 105–108.

his chapter on English slums, but it was merely the last stone of a gigantic pyramid, not a traveler's description of a unique sight.

Tocqueville's epitome of Manchester symbolically and significantly never emerged from his notes to be integrated in a larger work. Manchester impressed him and raised important problems in his mind, but the writings of at least one French critic of English industrialization, Alban de Villeneuve-Bargemont, had already thoroughly prepared him for a picture of industrial feudalism. It was never the core of an experience for him, and certainly from the very first moment he did not view it as the symbol of England's present or future condition. His first note on Manchester bears the title "Caractère particulier de Manchester"—the special character of Manchester—and this judgment became fixed in his mind as he attempted to grapple with the "new aristocracy," which this chaotic city forced him to consider. The following year, in his notes on Machiavelli's history of Florence, he was to warn against accepting the industrial centers of England as the true image of a modern democratic society, "as if it were said that Manchester or Liverpool, or any other great center of industry and commerce which encloses in its midst colossal fortunes and unknown miseries, presents a society whose social state is democratic. There can be cities of this kind among a democratic people, but to wish to judge a people itself by its cities would be unjust and absurd." [21]

This point will be further developed in considering the impact of England on Tocqueville's economic thought. It must suffice here to state that Manchester did not seriously affect his general impression of England. It did arouse him to an awareness of a new social relationship, one which he deemed especially dangerous to political life. In Birmingham he obtained his information on working-class conditions from outside their ranks—from a lawyer, a municipal history, and a manufacturer; in Manchester, again from a manufacturer. He fortunately met one man, however, who

[21] *Oeuvres* (B), VIII, 446, Aug. 9, 1836. For Engels, of course, Manchester was the "classic type of a modern manufacturing town."

was an authority on workers' conditions, Dr. James Phillips Kay.[22] Kay was the author of a pioneer study on *The Moral and Physical Condition of the Working Classes in Manchester* (1832), and was about to become an assistant commissioner of the poor when Tocqueville met him. He gave Tocqueville an indication of the immense political, economic, and social isolation of the classes of Manchester from each other. This condition seemed a far cry from Birmingham's famous political union and its infinity of small industrialists. In Manchester the extremes of wealth and poverty acted as a significant deterrent to the slow continuous action of government, and political life in the ordinary sense seemed absent.

The *Démocratie* of January 1835 had dismissed the rich in America as a lingering relic of the past. Beaumont's *Marie* of the same month had taken issue with English travelers who affirmed the existence of an aristocracy of wealth in America. The future seemed to point unerringly toward limitless equalization. The English journey placed a small question mark over the inevitability of this tendency, reinforcing suspicions already aroused in Tocqueville by French critics of the new industrialism. In June 1838, in a note for his *Démocratie,* he tried to fit the industrial aristocracy into the general pattern described by his study by viewing it as a passing historical development which simply recapitulated that of the landed aristocracy. In a marginal note, "What I say of master and worker," he wrote: "All societies at birth begin by organizing themselves aristocratically. Industry is at this moment obeying that law." [23] Did this mean that industry eventually would democratize itself by reform or revolution along the lines of a *morcellement* or

---

[22] According to *Oeuvres* (M): *Voyages Angleterre,* 79n, Tocqueville in his notes on Manchester quoted a "Dr. Key," on the working class in that city. He is not further identified by the editor. Tocqueville undoubtedly meant Dr. James Phillips Kay. Beaumont included Dr. Kay on a list of people he had met (Yale Mss(B) C.X.3: *L'Irlande,* notes). They probably met Kay through Nassau Senior. See Frank Smith, *The Life and Work of Sir James Kay-Shuttleworth* (London, 1923), 27–31.

[23] Yale Mss(T) C.IV.k: copy of notes for the *Démocratie* of 1840, paq. 7, cahier 1, June 12, 1838.

breaking up of great factories? Tocqueville remained too much in doubt to make any prediction at all as to the future.

Here lies the origin of Tocqueville's famous chapter in the second part of the *Démocratie* (1840), "How an Aristocracy May Be Created by Manufactures." Tocqueville pointed out the significance of factory specialization in brutalizing the worker so that he ceased to be fit for either political or intellectual activity. He also underscored the difference between the new industrial aristocracy and all those which preceded it, their lack of permanence and solidarity. Perhaps he was applying his theory that a hereditary landed class could achieve the basic coherence and continuity that an industrial class could never duplicate. But the lack of political ambition and leadership, of a sense of responsibility, impressed him most deeply: "Not only are the rich not firmly united among themselves, but there is no real bond between them and the poor. Their relative position is not a permanent one; they are constantly drawn together or separated by their interests . . . The one contracts no obligation to protect nor the other to defend, and they are not permanently connected either by habit or duty. The aristocracy created by business rarely settles in the midst of the manufacturing population which it directs; the object is not to govern that population, but to use it . . . It knows not how to will, and it cannot act." [24]

Thus Tocqueville came briefly to grips with the new manufacturing aristocracy, not bound like the old to act with or for its subjects. His description of the moral characteristics of industrial capitalism bore in many respects a close and prescient resemblance to those announced in the *Communist Manifesto* in 1848, but he regarded this new class as a "monstrous exception" to the general development of society.[25] Since it represented for Tocqueville only an eddy in the mainstream of the democratic revolution, it was discussed as a contrast to the state of society and not its point of departure or termination. The chapter on the manufacturing aristocracy in the

[24] *Oeuvres* (M): *Démocratie*, II, 166–167.

[25] *Démocratie*, II, 166: "Elle est une exception, un monstre, dans l'ensemble de l'état social."

Démocratie precisely paralleled the portrait of Manchester in his notes, appearing as an isolated aside in the main train of thought.

The phenomenon of great divisions in classes created by analogous gulfs in wealth was soon to reappear when Tocqueville and Beaumont reached Ireland. For the moment, however, it was the unifying, lubricating, and antirevolutionary effect of wealth on English political life in general which captured their imagination in Birmingham and which remained uppermost in Tocqueville's mind as he ended his English journey. Even in Manchester, the city of filth and wealth, he recorded: "*Prosperity, wealth, liberty* of England, which is explained by its weakness in a thousand [other things]." [26] It appeared that an enormous proportion of the resources of the human spirit in England were acquisitive. Wealth seemed to be an indispensable part of everything worthwhile as well as the most reliable index of character and intelligence.

The English, dominated by this single passion, had become the boldest sailors and manufacturers in the world. "For manufacture and trade are the best-known, most rapid, and the securest means of becoming rich. Newton said that he had found the world's system by thinking about it all the time. The English have found by the same method, the art of engrossing the world's trade." [27] But in engrossing the world's trade they had themselves become so engrossed in mercantile pursuits that revolutionary passions had been kept at a low pitch in those classes which might have acted as their French counterparts. "I know of nothing more opposed to revolutionary attitudes," Tocqueville observed in the *Démocratie* (1840), "than commercial ones." [28] But if he was to re-evaluate the significance of the predominant passion of the English, some revision of Tocqueville's view of the English aristocracy was obviously also in order.

The broadened consideration of wealth in England led to a revision of the rigid distinctions between aristocratic and demo-

---

[26] Tocqueville, *Journeys to England*, 109.

[27] *Oeuvres* (M): *Voyages Angleterre*, 90.

[28] *Oeuvres* (M): *Démocratie*, II, 260–261.

cratic states of society. The cash nexus operated as much to break down class barriers as to create new classes. Tocqueville was no longer so certain that the supposedly incompatible principles of aristocracy and democracy (in the sense of inequality and equality in various spheres of society) could not coexist through the social and economic fluidity allowed by mobile and expanding wealth.

One of the chief characteristics of an aristocracy, its scorn of the pursuit of wealth as an end, was not an outstanding feature of the English aristocracy—again an exception to the rule. It became difficult to discern "whether men grow covetous from ambition or ambitious from covetousness, where men seek to get rich in order to arrive at distinction and seek distinction as a manifestation of their wealth." [29] Tocqueville still attempted to place the English aristocracy somewhere in the scale between the extremes of aristocracy and democracy. England was accorded a special transitional status in which it was difficult to say whether it represented the end of an aristocratic society or the beginning of a democratic one.

Even before Birmingham, Tocqueville and Beaumont had begun to revise their conception of the relation between the English aristocracy, wealth, and landed property. By the end of the voyage their picture was quite different from the one of 1833. It was no longer a "feudal nobility" which had reasserted itself completely after the tempest of 1640. The old ruling class seemed to have had the unique wisdom to recognize its need of the commercial elements in time. In the bartering of political and economic power a new aristocracy of wealth arose, blending with the old. Tocqueville assumed that this particular revolution had been consummated generations before.[30] The revolution of the aristocracy of wealth was as close as Tocqueville and Beaumont came to a "point of departure" in 1835. Yet they did not call it a point of departure or assign to it the total significance which they had accorded to

[29] *Démocratie*, II, 343.
[30] Tocqueville, *Journeys to England*, 114–115. See also Yale Mss(B) C.X.3: *L'Irlande*, notes, "Rich and Poor—Aristocracy of Wealth in Birmingham," and Yale Mss(T) C.V.k: copy of notes for the *Démocratie* of 1840, paq. 7, cahier 1, p. 88.

democracy in America. Too much in England remained unexplainable by this peculiar aristocratic revolution.

Their references to an accomplished revolution in England also reflected a growing conviction that changes in the English social system were not bound to follow uniformly the pattern which Tocqueville had designated in 1833 as the "French" or democratic spirit. Tocqueville and Beaumont's ideas about both the imminence and nature of the democratic revolution in England were responding to the same pressures which broadened their conception of the aristocracy. Even in the first flush of their arrival in London, when every conversation and excursion was designed to discover any sign of increasing political, economic, and religious antagonisms between social classes, Tocqueville had concluded that the "democratic revolution which has taken place among us will, sooner or later, occur in England. But it seems to me that it will not be effected in the same way, and will proceed along other paths." [31] This not only meant, as in 1833, that England would favor peaceful reform, but that alignments of interests in England were quite different from those in his own country.

Both Tocqueville and Beaumont were taken with the vitality of English religious passions, which echoed the turbulence of the reformation to a nineteenth-century Frenchman. They wondered briefly if religious divisions in England might not form the nucleus of a broad democratic party, with the rich entering the Established Church while "great numbers" of the poor and middle classes joined the ranks of the dissenters. Evidently, while resigning themselves to the fact that no great parties would coalesce over the inheritance laws, they were still hunting for a single unified ideological basis for an ever widening democratic movement.

They also took up Tocqueville's old search for the leaders of the revolution among the "rear guard of the aristocracy" and

[31] Tocqueville to Molé, London, May 19, 1835, *Oeuvres* (B), VI. Beaumont, probably with Tocqueville, had been to a gathering of dissenters the day before (see Yale Mss(B) C.X.3: *L'Irlande*, notes, "Dissenters," May 18, 1835).

eagerly listened to the Whigs and Radicals who would constitute, willingly or unwillingly, the general staff of the immense, unorganized, democratic army. But the generals proved as perplexing as the masses in avoiding their assigned role. Tocqueville was quite prepared for the reluctance of the Whigs at Holland House to acknowledge the "tendency of events" and their inevitable consequences. He concluded that they had used the egalitarian instinct as a tool, without substantially changing the social order, until the instrument was becoming stronger than the hand which directed it. The ignorance of the Whigs as to how nearly democracy was upon them fitted Tocqueville's theory of the difficulty which aristocratic societies experienced in formulating general ideas.

From the Radicals whom he and Beaumont met at Senior's home and elsewhere, however, one looked for bold plans for the total reconstitution of society. They would not have been at all surprised to find a taste for violence and counted at least on vehement impatience with the intolerable delays of the parliamentary system. But when the Radicals themselves were unsure that anything more than piecemeal reforms could be expected in England in the foreseeable future, their French interlocutors took a second look at their prospective revolutionaries. And when an avowed democrat like John Stuart Mill insisted that reform agitation almost always separated resentment against the abuse of a privilege from admiration for the brilliant lives led by those who enjoyed them, Tocqueville and Beaumont quietly began to jot down notes on "new points of view." [32] It was apparent that the process of dividing every idea or social fact in England into aristocratic or democratic "tendencies," in terms of their old definitions, was hampering their analysis. Their general concepts were distorting instead of sharpening their perspective. There was only one solution. They had come to England to understand as well as to fill in the details of a theory

---

[32] Yale Mss(B) C.X.5: *L'Irlande,* notes, "Esprit de légalité—esprit aristocratique," conversation with John Stuart Mill, May 19 [1835]. Also C.X.3: *L'Irlande,* notes, "Réforme," May 29 [1835], conversation with John Roebuck: "No radical thinks an *émeute* can lead to uniform progress."

of social evolution, to complete their political education as well as to confirm it. Theory had to yield to evidence and account for it if the English experience was to be of any value.

Confident that their conception of the world democratic revolution was still valid in a broad context, Tocqueville and Beaumont began to modify their categories of 1831–1833. As long as they considered England as a transitory social phenomenon, passing from a general stage in the past to another general stage in the near future, they were viewing a country whose institutions were a relic transforming itself into a society quite like those already in existence in France or America. English institutions were interesting only as a check on position and velocity in the historical process.

Once they conceded that the England of the present was a novel experience, that its institutions and customs had immense importance aside from a position in time, they began to view it as they viewed America and France, as a nation with a present whose historic tendencies would sometimes coincide with, and sometimes diverge from, the general pattern. As Tocqueville wrote to Beaumont just after the journey, "One is really aroused only by what partially coincides and is new and original in some way. The English have taken our ideas, but they have in some manner ground them in their own mill, and they are trying to make them triumph and to apply them in their own way. They are at bottom European, but English in style." [33] The differences might have their own comparative value, and the uniformities would be even more significant.

The subtle interplay of uniformity and difference, of general historical tendencies and peculiar institutional adjustments, emerged most clearly in what Mill, reflecting Tocqueville's influence, called "the fundamental problem of centralization and local government." The impact of the English journey on the culminating theme of the *Démocratie* in 1840, and on the point of departure of the *Ancien Régime* in 1856, was decisive.

[33] Letter of Nov. 15, 1835, *Oeuvres* (B), VII.

V ✧ *England 1835: Centralization, Decentralization, and the Spirit of Liberty*

BEFORE 1835 Tocqueville treated the issue of centralization and its alternatives only as a matter of comparative administration. In America he was convinced that "the system of decentralization has been and still is the strength of England." [1] There was no suggestion by any of his English respondents in 1833 that a threat to the administrative structure existed in England any more than it did in the United States. The Radical Sir John Bowring had told him that England was "the country of decentralisation" and regarded this as the chief cause of the substantial progress in civilization made by England. [2] Lord Radnor and Tocqueville discussed the problem of democratization of local government in terms of demands for local electoral control of the counties and breaking the class monopoly of the justices of the peace. Radnor gave him no hint of a threat to the office from any quarter, either through demands for local or centralized control. When Tocqueville himself contrasted local diversity in England with local uniformity in France in 1833, he spoke in terms of the French mentality, which needed uniformity in the smallest things, as opposed to an English sentiment for extreme diversity. Neither quality was linked to a particular social condition nor bound in any ironclad way to national evolution. One had only to present the relative merits of each system of administration.

---

[1] Yale Mss(T) B.II.b: "De la centralisation," Washington, January 1832 (copy), p. 7.
[2] Tocqueville, *Journeys to England*, 61–62.

In this spirit the *Démocratie* of 1835 analyzed centralization in the United States and France, drawing a distinction between centralized government and centralized administration. Centralized government was constituted when the directing power of a nation was concentrated in a single place. Centralized administration referred to a similar concentration of local decisions and executive power. Tocqueville clearly stated his preference for decentralized administration on the basis of a comparison between French and American systems. The American pattern of local government was less efficient than the coordinated system directed from Paris, but it diffused "through the whole society a restless activity, a superabundant force, an energy which never exists without it and which can, however unfavorable the circumstances, produce wonders." [3] The *Démocratie* of 1835 dismissed fears of the concentration of the sovereign power in the United States. In its summary of the sentiments that were intimately connected with democratic and republican institutions in America, centralization was explicitly excluded from the ensemble of customs, laws, and ideas: "Many among us [in France] think that in the United States there is a climate of opinion which favors centralization of power in the hands of the President and the Congress. I submit that a contrary movement is obvious. The federal government, far from menacing the sovereignty of the states, continually tends to weaken, and the sovereignty of the Union alone is in peril. That is the situation at present." [4]

Centralization was envisaged not as a product of a universal egalitarian revolution, but as the product of peculiar historical circumstances which varied from country to country. Even concerning France, Tocqueville and Beaumont were hopeful in their joint prison report of 1833 that political life "will enter increasingly into action at the departmental level, and that administrative interests will increasingly tend to become localized." [5] In

[3] *Oeuvres* (M): *Démocratie*, I, 255.
[4] *Démocratie*, I, 412; see also 413ff.
[5] *Système pénitentiaire*, 175–176.

the *Démocratie* the permanence of provincial liberties and administrative decentralization in the whole English-speaking world seemed assured. Whatever the attacks on aristocracy in England, Tocqueville had failed to discover anyone who extended an attack to local liberty.[6]

In 1835, it was again Nassau Senior who served as the medium through whom Tocqueville became acquainted with a new tendency in English administration. Shortly after the publication of the *Démocratie,* Tocqueville requested a copy of the Poor Law Amendment Act of 1834 from Senior in order to prepare a paper on pauperism. Senior promptly complied, sending not only a copy of the act, but the famous report of the Royal Commission of Inquiry on the Poor Law, which preceded it, only mentioning in passing that he was the author of the bulk of both.[7] Probably no other English documents were so seminal to Tocqueville's thought.

The Poor Law Amendment Act was the first great step in the reform of local government following the Reform Bill of 1832. It was an attempt to relieve the growing burden of poor relief on the ratepaying class. The administrative reforms, as far as the Whig government was concerned, were more a stopgap reaction to the breakdown of parochial machinery than a generally accepted theory of centralization. Nevertheless it was a precedent-making innovation in English public administration. It provided for the election of local boards of guardians, with the franchise extending to all ratepaying occupiers. The boards of guardians operated in more convenient administrative units (unions of parishes), not in the historic ones. The guardians functioned through paid officials, striking at the principle of unpaid local offices. Finally, the administration of the law was put under a central commission operating by means of orders and inspection. In its limited sphere, the amendment was an attack on the aristocratic monopoly of administrative

---

[6] *Oeuvres* (M): *Démocratie*, I, 98.

[7] According to J.-P. Mayer (*Journeys to England,* 205n), Tocqueville's working library at the Château de Tocqueville contains a copy of *An Act for the Amendment and Better Administration of the Laws relating to the Poor in England and Wales* (London, 1834) bearing the inscription "M. de Tocqueville from W. N. Senior."

functions in local government. The basic administrative principles, central control, locally elected bodies, and paid officers had a discernible intellectual pedigree.

The attempt to revitalize local administration and responsibility while establishing central control for the national interest joined two strands of thought in the program of philosophical radicalism. The central board was the answer of those reformers who placed their hopes in scientific legislation to the loose framework of unsystematic and haphazard adjustment which had kept England suspicious of all central authority for over a century. Resting on the argument that centralization was necessary to deal with a national problem on a national basis in the face of widespread local maladministration, the Radicals had managed to win the support of the reform cabinet for its application in the new poor law. Senior and Edwin Chadwick were the two leading lights of the royal commission appointed in 1832. Chadwick had been Bentham's literary secretary in 1830, while the latter was engaged in writing his *Constitutional Code,* and succeeded in introducing many of Bentham's ideas into the Report of 1834 and the act that resulted from it. Senior became committed to the introduction of centralized inspection and control and was the chief author of both the report and act, although his chief goal in 1834 was the abolition, or at least the amelioration, of the economic problem.[8]

Another element of Benthamite thought went into the reform of the poor law. Bentham's *Constitutional Code* provided for sublegislatures elected by districts to vote laws of local interest as a complement to centralized ministries. Whether the inclusion of unpaid elected boards in the bill was a reflection of his principles or only a tactical move to cut down administrative expenses and political opposition,[9] the result bore a striking resemblance to Bentham's half elective and half administrative system. Above all

[8] See Webb, *English Poor Law History, Part II,* I, 90–100, and Marian Bowley, *Nassau Senior and Classical Economics* (London, 1937), 317ff.

[9] S. E. Finer, in *The Life and Times of Sir Edwin Chadwick* (London, 1952), 79, shows that Chadwick himself would have abolished local administration altogether but for the expense. See also Elie Halévy, *The Growth of Philosophic Radicalism,* transl. Mary Morris (New York, 1928), 431–432.

it was a new departure in executive control and a direct curtailment of the powers of the aristocracy in their role as justices of
the peace.

Tocqueville and Beaumont arrived in England at a moment
when the extension of the scope of poor-law administration was
very much an issue. They were immediately so struck by this combination of principles and by the apparent ease with which Parliament had acquiesced to them that they saw in administrative centralization the hidden corollary of the democratic revolution. After
a conversation with Reeve on poor-law and prison reform, Tocqueville noted: "Centralization, a democratic instinct; instinct of a
society which has succeeded in escaping from the individualistic
system of the Middle Ages. Preparation for despotism. Why is
centralization more suited to the habits of democracy? Great question to *dig into* in the third volume of my work, if I can integrate
it there. A *fundamental* question." [10] Soon after, he was uniting
the growth of democracy and centralization in his thought by such
expressions as "symptom of democracy and centralization." Centralization was no longer envisioned as a self-contained and historically inert phenomenon, but a dynamic, and all-enveloping
movement linked to the egalitarian process itself.

Toqueville found himself on the path which was to take him
on a lifelong study of the role of centralization in the development
of Western society. On this subject especially the *Démocratie*s of
1835 and 1840 are different works. Among his notes to the 1840
edition was the reminder to "admit my error" about some of the
implications of his earlier comments on centralization, while the
rough drafts cited England as conclusive evidence in favor of his
new theory. [11]

Meanwhile, alarmed by the "centralizing mania which has seized
the democratic party" [12] in England, Tocqueville anxiously raised

[10] *Oeuvres* (M): *Voyages Angleterre,* 49; see also p. 69.
[11] Yale Mss(T) C.V.k: copy of notes for the *Démocratie* of 1840, paq. 7, cahier 1,
p. 184; see also C.V.g: copy of rough drafts for the *Démocratie* of 1840, paq. 9,
cahier 2, pp. 43, 52–53.
[12] *Oeuvres* (M): *Voyages Angleterre,* 69, June 29, 1835.

the problem with his most enthusiastic Radical admirer, John Stuart Mill.[13] Mill had been hitherto more impressed by the jobbing, mismanagement and inefficiency of English local government than by the potential political dangers of centralization. The division of power between local and central administration seemed largely a question of relative efficiency. Ironically, had the two men met before Mill had read the *Démocratie,* the Frenchman might have judged that the Radicals were in danger of succumbing completely to pernicious Continental ideas. Mill revealed in his autobiography that it was Tocqueville who "led him to attach the utmost importance to the performance of as much of the collective business of society as can safely be so performed by the people themselves." [14] The *Démocratie*'s description of local government as a source of civic education and as a possible bulwark against the tyranny of the majority or of the central government placed the question of public administration in a new perspective.

Mill was not ready, however, to admit that England was in any real danger of a bureaucratic inundation, in spite of the new tendency toward centralization. He separated the antiaristocratic tendencies of the new poor law from the crushing of local government, insisting that "if democracy were *organized* in our parishes and counties so that it could manage the tasks of government, I am sure that we would leave them quite independent of the central government." [15] Tocqueville wondered if his Radical friends realized that the destruction of local government along with aristocratic abuses might be part of a basic democratic instinct.[16]

To both men this brief meeting had lasting significance. As early as his initial review of the *Démocratie* in October 1835, Mill carefully dissociated American municipal decentralization from

[13] *Voyages Angleterre,* 53–54, May 26, 1835.
[14] John Stuart Mill, *An Autobiography of John Stuart Mill* (New York, 1924), 134–138. See also Iris Wessel Mueller, *John Stuart Mill and French Thought* (Urbana, 1956), 160–162.
[15] *Oeuvres* (M): *Voyages Angleterre,* 53.
[16] For the development of this idea for the *Démocratie* see Yale Mss(T) C.V.k: copy of notes for the *Démocratie* of 1840, paq. 7, cahier 2, p. 27, Feb. 27, 1838.

aristocratically dominated English local government, while emphatically declaring his commitment to the small political unit
as a bulwark against despotism. He was still wrestling with the
problem of centralization when he wrote *On Liberty* and *Considerations on Representative Government* a generation later.[17]
Tocqueville in turn began to consider the principles behind reform,
especially poor-law administration, and to revise his estimate of
how the English, at least, were mitigating their innovations in
centralization by judicial control and elected local officers. Even
the poor law, he discovered on analysis, included the principles of
judicial control and the retention of a local inspectorate. In his
outline of the law Tocqueville, as usual, attempted to draw some
general conclusions: "Let us stop a moment to say a word about
this organization which is characteristic of the English race, and
which can be found in almost all the institutions created by it in
the New World. Three elements are mingled here:

1. Choice of the executive power
2. Election
3. Control by the judicial power." [18]

The three elements appeared to Tocqueville combined in a manner
which assured an active but not tyrannical administration, calling
into play the publicity of yearly reports, appeal to the courts, and
elected local officials.

When Tocqueville and Beaumont became aware that the new
poor law embodied more than simply centralized administration,
they saw a new principle of harmony between central control and
local participation, which opened exciting possibilities for adop-
tion by France. Poor-law administration seemed a timid system of

---

[17] See John Stuart Mill, "De Tocqueville on Democracy in America," *London
Review,* II (October 1835), 85–129; Mill, "Democracy in America," 1–4, 7; Mill
to Charles Dupont-White, April 6, 1860, *The Letters of John Stuart Mill,* ed. Hugh
S. R. Elliot (London, 1910), I, 234–235; and Mueller, *John Stuart Mill,* 236–238.

[18] *Oeuvres* (M): *Voyages Angleterre,* app. 1, section 3, "The Poor. Examination
of the Law of 14th August 1834," p. 230. This note is unfortunately not dated.
Internal evidence from it and from contiguous notes leads me to believe that it was
composed on or about June 1, 1835, at the same time that Tocqueville was investigating the English judicial system.

"mixed centralization" quite unanalogous to "centralization as we know it in France." It was nothing less than the model of English genius. Tocqueville, in his last note on centralization in England, concluded: "Find a means: 1. of rendering the centralizing power subject to publicity; 2. of having its *local* decisions executed by *elected* authorities, and I will let you extend the sphere of its power as much as you wish . . ." [19] In Beaumont's *L'Irlande,* the act of 1834 was the perfect adjustment of Whig England to the democratic and centralizing demands of the epoch: "Is it not fortunate," wrote Beaumont, "that a people who must reform its institutions can give the central power enough force to slowly accomplish its task, while withholding enough power to avoid tyranny." [20]

Their views of centralization in England had come full circle. Initially the new poor law seemed only a symptom of centralization opposed to the spirit of local liberty and aristocratic diversity. This inference eventually merged with Tocqueville's extrapolation of French development in the *Démocratie* and the *Ancien Régime.* The poor law itself, however, was a catalyst which triggered a second revolution in Tocqueville's thought. A new stage of interpretation came with further study of the law itself and with Mill's caution that England was far from moving toward massive centralization.[21] In a new context it pointed to an answer as well as to a problem of universal significance. Having come to England to complete their study of the egalitarian revolution, they were now grappling with an administrative revolution.

The reassessment of the political role of the great estates and of the Poor Law Amendment Act of 1834 in England entailed a long second look at the system of public administration. Early in June,

---

[19] *Oeuvres* (M): *Voyages Angleterre,* 84.

[20] *L'Irlande,* II, 309. The evolution of their thinking on the administration of a penitentiary system in France shows the effect of the English visit on their principles of public administration. Compare *Système pénitentiaire,* 174ff, and Tocqueville's later report to the Chamber of Deputies on a law to reform French prisons, in *Oeuvres* (B), IX, 369–371.

[21] Nassau Senior does not seem to have introduced his two visitors to Edwin Chadwick. Perhaps he feared their reaction to the very embodiment of the *esprit administratif* in England.

midway in the journey, a long conversation with a young London Radical named Sutton Sharpe gave Tocqueville a new conception of the myriad of English local authorities.[22] The churchwardens, surveyors of the highways, constables, and overseers of the poor, all officers of the parish; the freemen, aldermen, and mayors of the municipal corporations; the lord lieutenant and high sheriff of the county; the local acts' commissioners and the turnpike trustees, were all now ranged beside the justices of the peace. Sharpe used the words "in general" so often in his attempts to precisely describe an office or function that Tocqueville remarked in the margin of his notes, "I must say once and for all that the words *in general* are always understood in questions and answers. The exceptions are *always* very numerous."[23]

Naturally the number and diversity of English local officials was an obvious contrast with the picture of 1833. But there was one general principle which was imparted to Tocqueville amidst the bewildering sequence. Every time Sharpe was asked about the means for controlling an authority, of settling matters of competence, or of removing an official, he referred Tocqueville to judicial procedures which could be undertaken by any individual. Every decision led back to the courts. Tocqueville commented further in the margin of his notes: "Administrative action by the judicial power, *its growing importance in my eyes.*"

Whether it was the sudden release from the London social round or simply the stimulus of a new environment, the trip to Birmingham again crystallized Tocqueville and Beaumont's views on a

[22] Yale Mss(T) C.XI.b: "Organisation politique," conversation with Sharpe, June 8, 1835. Sharpe also outlined the attack on some of the justices' functions which had taken place since 1825. This 18-page document is missing from both the Beaumont and Mayer editions of Tocqueville's *Voyages.* Sutton Sharpe (1797–1843) was a London Radical in close contact with the French literary world. A member of the London Ballot Union agitating for the secret ballot, and a close friend of the Grotes, he was particularly interested in judicial reform. Beaumont and Tocqueville met Sharpe through a letter of introduction from J. Taschereau. See Doris Gunnell, *Sutton Sharpe et ses amis français, avec des lettres inédites* (Paris, 1925), 225.

[23] Yale Mss(T) C.XI.b: "Organisation politique," 1.

vital point. Stimulated by the vigor and efficiency of Birmingham's municipal services, they looked more closely into the details of English local government and the notes on administration overshadowed even the observations on industrialization. Tocqueville plunged into William Hutton's *History of Birmingham,* investigated reports on the assessment of the poor rate, and studied an act of May 23, 1828, which prescribed the functions of the street commissioners of Birmingham.[24] One of the longest entries made on the journey was a summary of this local act. Nothing seemed more significant than the provisions for summary proceedings before a justice of the peace in instances of official malfeasance, the directing of appeals against assessments through quarter sessions, and the direct role of the courts at Westminster in adjudicating specified actions against the commissioners.

Before he left the city he hastily recorded a whole set of new "Ideas concerning Centralization and the Introduction of the Judicial Power into the Administration." There was the evident excitement of one who has discovered a hidden disease and a possible cure almost simultaneously. The note began: "Concerning the introduction of judicial power into the administration. Concerning its necessity. The different means used by peoples to introduce it. The subject needs a *book,* not a chapter, to cover it, and one of the most important books imaginable. The necessity of introducing the judicial power into the administration is one of those *central* ideas to which I am led by all my investigations concerning the sources of political liberty."[25]

Two months in London and two weeks in the North did not really allow Tocqueville time to study the functioning of the judiciary or any local body in detail, but without attempting to

---

[24] See Hutton, *A History of Birmingham* (Birmingham, 1781; 6th ed., 1835), and Tocqueville, *Journeys to England,* 100–103. See also Yale Mss(B) C.X.l: *L'Irlande,* notes, "Birmingham." The street commissioners of Birmingham were too efficient to be typical of municipal government in England in 1835. Tocqueville also read reports of the corporation commissioners of Liverpool (see *Oeuvres* (B), VIII, 369).

[25] *Oeuvres* (M): *Voyages Angleterre,* 68, June 29, 1835.

make a comparative study of municipal administrations he was certain that he possessed general institutional principles which were thriving in the Old World as well as the New. The government of Birmingham recalled America no less than did her bustling economy. "The Americans must be *re-examined* for the same question," he wrote in the margin of his discussion of judicial power, "Analogous principles *perhaps* more simple and rational." This English and American judicial control had to be introduced to the Continent as the *"general principle of free peoples."* [26]

In one way, judicial control in England was an even more valuable example than the American system. America was decentralized and free. Its legal and political institutions were less encumbered by the weight of centuries of haphazard development. But much of America's ability to enjoy local self-government and the political benefits of its judicial system could be attributed, as Tocqueville himself had often done, to her uniquely isolated condition. Political life in America seemed to flourish at the expense of her foreign policy and status as a world power. England was not only free, but was also a great power with an uncontested world empire and naval pre-eminence. The possibility of a combination of power and political liberty and the conviction that they were causally related were to become one of the cornerstones of Tocqueville's political faith.

Toward the end of the journey he attempted to capture the combination of strength and freedom in a single paragraph. "Principle of *centralization* and principle of *election of local authorities:* principles in direct opposition. *Introduction of Fines* as administrative methods; *agency of the tribunals,* intervention of *third parties:* the only way of combining the two principles to some extent, since the first is essential to the power and existence of the State, the second to its prosperity and liberty. England has found no other secret. The whole future of free institutions in France depends on the application of these same ideas to the genius of our laws." [27]

[26] *Voyages Angleterre,* 70.
[27] *Voyages Angleterre,* 84.

Tocqueville's traveling companion was destined to assume the task of presenting these ideas to their fellow countrymen. In *L'Irlande* (1839), Beaumont contrasted the chaos of administrative bodies in England with the rational hierarchy of authorities in France.[28] The English court system, centered in Westminster, generally formed the only network of appeals, outside the general legislative control of Parliament, for determining the competence and limits of actions by local or statutory authorities. Beaumont, modifying Montesquieu's theory of the functional separation of powers in the English constitution, emphasized the mixture of administrative and judicial functions and the resulting turn given public administration by the judicial frame of mind. The result was a profound difference in conceptions of administration in England and France. The French system led to prescriptive decisions from Paris. The Westminster courts, even in their administrative capacities, could act only on the legal initiative of an interested party. A ratepayer illegally assessed, or a member of a municipal corporation denied his voting privilege, could within the process prescribed by common law, without administrative formalities, carry his claim to the regular courts.

In his analysis Beaumont minimized two important assumptions of the system: that the society must contain numerous individuals wealthy enough to assume the burden of litigation, and that they be habituated to its frequent use. Actually, the expense of the process discouraged all but the most obstinate and opulent plaintiffs.[29] The expense, delay, and uncertainty of the whole system of appeals was perhaps as much a depressant to the legal activity of the lower classes as it was a rare stimulant to the initiative and independence of the prosperous. For Tocqueville and Beaumont, however, both the peculiar disadvantages of English judicial practices and those inherent in the very nature of the system were lesser considerations. In his "deduction of ideas" in 1835 Tocqueville

[28] I, 302–307.
[29] See Webb, *Statutory Authorities,* 393ff, and David Roberts, *Victorian Origins of the British Welfare State* (New Haven, 1960), 17.

repeatedly returned to the judiciary as something besides an impartial institution for settling disputes and protecting the individual against the abuse of public office. The courts threw the light of the open hearing on administrative decisions, affording an arena for endless individual action, whether to make the administrative power act or to guarantee against its excesses.

Beginning with the process of public administration Tocqueville, as usual, moved to the spirit of administration, and then to the spirit of society. Here he saw a profound gulf separating England and France. The English spirit, its laws, habits, and customs rebelled against the natural tendency of the age toward bureaucratic centralization. Regardless of the unique historical circumstances that produced it and the chaotic complexity that hindered it, the English conception of society as reflected in its administrative procedure was compatible with the existence of political liberty. Above all, it alone was "capable of making citizens, or even men." [30]

In the French administrative process Tocqueville saw the outstanding expression of a tendency which threatened to permeate every corner of society, engulfing it in a web of small, complicated, inescapable, and uniform rules. The bureaucratic spirit sought to guide and guarantee its citizens without primary concern for their participation in decision making. At the center of the bureaucratic society lay the exemption of administrative litigation from the ordinary courts. This *justice reservée,* which he viewed as the most significant comparative feature of *droit administratif* in France, impeded the citizen, in his individual capacity, from proceeding against administrative actions.

Tocqueville was one day to warn against the concept of *justice reservée* in the *Démocratie,* the Academy, and the Chamber of Deputies, citing in support of his position the overwhelming sentiment in the English-speaking world that the French administrative system was ultimately incompatible with political liberty. [31] He made

---

[30] *Oeuvres* (M): *Voyages Angleterre,* 69.
[31] See *Moniteur,* April 20, 1843, 851; *Oeuvres* (B), IX, 71–74; and *Oeuvres* (M): *Démocratie,* II, 314–315.

no attempt, however, to conduct a broad legislative assault upon *droit administratif* in France. This was partly due to his belated realization that the famous Article 75 of the Constitution of the year VIII, making legal proceedings against any official contingent on the express permission of the Council of State, was in practice modified after 1815 by the growth of judge-made law and case precedents. Executive discretion in most proceedings became almost a legal fiction. During the latter part of the July Monarchy and the Second Republic *droit administratif* did not capitalize on the potentialities for arbitrary action in the original Napoleonic system. After Louis Napoleon's seizure of power, however, Tocqueville's basic political distrust of the French administrative system came to the fore again. The introduction of secret administrative political trials and the continuous use of Article 75 in the early years of the Second Empire formed the contemporary setting for his search for the roots of administrative despotism in the *Ancien Régime*.[32]

Equally as significant was the influence of Tocqueville's emphatic separation of French and English administrative principles on A. V. Dicey, and through Dicey on the development of comparative constitutional theory in England. "The nature and the very existence of *droit administratif*," declared Dicey in his *Law of the Constitution* in 1885, "has been first revealed to many Englishmen, as certainly to the present writer, through the writings of Alexis de Tocqueville."[33] For Dicey, the *Démocratie* and the *Ancien Régime* pointed to a fundamental difference between England and France of the conceptions and rules that dominated the relations of administrative authorities and individual citizens. Although he later modified much that he had taken from Tocqueville, in order to account for the administrative evolution of both countries toward the end of the century, Dicey retained Tocqueville's fundamental dualism through the last revision of his work, in 1908.

---

[32] Tocqueville and Senior, *Correspondence and Conversations,* II, 19–20, conversation of January 8, 1852. See also A. V. Dicey, *Introduction to the Study of the Law of the Constitution,* 10th ed. (London, 1959), 359–360.

[33] Sixth ed. (London, 1902), 490.

Dicey himself only gradually became aware of the extent to which the socially responsible state required the efficiency of new administrative processes as well as of politically responsive citizens. Tocqueville was never able to operate in a context where political liberty was the assumed framework within which the balance of administrative discretion and individual rights could be adjusted. There was little in the evolution of France before 1859 to weaken his conviction about the political liability of the combination of administrative centralization and the French judicial system.

The growth of administrative law in England and the progressive acceptance of the principles of judicial autonomy and of the state's liability toward individual citizens in France has tended to make the two systems converge and has filled the juridical abyss which Tocqueville envisioned in 1835. It is still possible to argue with a recent commentary that "however nearly the French and English systems approach each other in practice, the one seeks to afford remedies for illegal administrative action, whereas the other hopes by setting up standards of conduct and by deterrent action to ensure that remedies will not be needed." [34] But if Tocqueville were to make his comparative analysis today, he might well emphasize the general concordance on both sides of the Channel concerning the rule of law as opposed to more fundamentally divergent concepts elsewhere in the world. He was less concerned with specific differences in the judicial process than with those elements which were empirically compatible with a free society. Political liberty seemed to him a precarious venture where there was no appetite for the intervention of an independent judiciary in the political realm—"the most salient feature of a free people."

The English journey of 1835 was something more than a harvest of new ideas. The observations on industrialism, centralization, and judicial intervention were really the residues of a profound psy-

---

[34] F. H. Lawson, "Dicey Revisited," *Political Studies,* VII (1959), 126; this is a vindication of Dicey's (and, to an extent Tocqueville's) conception of *droit administratif* in France in its historical context.

chological experience. The actuality of political life in England
and the sheer multiplicity of human activity evoked from Tocqueville and Beaumont a response that could only be impressionistically
recorded. "The spirit of English legislation," wrote Tocqueville,
was

an incomprehensible mixture . . . of innovation and of routine, which
perfects the details of laws without noticing their principles . . . which
exhausts its skill in mending, and does not create except, so to say, without knowing it and by chance; the most restless for improvement and
the well-being of society, but the least systematic seeker for these things;
the most impatient and the most patient; the most clear-sighted and the
blindest; the most powerful in some things, and the weakest and most
embarrassed in some others; which keeps eighty million people under
its obedience three thousand leagues away, and does not know how to get
out of the smallest administrative difficulties; which excels at taking
advantage of the present, but does not know how to foresee the future.
Who can find a word to explain all these anomalies?[35]

The spirit of individuality seemed haphazardly combined with
the ability to form associations together for every purpose. Even
more bewilderingly, these Englishmen combined two tendencies
which appeared contrary to Tocqueville: the spirit of association
and the spirit of exclusion. The first was exemplified in the endless
pooling of efforts to attain ends which "in France we would never
think of approaching in this way. There are associations to further
science, politics, pleasure, business." On the other hand, how could
the spirit of exclusion be so highly developed in the same people
and so often combined in the same organization? "Example, a club:
what better example of association than the union of individuals
who form the club? What more exclusive than the corporate personality represented by a club? The same applies to almost all
civil and political associations, the corporations . . ."[36] Beaumont
was equally surprised and amused at how the Tories, who had

---

[35] Tocqueville, *Journeys to England*, 82–83. See also Yale Mss(B) C.X.3: *L'Irlande*,
notes, "Caractère anglais," May 20 [1835].
[36] Tocqueville, *Journeys to England*, 88. See also Yale Mss(B) C.X.3: *L'Irlande*,
notes, paq. "Associations politiques et civiles."

been so antagonistic to political associations a few years before, were mobilizing for the postreform era more quickly and efficiently than the Radicals in forming conservative societies throughout England. Without fully realizing it the two had stumbled on one of the most important and novel processes of the era—the conversion of social clubs into the structural cells of local political parties. In the words of a recent historian, "In both the main parties of the period, the provision of a club as a social bond of union was inextricably entwined with the organization of central machinery for the supervision of the register and the conduct of elections." [37] It was the reaction of English political life to the fluid electoral situation created by the first Reform Bill.

Tocqueville was firmly convinced that the absence of "the spirit of association" was one of the greatest drawbacks of the French political system. He had already declared in the *Démocratie* (1835) that the American habit of association as a means of persuasion rather than of direct action was not widely held on the Continent. He emphasized the danger of importing an unrestricted right of political association into France. In the second part of the *Démocratie* (1840) he linked the exercise of free political life more intimately to the spirit of association. It was not really possible to separate political and civil associations. No society could hope to achieve a continual organization of scientific, industrial, or intellectual endeavor without the political activity that generalized the habit and taste for common action. The future of liberty and of civilization itself required that the art of association be developed and perfected "as rapidly as the extension of the equality of conditions." If, even after England, Tocqueville still hesitated to grant the political expediency of an absolute right to political association, the whole weight of the argument had shifted. The heavier and more continuous the restrictions on such a right, the greater would be the chances of permanently maiming the society. "Taking the

[37] Norman Gash, *Politics in the Age of Peel: A Study in the New Technique of Parliamentary Representation, 1830–1850* (London, 1953), 394.

whole life of a people," he concluded, it would be easy "to demonstrate that freedom of political association is favorable to the well-being and even to the tranquillity of its citizens." [38]

The raucous public meetings where Tocqueville had once observed the degrading saturnalia of English liberty and heard the rumble of revolution were accepted after 1835 as the very lifeblood of her politics. In France, Beaumont noted, a parliamentarian spoke to sway the Chamber of Deputies, and succeeded or failed within its confines. His English counterpart spoke to Parliament, but for the public. As political power was awarded on the hustings, speeches were always directed primarily toward it, and at every public meeting an Englishman learned the use of his political rights and accumulated a store of political habits.

The frequency of political rallies, however, varied with events and elections. In one institution, the parish vestry, Tocqueville and Beaumont noted the continuous personal confrontation between all the members of the community, regardless of the great social distance between them. "One must go to the meetings of a Vestry," wrote Beaumont,

to judge what extraordinary liberty can be joined to inequality. One can see with what independence of language the most obscure English citizen expresses himself against the lord before whom he will bow presently. He is not his equal, of course, but within the limits of his rights he is as free, and he is fully aware of it. His right is that of discussing the interests of the parish and this right he exercises not only freely but with a propriety and, sometimes, an ability which is surprising in an orator whose blackened hands and coarse clothes declare him to be an artisan or a man of the lowest class. The ensemble of English institutions is doubtless an aristocratic government, but there is not a parish in England which does not constitute a free republic.[39]

[38] *Oeuvres* (M): *Démocratie,* II, 117ff.

[39] Beaumont, *L'Irlande,* I, 295–296. See also Yale Mss(B) C.X.3: *L'Irlande,* notes, "Discussion parlementaire—Publicité," May 19, 1837. Another note on a political trades-union meeting commented, "An excellent school for liberty" (*ibid.,* July 26, 1837).

The parish, then, was the fundamental unit of public participation, the center of a multitude of interests vital to everyone in the community. For Tocqueville it was a complete democracy at the base of the social edifice.[40] When Beaumont later declared in *L'Irlande* that the democratic parish had never submitted to a conqueror, he was not just turning a phrase. He and Tocqueville had adopted a whole theory of English political development revolving around the parish. Tocqueville felt that there might be a historical explanation for the tremendous disparity of basic principles which seemed to inform different English institutions. He accounted for England's aristocratic and democratic constituents in terms of "Saxon" and "Norman" institutions. The Saxon principle was basically the democratic principle and all that was "democratic in English society dates from that time." [41] This accounted for the foundation of the parishes and the hundreds on the basis of a common representation of interests. The Normans, that is, the county magistrates, had thrown a blanket of absolute power over the democratic substratum without destroying it, and now of course a renaissance of the Saxon-democratic principle was at hand with the passage of the Reform Bill.

What is significant is not a key to English history, to which Tocqueville and Beaumont made only brief reference in their works, but the depth to which they had been impressed by this unexpected vitality on the most inconspicuous level of the English polity in an aristocratic society. The observed activity and the antiquity of the parish seemed to testify to a historic connection. The Saxon principle served to explain why England found accessible the institutions and habits by which it could absorb the shock of electoral reform with relative ease. The universality and the continuity of political life were thus integrated into Tocqueville and Beaumont's analysis.

Tocqueville's later rediscovery of the parish as a political unit on

[40] Yale Mss(T) C.XI.b: "Organisation politique," conversation with Sharpe, June 8, 1835.
[41] Yale Mss(B) C.X.5: *L'Irlande,* notes, paq. "Eléments saxons et normands—Idée Générale: Tocqueville disait hier . . ." and "Eléments saxons et normands . . ." See also Beaumont, *L'Irlande,* I, 397n.

the Continent as well was to alter his conception of the development of political life in Europe. The Introduction to the *Démocratie* (1835) had pictured a social condition where men were bound to each other by force and faith as lord and vassal, seigneur and serf. From this politically inert beginning, the progressive subdivision of political power and its increasing complexity and vigor constituted a smooth historical pattern. Far different was to be the depiction of political life in his *Ancien Régime,* where the diversity, activity, and balance of medieval social classes constituted the healthy polity from which emerged a France alternating politically between somnambulance and epilepsy.

It may have been comforting to believe that with such a firm historical root as the parish, English political life and democratic forms were not just recently introduced to each other. Unfortunately, Tocqueville and Beaumont's encounter with parish government deceived them, for it occurred in the one area in England where the parish was most democratic and vigorous. They were led astray on two important points: the historical antiquity of parish democracy (not to mention the vestry meeting as a known institution) and its role as the cell of local government in England. Their personal observations and verbal sources were probably confined to the London area,[42] and when, in customary fashion, Tocqueville later asked Henry Reeve to supply information on the structure and function of the parish unit, he complied with a description of a metropolitan parish. It is no wonder that Tocqueville wrote to Reeve of the "complete confirmation of my ideas in this matter. I conceived them during my stay in England and feel immense pleasure in discovering that all my first impressions were right."[43]

[42] See Yale Mss(T) C.XI.b: "Organisation politique," conversation with Sharpe, June 8, 1835. Sharpe's only specific citation was the parish of St. Marylebone (written "Mary-le bonne" by Tocqueville), and no historical data were supplied. See also F. H. W. Sheppard, *Local Government in St. Marylebone, 1688–1835* (London, 1958).

[43] Letter of April 17, 1836, *Oeuvres* (M): *Corr. angl.,* I. Tocqueville received a letter on the parish, dated March 29, 1836, from a resident of Hampstead, almost certainly Reeve; it was based on St. Andrews, Holborn, in London, and referred to

The metropolitan parishes in England had been given a new democratic structure by Hobhouse's Act in 1831. It had included among the parochial electors every person, male or female, who paid rates, however low the assessment. It provided for annual elections and one vote per ratepayer by ballot. Projecting the re-formed London parish on all of England, it is no wonder that Tocqueville wrote to Reeve, "You have only to generalize and extend what we must create," or that Beaumont concluded of the vestry meeting, that the sentiment of the majority was law there.[44]

Historically, neither the London parishes nor the parish struc-ture elsewhere in England merited the pure democratic pedigree Tocqueville and Beaumont assigned to them. Beaumont, in *L'Irlande,* outlined the functions, structure, and scope of parish government in terms that were already outdated in 1835. He listed the extensive vestry functions in poor relief just when they had ceased to exist. It was in fact the administrative and economic breakdown of the parishes under the burden of the Elizabethan poor law which had led to the removal of its most important func-tion. Finally, Beaumont had no idea of how often the participants in the open vestry, aided by the Stourges-Bourne acts (1818–19), talked, shouted, and polled parish administrations to death.

The divergent conclusions which could be drawn from the role of the parish in the English constitution is remarkably illustrated by John Stuart Mill's review of the *Démocratie* in October 1835. Combining the Radical attack on mismanagement in English local government with Tocqueville's point of departure for America, he underscored the spontaneous generation and complete original-ity of the New England township. The justice-dominated "feudal" English rural parish bore absolutely no relation to the latter, and the democratic forms of the large open vestries were usually the

---

"democratic" parish rates and "aristocratic" county rates (Yale Mss(T) C.V.a: copy of notes for the *Démocratie* of 1840, paq. 8, p. 41).

[44] Tocqueville to Reeve, April 17, 1836, *Oeuvres* (M): *Corr. angl.,* I; Beaumont, *L'Irlande,* I, 295. Tocqueville gathered from Sharpe only that the select vestry was the representative principle applied to parishes which were too large for the open vestry.

mask for a jobbing oligarchy. Rather than being the root of public life, the parochial system proved to Mill that in England it would be useless to call "upon the people themselves to bestow habitually any larger share of attention on municipal management than is implied in the periodical election of a representative body." [45] For Mill, the greatest public service which the parish could perform was to dissolve quietly into the new Poor Law "unions" and their popularly elected boards of guardians. The old parish unit was not destined to be the nucleus of local government in England.

Tocqueville and Beaumont naturally assumed that the reform movement spreading to other areas of local government in England was but "an extension of the democratic parish principle." [46] They left England just too early to observe the transformation of the municipal corporations, but they were well aware of the nature and intent of the reform. The Municipal Corporations Act of 1835 abolished the self-electing bodies, which Tocqueville condemned as a dangerous aristocratic institution, giving only the appearance of popular government. Second, although it aimed at systematizing the structure of English municipal government, it was untainted by any touch of centralization or even coordination in the manner of the Poor Law Amendment Act. When at the end of 1835 municipal elections took place under the new law, Tocqueville and Beaumont, who were back in France, saw it as one more stride in the great democratic resurgence in English local government, along the lines of deep-rooted decentralist habits. [47]

A momentous shift had occurred in Tocqueville's attitude toward local government from the time when he believed the justices of the peace to be the sole administrators of the country. At least a portion of English institutions seemed much more democratic than those of France. The "republican" element in the English constitution, alluded to by Beaumont in his description of the parish,

---

[45] "De Tocqueville on Democracy in America," 101.

[46] Yale Mss(B) C.X.5: *L'Irlande*, notes, "Réforme des bourgs et des corporons municipales," conversation with George [Cornewall] Lewis, London, June 18 [1835].

[47] Tocqueville to Senior, Jan. 27, 1836, *Correspondence and Conversations*, I, 15.

became the means by which they resolved the problem of the long coexistence of democratic and aristocratic elements in English society. One of Beaumont's notes, entitled "République," made the direction of their thought clear. The proximity of a free republic to a free aristocracy was the central point: "An aristocracy is nearer to a republic; a monarchy to despotism." The element of political participation outside parliamentary elections was the decisive factor to the two travelers. An aristocracy employing the political potential of the parish meeting and the court system to bring the masses indirectly into the "conduct of affairs" caused "the principles of government and the habits of liberty to enter into the masses." [48]

Tocqueville went even further. The republican element of the English political system became his chief point of contrast with Switzerland when he made a tour of that country in the summer of 1836. "I will not compare Switzerland to the United States," he wrote, "but to Great Britain, and I will say that when one examines or even only travels through the two countries, astonishing differences between them can be observed. All in all the kingdom of England seems much more republican than the Swiss Republic." He saw the difference in both the institutions and the customs, in the revolutionary abuses made by the Swiss of the free institutions he had observed in England. The entire practice of self-government in Switzerland was sporadic and intermittent, and Tocqueville missed "that thirst for political rights, that need to participate in public affairs which seems to torment the English incessantly." [49]

The more he discovered of the republican element in the bosom of the English aristocracy the more he was inclined to regard the development of civic spirit in the Anglo-American world as an unbroken evolutionary process. The *Démocratie* of 1840 no longer assigned so much importance to the isolated condition of the Amer-

---

[48] Yale Mss(B) C.X.1: *L'Irlande*, notes.

[49] *Oeuvres* (M): *Voyages Angleterre*, "Voyage en Suisse" (1836), 175–176. The whole complex of ideas on "republican England" and parish democracy may have been first suggested to them by a reading of A. de Staël-Holstein's *Lettres sur l'Angleterre* (Paris, 1825), letter 7.

ican colonists in the growth of civic institutions, and now placed inherited liberty at the American point of departure: "Thus among the Americans it is freedom that is old; equality is of comparatively modern date." [50]

In England, Tocqueville found himself identifying with political society in a way he never found possible in his own country. The second voyage to England marked the moment of real optimism in his prognosis for a free democratic evolution in Western civilization. Under the spell of English political institutions, he hoped that the transition to democracy might be easier and more lasting than he had so far believed. It was the Radicals who really fired the enthusiasm of the French liberal. Their political methods affected him far more than their ideas. Whatever verbal similarities there were between English Radicals and French democrats, as political men they were worlds apart. "Everything I have heard said among [English] Radicals," he wrote, "is filled with real respect for the principle in whose name they act. I have never observed them wishing to impose on the nation a political condition (even for its own good) not of its own choice. The whole question is to win the majority and I have never noticed the idea of doing it other than by legal methods." [51]

He also found a deep, though not superstitious, respect for property among the Radicals, and a conviction, which Tocqueville deeply shared, that this was the primary basis of a civilized society. Enthusiastic sectarians abounded, and where the *esprit philosophique* was strongest, there was still a firm belief in the political necessity of religion and a real respect for it. Among the French counterparts of the Radicals, he saw scorn for law in practice and theory, an anti-Christian bias, and the most "antisocial" philosophic doctrines.

A last difference which Tocqueville perceived best shows what put him at ease with both democrat and aristocrat in England.

[50] *Oeuvres* (M): *Démocratie,* II, 305.

[51] *Journeys to England,* 86. See also Yale Mss(B) C.X.3: *L'Irlande,* notes, paqs. "Réforme," "Radicaux," May 29 [1835].

The Radical leaders in England were, in general, financially secure ("wealth having been until now the necessary preliminary to everything"), well versed in economics, history, and politics, and though their demeanor was not aristocratic, "it is clear that they are *gentlemen*." Turning to France, Tocqueville found the radical almost always impoverished, ignorant of political science, respectful only of force, and dealing in empty generalizations.

In England he could see himself allied to a serious reform group. He moved in its political milieu with a balance which he was never to strike in his own land. "In brief," he concluded, "at present I think that an enlightened man of good sense and good will would be a Radical in England. I have never met these three qualities together in a French radical." It is no accident that Tocqueville in his *Démocratie* (1840) declared that the utilitarian ethic of enlightened self-interest was the most suitable moral philosophy of contemporary civilization, and that whatever its imperfections it was indispensable in a democratic age.[52]

Before he left England, Tocqueville confessed to Mill that he had arrived hostile to the "democratic party" because of developments in France. The longer he remained in England the more he agreed with the goal of the English Radicals, which was legally and intellectually to place the majority of citizens in a condition of being able to govern. "I am myself a democrat in this sense," he wrote.[53] He chose to side with democratic liberty because of its promise of universal extension and because it alone might prevail in the new world. It universalized that republican element of common participation in political life which was the supreme good of liberty.

That he did not see this notion of liberty fully triumphant yet in England did not greatly disturb Tocqueville, since the functioning of political processes in England was already far beyond the level of any of its Continental neighbors. When Beaumont con-

---

[52] See Yale Mss(T) C.V.k: copy of notes for the *Démocratie* of 1840, paq. 7, cahier 1, p. 184; *Oeuvres* (M): *Démocratie*, II, 127, and *Corr. Gobineau*, Sept. 5, 1843.

[53] Tocqueville to Mill [June 1835], *Oeuvres* (M): *Corr. angl.*, I, 294.

firmed in his voyage of 1837 what both had already suspected in 1835, that the aristocracy had stemmed the reforming tide, it did not occur to either that this was a setback to the cause of European liberty.

What most excited Tocqueville in England was no longer the drama of aristocracy besieged or democracy on the march, but the unity, activity, and prosperity created by political liberty. The mutual exclusiveness of "aristocracy" or "democracy" as fundamental principles of society became muted before the spectacle of political liberty. The note on which he concluded his trip was both a testimony to what he had witnessed and a rededication of his goals. At no other point, except perhaps in the *Ancien Régime,* did his fervor for liberty reach a similar pitch. After an intense discussion with Beaumont, Tocqueville epitomized his voyage: "Liberty in the political world holds the same place as the atmosphere in the physical. The earth is filled with a multitude of beings differently constituted, but all live and prosper. Alter the conditions of the atmosphere and they suffer. Put them elsewhere and they die . . . Change your laws, vary your customs, alter your beliefs, corrupt your forms; if you come to that point where man has full liberty to take actions which are not bad in themselves and the certainty of enjoying the consequences of these actions you will achieve your goal. It is single, the means are many." [54]

When Tocqueville and Beaumont left England early in July 1835, it marked the end of the fullest experience of their lives. More than twenty years later Tocqueville vividly recalled to Beaumont how weeks had passed before his agitated mind became calm enough to permit him to resume an ordinary existence. But the excitement of England left more than a painful loneliness in its wake. No comparable period, except the visit to New England four years earlier, could compare with it for the sheer outpouring of ideas which were to dominate their thought and action. The

[54] *Journeys to England,* 117. Beaumont's parallel note also referred to the "atmosphere of liberty" in England (see Yale Mss(B) C.X.5: *L'Irlande,* notes, paqs. "Liberté en général-Despotisme, Idée générale," Dublin, July 8 [1835].

creation of local institutions and a broader political role for the
judiciary were more than ever integral parts of their political program. In 1848, as members of the drafting committee of the Second
Republic's constitution, Tocqueville and Beaumont helped to salvage the principle of the irremovability of judges from the wreckage
of the July Monarchy, and Beaumont wrote the articles on the
Court of Appeals. By the end of his life Tocqueville was also
regarded as the chief inspiration of the decentralist movement in
France.[55]

Tocqueville's notes of 1835 on decentralization and on the political bases of power and liberty were the most eloquent testimony
of the impact of England, but he made no effort to summarize his
journey as he had done in 1833, or to rework and publish his observations. It was left to his traveling companion to include a
portion of the notes on England in the posthumous edition of
Tocqueville's works. In a sense Beaumont was repaying a courtesy,
for Tocqueville's abstinence was probably due in part to a reluctance to encroach on his friend's territory. Tocqueville released
nothing to the public which would interfere with Beaumont's
study of England and Ireland.

There was another significant reason for Tocqueville's hesitation
to act as the prophet and analyst of English society. Basically he
found himself much further from a single point of departure in
1835 than in 1833. The more he traveled the greater did the confusion of contrary tendencies in English development become, and
the visit to the North had definitely shattered the older image of
aristocracy that he held in 1833. Suppressing a rumor that he intended to write a book about England, he wrote to Count Louis
Molé soon after his return:

I think I have gathered in England a certain number of new thoughts
which could be useful to me one day; but I never had the notion of
writing on the country I was traversing. I add that if I had had this

---

[55] See Yale Mss(B) D.IV.1: notes for the Committee of the Constitution of 1848;
Tocqueville, *Souvenirs,* 172; and [J. S. Mill], "Centralisation," *Edinburgh Review,*
CXV (April 1862), 325.

thought in starting out, I could not have returned with it. One must be gifted with a great philosophical impertinence to conceive oneself able to judge England in six months. One year always appeared to me much too short a time to be able to suitably judge the United States; and it is infinitely easier to acquire clear and precise notions of the American Union than of Great Britain. In America all the laws develop more or less from the same thought. All society, so to speak, is based on a single fact; everything unrolls from a single principle. One could compare America to a great forest pierced by a multitude of straight roads which end in the same place. It is only a question of reaching the hub, and all is revealed in a single glance. But in England the roads intersect, and it is only by following each one that one can get a clear idea of the whole.[56]

Beaumont, also, feared to tread heavily on the unending paths of the British social state, and in his *L'Irlande* apologized for any errors on the British constitution, referring to it only in relation to the problems of Ireland. Perhaps what most puzzled Tocqueville and Beaumont was the unsystematic nature of the revolution in English local government. In America, and especially in France, they had begun to think of the democratic revolution as a movement toward systematization and rationalization in laws and institutions as well as toward a new basis of popular sovereignty. English reform with its centralizing Poor Law Amendment Act and decentralizing Municipal Corporations Act was hopelessly chaotic. New principles replaced old, but the heterogenous complex of overlapping local authorities was not straightened out into any systematic organization. Responding to this haphazard revolution Tocqueville and Beaumont were at least agreed in sensing a profound alteration in local government along the lines of elective representation and a franchise extending to all who were taxed for public services.

There is an irony in their enthusiasm for the robust English polity. When, in 1922, almost a century after the journey, Sidney and Beatrice Webb wanted to epitomize the spirit of English local

[56] Letter of August 1835, *Oeuvres* (B), VII. He was adding his 1833 journey as well as the month in Ireland.

government in 1835, they quoted not Tocqueville's notes on England, but his later autopsy of the narrowly bourgeois government of the July Monarchy.[57] Where the Webbs saw middle-class mentality as supreme on both sides of the Channel, Tocqueville, when he wrote the passage they cited, believed that the English were being spared France's fate precisely because the bourgeois had not destroyed the citizen.

The reason they found his analysis of France so appropriate is clear. Tocqueville rightly saw in 1835 a political resurgence in local government. The granting of the vote to the lowliest resident ratepayer, however, was interpreted as an extension of political power to what he termed "the most democratic class" in the nation.[58] It meant the reorganization of local government, in favor of the active citizen, against the claims of religious, corporate, and proprietal privileges. Tocqueville and Beaumont did not attempt to estimate what portion of the population was still beneath the most democratic class. They bypassed the element common to the Reform Bill of 1832, the Poor Law Amendment Act, Hobhouse's Act, and the Municipal Corporations Act—the property qualification. The "aristocracy of wealth" had permeated English local government also, in harmony with its broader social condition, and the demand for cheap and efficient government was as potent as the upsurge of the civic spirit.

In an era when few English Radicals looked beyond a ratepayers' democracy, the vision of two itinerant Frenchmen was inevitably limited by their sources. This was one real disadvantage connected with Tocqueville and Beaumont's easy and continuous contact with the leaders of politics and society. In viewing class relations and social forces in England their perception became progressively

---

[57] Webb, *Statutory Authorities*, 480–481; Webb, *The Manor and the Borough* (London, 1908), 692. See Tocqueville, *Souvenirs*, 26–27 (written in July 1850).

[58] Tocqueville to Senior, Jan. 27, 1836, *Correspondence and Conversations*, I, 15; see also C.V.g: copy of rough drafts for the *Démocratie* of 1840, paq. 9, cahier 1, p. 171, as well as Beaumont, *L'Irlande*, II, 301–302; and *Oeuvres* (M): *Démocratie*, II, 260. The Webbs estimated that in 1836 only one householder out of four could cast a vote (*Statutory Authorities*, 474).

weaker as they moved downward. With the possible exception of Dr. Phillips Kay, their information on the conditions and outlook of the working classes came from manufacturers, Radical intellectuals, and parliamentarians. As Tocqueville said, all were gentlemen. There was no attempt to penetrate the gap which separated the lower rungs of the working class from the Radicals. Believing that the tastes, the passions, and the outlook of the middle classes would be normative for all European society, it was no accident that Tocqueville went no further to complete his political education. During his last trip in 1857 Tocqueville was to regret not having made personal contact with members of the lower classes. His keen ear for the state of relations between classes never heard the full range of English protest. The Owenite cooperative movement and the trade-union movement were nowhere discussed or even mentioned. The trip of 1835 coincided with an ebb in working-class agitation, and the London Radicals were taken to be the spokesmen of the whole range of democratic aspirations.[59]

All the same the spoils of the eleven-week expedition were immense. Tocqueville and Beaumont had undertaken a complete revaluation of what aristocracy and the democratic revolution meant in their English context. Wealth was freed of its too intimate link with land, and the extension of political participation was seen to be as deeply rooted in native institutions as in ideological influences from abroad. Of equal significance was their renewed respect for the agility of the English aristocracy in deflecting and controlling the political and social transformation of England. The possessors of the new industrial and commercial wealth were being absorbed into the ruling class. The extension of the electoral principle had likewise failed to destroy wholly the leadership of the aristocracy in national politics or their continuing influence in the county as justices of the peace.

Their view of England was incomplete, but the final image was only intensified by that incompleteness. Perhaps because they had

---

[59] In contrast see C.-G. Simon's study of working class conditions and ideology, *Observations recueillées en Angleterre en 1835* (Paris, n.d.).

arrived during one of the most prosperous years of the century, perhaps because of the political vitality of London, perhaps because of the booming North, perhaps because of the unquestioned acceptance of gradualism among all political parties, or perhaps because of subtle experiences which never found their way into their notes, Beaumont and Tocqueville departed with a feeling that they had passed through the most powerful, the most active, the most successful social entity on earth.

VI ❖ Ireland 1835: The Alienation of Aristocracies

TOCQUEVILLE and Beaumont left Liverpool on July 5 or 6, 1835, in transit from one of the most stable polities of their time to a volcano. The Irish Sea proved to be a chasm wider than the ocean which separated England and America. Well before the crossing, they were prepared for the great failure of the English political genius. Almost every thinking Englishman with whom they had talked had at hand a prepared analysis of the Irish question, and whatever their differences there was universal agreement on one point: Ireland was like a never ending nightmare, and no matter how one twisted and turned, a solution seemed beyond reach.

The two Frenchmen thus arrived in Dublin provided with general background on the Irish dilemma. In London, Tocqueville had recorded a conversation between John Revans, secretary to the Irish Poor Law Commission, and Nassau Senior on the problem of poverty in Ireland. Revans simply characterized the situation as horrible.[1] Senior had himself become involved in the Irish question as early as 1830. He believed the condition of the lower classes in Ireland to be worse than that of countries much less favored by nature. Beaumont likewise sought out George Cornewall Lewis while Lewis was preparing his study of local disturbances in Ire-

[1] Tocqueville, *Journeys to England,* 118. John Revans had succeeded George Taylor as secretary of the Royal Commission on the Poor Law in July 1832. He became secretary to the Irish Poor Law Commission in 1835, and an Assistant poor-law commissioner in England three years later. Tocqueville described him as "a very intelligent young man who belongs to the Radical Party."

land and the "war for the means of subsistence" among the poor.[2]
In John Stuart Mill, they encountered someone who understood
the Irish problem better than most of his contemporaries and who
recommended the sweeping abolition of abuses, whch they were to
come to regard as the first need of Ireland.

As in America, first impressions were decisive. The very moment
Tocqueville and Beaumont arrived in Dublin they thought themselves in a new world, a feeling which deepened as they moved
through the south and west of Ireland. A "visit to the Poorhouse
and the University" on the same day set the theme for the entire
trip—the shocking and unending contrast between wealth and
poverty. The interior of the poorhouse in Dublin was one of the
most hideous and disgusting extremes of wretchedness Tocqueville
had ever seen. The dehumanization of the paupers appeared complete: "They sit on wooden benches, crowded close together and
all looking in the same direction, as if in the pit of a theatre. They
do not talk at all; they do not stir; they look at nothing; they do
not appear to be thinking. They neither expect, fear, nor hope anything from life." [3] On leaving the poorhouse to go to the university,
he came upon two paupers going with a wheelbarrow from the
poorhouse to get the garbage of the rich to make soup. The subsequent description of the university, with its immense garden, its
magnificent palace, its church, and its liveried lackeys, revealed a
note of moral indignation which was to pass into Beaumont's
L'Irlande.

The entire journey through Ireland was a dreary repetition of
the first violent contrast. "Only magnificent chateaux or miserable
cabins are to be seen in Ireland," wrote Beaumont. "There are no
buildings between the palaces of the great and the huts of the indigent." [4] The landscape itself echoed the antithesis of splendor

[2] Lewis, *On Local Disturbances in Ireland and on the Irish Church Question*
(London, 1836), 338. See also Nassau William Senior, *Journals, Conversations, and
Essays relating to Ireland* (London, 1868), I, 18ff.

[3] *Journeys to England*, 121, July 9, 1835. By "University," Tocqueville probably
meant Trinity College.

[4] *L'Irlande*, I, 198. See also Tocqueville's descriptions in *Journeys to England*,
136–138, 158–159, 185–189.

and indigence. On one side of a highway lay only sterile marshes, and the bare and uncultivated fields of the poor stretched endlessly to the horizon—a symbol of its inhabitants' lives. On the opposite side of the road the estate of the landlord flaunted its rich and fertile fields and forests before the observer. Tocqueville, in a letter to France, confessed his inability to portray fully the miserable condition in which the population of the country existed. He could only compare them to the pitiful remnants of certain tribes in America. Beaumont too was reminded of the Negroes and Indians, who had been central to his novel of racial oppression, *Marie*.[5] Tocqueville and Beaumont climaxed their itinerary by a visit to Newport-Pratt in Connaught. This village was in the throes of a famine and its population in danger of dying of hunger. The contrast between opulence and privation again left a deep impression. "You have seen two hundred unfortunate people," the priest of Newport told him, "who are in constant danger of starving to death and who hardly keep alive at all. On the nearby meadows the Marquis of Sligo has a thousand sheep and several of his granaries are full."[6]

The travelers were also struck by the deep religious animus which reinforced the economic rift between rich and poor. The early nineteenth century had witnessed a renaissance of Irish Catholicism. Absorbed in the attempt to secure a basic ecclesiastical foundation, the main work of the Irish clergy was practical rather than speculative. With the slow return of political rights of the Catholic population the Irish clergy benefited by past identification with their suffering communicants.

For Tocqueville, the democratic political orientation of even the upper clergy was the most striking feature of the Irish Church. After a dinner with the Bishop of Carlow, at which an archbishop, four bishops, and several priests were present, he noted that they were "clearly as much the leaders of a Party as the representatives

---

[5] See Tocqueville to Mme. la comtesse de Grancey, Kilkenny, July 26, 1835, *Oeuvres* (B), VII, and Beaumont, *L'Irlande*, I, 205.

[6] Tocqueville, *Journeys to England*, 190. Beaumont's account of the famine appears in *L'Irlande*, I, 377.

of the Church." [7] Many of the Irish priests were even skeptical about the value to religion of upper-class support. The parish clergy derived mainly from the peasant class and stayed closely tied to them by the fact that they remained a relatively impoverished group. The influence of the clergy in political questions was at its height.

Among the Catholic hierarchy to which they had easy access Tocqueville and Beaumont found the necessary national unity which accorded with their desire to see religion and liberty acting together in mutual cooperation. In Tocqueville's descriptions of the Protestant and Catholic clergy, the same stark contrast which infused his description of the economic extremes in Ireland was extended into the depiction of their physical and moral condition. He devoted a large and well-edited note to an evening spent with a Catholic priest, vividly describing his humble dwelling and his muscular healthy appearance as reflections of an active life among the people. He accompanied the priest on his rounds, past men stricken with idleness for lack of work, and to the schoolhouse, where the new spirit of vitality infused children in rags.[8] A minister of the Established Church was then sketched against the background of his gothic mansion at the top of the hill, far from the mass of cottages visited by the priest. He was frail in appearance, just returned from Italy where he had gone for his health. It was Sunday, but the church was shut. The wealthy Protestant minister, like his tiny congregation, was isolated from the people. He was utterly dependent on the aristocracy, the Established Church, and endowed revenues.

Tocqueville and Beaumont thus found themselves in a society hopelessly divided by wealth and religion. The English spirit of exclusion had here become magnified into class isolation. They were well aware, however, that they had not come upon a static situation. Beaumont's comparison of the social condition of the Irish to the Negro slave did not preclude his awareness of an im-

---

[7] *Journeys to England,* 130. See also Robert B. McDowell, *Public Opinion and Government Policy in Ireland, 1801–1846* (London, 1952), 31–32.

[8] *Journeys to England,* 160–173.

portant difference. The impoverished Irishman, as yet without full liberty, was on the path to breaking his fetters. The Catholic emancipation in 1829, followed by the French and Belgian revolutions, was having continuous repercussions in Ireland. The peasants had refused to pay their tithes to the Established Church and O'Connell's political union was a force in the London government as well as in Ireland. The abuses of legal tyranny, religious persecution, and absentee landlordism appeared to be ready for a great retribution. The wall of exclusion which had barred the Catholic population from political life was crumbling under the steady pressure of mass agitation in Ireland and the less dependable pressure of the London government under the Whigs.

While the two travelers had discovered no single principle in English political life to which they could logically relate all aspects of its society, before the end of their Irish trip they felt that they had discovered the key to Irish history. It was a primeval and continuing injustice which had turned Ireland into a tragic caricature of England. Beaumont had unearthed the point of departure for a new study of the oppressed and ample material for a comparative analysis of ruling classes. One evening about midway in their journey they attempted to consolidate their ideas. After a prolonged discussion, each composed his own version of the contrast between the English and Irish aristocracies. Beaumont's account finally appeared as the second chapter of his work: "A bad aristocracy is the first cause of all the evils of Ireland. The vice of this aristocracy is to be English and protestant." [9]

Basically, their theme was the antithetical development of two ruling classes with respect to the masses. Both had settled upon the territory of an alien people with its own laws and customs. The English aristocracy had mixed with the conquered nation, taken its language, adopted part of its customs, fought against the king, and, wrote Beaumont, "united itself to the people by ties of mutual interest." It had never ceased to maintain its contacts with the peo-

[9] *L'Irlande,* I, 211–220.

ple as leaders and rulers, and opened its ranks, sacrificing half its revenues to abolish poverty, giving its people political and civil liberties, the glory of empire, and world maritime supremacy. England, Tocqueville's version asserted, was "a nation among whom the upper classes are more brilliant, more enlightened and wiser, the middle classes richer, the poor classes better off than anywhere else." [10] This image, heightened for effect, was to pervade Beaumont's *L'Irlande,* which found it doubtful that the poorest man in England was not better off than the most fortunate Irish peasant.

The English aristocracy was nebulous, active, and in continuous personal contact with the ruled, "never ceasing to be superior, in talents and virtues as in wealth and political power," participating in all assemblies, directing all undertakings, and participating in the commercial and industrial expansion of the society.[11] The Irish aristocracy, also beginning in conquest, kept its own language, laws, and customs, even protecting itself from intermarriage. Religion, the most powerful social tie, became a focus of social and legal tyranny. But above all, observed Beaumont, this aristocracy continued to be English at heart and tied itself to the destiny of England. Supported by English artillery it had had little use for Irish loyalty.

To the lack of a genuine polity and the difference in religion, Beaumont added a third alienating factor in Ireland—the tremendous economic gulf between the upper and lower classes. The Irish aristocracy possessed great proprietary holdings, resembling its counterpart in England save for its lack of aptitude for the scientific improvement of agriculture. But the Irish had no industrial alternatives to the acquisition of wealth and power. Moreover, this was a direct result of the complete political dependence of the Irish ruling class on English support. The Irish had been forced to consent to industrial and commercial subservience to English economic development. "The two societies," concluded Tocqueville's essay ". . . were both founded on the principle of aristocracy. The two

---

[10] *Journeys to England,* 156. His essay was dated July 26, 1835.
[11] Beaumont, *L'Irlande,* I, 212.

aristocracies of which I have been speaking, have the same origin and manners and almost the same laws. But the one has for centuries given England one of the best governments that exist in the world; the other has given the Irish one of the most detestable that could ever be imagined." [12]

From their comparison of the aristocratic principle in England and Ireland, two studies of the problem of class alienation were to emerge. While Tocqueville turned his conclusions to a contrast between the French and English aristocracies which would culminate in the *Ancien Régime,* Beaumont continued the investigation of Ireland, determined to extend his conclusions into a full-length study. After another journey to the two islands in 1837, he was ready to expand his essay into *L'Irlande sociale, politique et religieuse.*

Appearing in 1839, the work was well received in both England and France, and was even compared to Tocqueville's monumental study of America. While it was of less universal interest, it has been recognized as a classic portrait of Ireland in the age of reform.[13] It was immediately translated into English. The comparison of the British constitution in England and in Ireland was so well wrought that the *Dublin University Magazine,* the organ of Irish Toryism, considered foreign authorship impossible and was convinced that Beaumont had been given a ready-made exposition by a Dublin radical. Mill found Beaumont more accurate on both England and Ireland than "any foreigner I know of," and almost all Englishmen. He and George Grote were only a little disturbed by the glow cast on the English aristocracy.[14]

[12] *Journeys to England,* 157–158.

[13] See P. Duvergier de Hauranne's review, "L'Irlande sociale, politique et religieuse, par M. Gustave de Beaumont," *Revue des deux mondes,* ser. 4, vol. XXII (April 1840), 15; John L. Hammond, *Gladstone and the Irish Nation* (London, 1938), 13, 24, 37; and Nicholas Mansergh, *Ireland in the Age of Reform and Revolution: A Commentary on Anglo-Irish Relations and on Political Forces in Ireland, 1840–1921* (London, 1940), 22ff.

[14] Grote to Beaumont, Aug. 1, 1839, and Mill to Beaumont, Oct. 18, 1839, Yale Mss(B) C.XI.c.

Two solid volumes, with a penchant for occasional romantic overemphasis and epigrammatic phrases, summed up the English domination of Ireland. The study began with a brief historical account of the wars of conquest and of religion, and the legal persecution of the eighteenth century. The point of departure was the never ending and never complete struggle between two peoples, as harmful in its incompleteness as in its cruelty.

Beaumont then traced the differences between England and Ireland in every phase of political, economic, and social life. As the aristocracy was the strength of England and the "cancer of Ireland," so Ireland was presented as a political and social caricature of England. It was a classic demonstration of the "spirit of the laws," which made the essential difference between England and Ireland. To conclude that the Act of Union had really made the two countries alike was, as Beaumont correctly observed, "deceptive analogy." He did not deny that the English, by uniting the two nations in 1800, believed they were giving the best constitution in Europe to Ireland and sharing England's political experience and economic initiative as the foremost capitalist society in Europe. The calamity was, as a later historian wrote, that "there was no nation in Europe, whose best, as it happened, was so bad for the Irish peasant." [15]

The Act of Union was unable to unite England and Ireland, not only because the spirit of the British constitution could not be imposed on a population engaged in semicivil war, but because it was, more than any other constitution, a mass of customs, traditions, and statutes. "If the observance of a law can be prescribed for a people, one cannot attach custom to it; that complex of facts is the result of a thousand preceding facts, an experience repeated so often that it becomes law through use." [16]

Every aspect of political life dependent on custom had, according to Beaumont, become warped into a mockery. English legal persecution in Ireland had a terrible logic, contrary to the intent of the law in Britain, and as the spirit of the laws was perverted, every

---

[15] Hammond, *Gladstone and the Irish Nation*, 7.
[16] Beaumont, *L'Irlande*, I, 183–184.

moral and political concept also suffered. The court system which worked so well in England fostered class antagonism instead of a respect for judicial impartiality. The Irish peasantry resorted to their own code of violence to counteract dispossessions. Witnesses were either killed by rural terror or bribed by the government. "But who will admit the sincerity of a witness deposing under the combined influence of the money he receives and of the death he fears?"[17] Once the social tie had been broken, the magistrate no longer saw in the accused peasant a fellow citizen invoking the sacred rights of the constitution, but a savage enemy who had to be exterminated.

The county and municipal governments and parish vestries were inanimate institutions in Ireland. Religious fiction and political exclusion were subtly woven together to the complete exclusion of those elements which Beaumont so admired in English local government. Parish government, whose meetings seemed to be the soul of republicanism in England, was impossible. Its first function was the maintenance of religion, and the law excluded Catholics from all vestry assemblies where the Protestant religion was concerned. The Established Church itself was only the ghost of a religious body outside Ulster.

The entire character of the masses had in some measure reflected the corruption of the body politic. Beaumont was as unsentimental as any Tory in describing the Irish peasant. Fresh from his description of the warping of American ideals by the institution of Negro slavery he did not deny that the victims of injustice might not suffer a psychological crippling, in reaction to centuries of suppression, outlasting the end of physical and legal privation.[18] If the Irish had had the good fortune, in the eyes of moralists, to be the oppressed rather than the oppressors, they had learned the lessons of violence and conspiratorial behavior which would far outlast the English tyranny.

Since Beaumont had found the prime cause of Ireland's evil in

---

[17] *L'Irlande*, I, 240–241. See also Tocqueville, *Journeys to England*, 148.

[18] See *Système pénitentiaire*, alphabetic note cc, and Beaumont, *Marie, ou l'esclavage aux Etats-Unis*, 4th ed. (Paris, 1840), 67–68.

the existence of a foreign and religiously antipathetic ruling class, his solution was obvious—the destruction of the Irish aristocracy. However extreme the suggestion appeared at first sight, it reiterated those already voiced in England by Radicals, including John Stuart Mill, and the means of destruction were by no means drastic. Beaumont accepted the framework of the British constitution as the one in which reform would have to be carried out, and dismissed the idea of repeal of the Act of Union as a dream. However fatal the British social system might be to Ireland, its geographic location irrevocably joined this gangrenous but strategic island to the entire Empire. In this he concurred with almost the entire body of English public opinion. England could never consent to having an independent Catholic and democratic island at her back. Moreover, Beaumont and Tocqueville both sympathized with the necessity for England to preserve her reputation as a great nation. The *Démocratie* of 1835 declared that "a people which proceeded to divide its sovereignty in the presence of the great military monarchies of Europe would, by this fact alone, seem to renounce its power and perhaps its name and existence." [19] Since the popularity of the English aristocracy partially depended on its empire building, it seemed axiomatic that, for its own survival, no English government could contemplate dissolving the Act of Union. Any people who too easily relinquished conquered territory would clearly be marked as a nation in decline. "What is an empire," asked Beaumont rhetorically, "which consents to dismember itself? Is not a power in decline which diminishes in extent, or does it not, in any event, appear to be? England, which refuses to lose Canada at any price . . . will certainly not abandon Ireland, which is a part of itself." [20]

This did not imply that the Irish could not proceed through openings in the British constitution itself to attain their ends. Ireland, thought Beaumont, possessed a real asset in those British rights which were skillfully being manipulated by the renascent Catholic-

---

[19] *Oeuvres* (M): *Démocratie*, I, 174.
[20] *L'Irlande*, II, 328. See also *Oeuvres* (M): *Ecrits politiques*, I, 214.

democratic movement. In the matter of administrative reform the Act of Union might turn out to be the best way of achieving rapid change. During the 1835 journey both Tocqueville and Beaumont sensed that reform from above could only come from London. Beaumont argued in *L'Irlande* that the special case of Ireland, combined with Whig domination in London, called for a high degree of centralized authority. It was the only possible mediator between two implacably hostile groups. Parliament had just initiated the abolition of colonial slavery, and Tocqueville was to argue for a similar approach to emancipation in the French West Indies.

The task of the British aristocracy in England was above all to destroy its own caricature in Ireland—to foster a political, religious, and social revolution within the framework of the English polity. The work of destruction would have to begin, Beaumont observed, in the vital area of land tenure. Another Irish parallel to English history, the enclosure movement, had turned into unparalleled disaster. A cycle of evictions and starvation had become endemic by the 1830's. The peasant landholding system secured for France seemed the answer to both Ireland's economic and political problems. Comparing their own country with both Ireland and England, Beaumont and Tocqueville were still convinced that, in general, landed inequality was a barrier to stable political evolution. If the English farm laborer happened to be poor revolutionary material, the Irish tenantry was in a state of permanent, if sporadic, social war. The independent French peasant offered the best social base for modern democratic societies. In one area, at least, France's future seemed better guaranteed than either of her island neighbors or even America.[21] Her peasantry was, in fact, to emerge as a bulwark against social change during the Revolution of 1848. Unfortunately for the two liberals, this solid investment against the Parisian proletariat produced equally lucrative returns for Louis Napoleon. As with other classes, elements of social stability turned out to be political quicksand. Tocqueville became less certain about

[21] See also Yale Mss(T) C.V.h: copy of notes for the *Démocratie* of 1835, paq. 3, cahier 4, p. 90.

the possession of land as an inherent source of desirable political attitudes.

For Ireland in 1839, as for France, there was no turning back. History had decided. Although Beaumont called only for legal simplification of sales and the removal of primogeniture, the goal was both clear and prophetic—"make laws which render land accessible, divide and splinter property as much as you can, for it is the only means, while overturning an aristocracy which must fall, to raise the lower classes; it is the only way to place the soil within reach of the people, and it is necessary that the Irish people become proprietary." [22] Ireland's revolution could be channeled, but it would be democratic and agrarian.

By this circuitous path, *L'Irlande* came back to the theme of England's democratic revolution. On his second trip to England, in 1837, Beaumont witnessed the ebbing of the reform movement. As Tocqueville concluded from his friend's reports the English aristocracy was still a worthy adversary of the egalitarian movement, the only one in Europe which met its enemy squarely and was "still standing firm." [23] The only breach that could be observed in its fortifications was the continued and unceasing agitation in Ireland. Already in 1835, although the Conservatives had captured a majority of the English constituencies, O'Connell's Irish bloc threw the balance of power to the Whigs. Beaumont's final emphasis in *L'Irlande* was on the stress that Ireland was placing on the aristocratic principle in England. The Irish question was beginning a century of ulceration within the English Parliament itself, and Beaumont foresaw that effective Irish discontent now introduced a new and volatile factor into British political calculations. [24] Britain might still, through Ireland, be concretely fitted into the world-

[22] *L'Irlande,* II, 234.
[23] See Yale Mss(B), undated copy of a letter of Beaumont to Tocqueville [May 1837], "Londres ou plutôt Kensington," p. 83, and Tocqueville to Louis de Kergorlay, Sept. 4, 1837, *Oeuvres* (B), V.
[24] A half century after Beaumont's work was published, Englishmen were still amazed at how his prophecies were fulfilled, "almost to the letter!" (Lord Ebury to Reeve, Feb. 13, 1886, Reeve, *Memoirs,* II, 344).

wide democratic movement. The quickening pace of reform in Ireland would rebound ideologically upon Britain at the very moment when England's aristocracy sought to disentangle herself from the legacy of class war. Thus *L'Irlande* foreshadowed Tocqueville's suggestion in the *Ancien Régime* that the most dangerous moment for a government was not when it was completely indifferent to suffering inflicted, but when it admitted its tyranny and attempted to rectify the mistakes of the past.

While Beaumont was suggesting the consequences of the democratic movement and aristocratic alienation in Ireland, Tocqueville was looking beyond the British Isles. Even his comparative essay in Ireland had ended with a note on aristocracy in general: "Aristocracy can then be subjected to particular conditions which modify its nature and its results, so that in judging it one must bear circumstances in mind." [25] Tocqueville was probably already thinking of the failure of the aristocracy of his own nation. The problem was discussed at length in an article he wrote at John Stuart Mill's request, for the *London and Westminster Review* in 1836, on the social state of France before the Revolution.[26]

The differences in context and tone of this article from the more complete analysis in the *Ancien Régime* twenty years later are reflected in the basic mood of optimism which Tocqueville carried over from his voyage to England in 1835. France was successfully enjoying the conditions of representative government, and the constitutional provision for individual rights seemed firmly established. However tenuously political liberty was planted in French

[25] *Journeys to England,* 158.
[26] Tocqueville, "Political and Social Condition of France, First Article," *London and Westminster Review,* III and XXV (April 1836), 137–169. The original and uncut French text has been published in *Oeuvres* (M): *Ancien Régime,* I, under the title "État social et politique de la France avant et depuis 1789." In this chapter, Mill's approved translation, which appeared in 1836, will be used in citations. For comparisons with the *Ancien Régime* in Chapter X, below, some attention must be given to the original French. A second article was promised to Mill but the project was dropped during the composition of the second part of the *Démocratie,* and was never resumed.

habits, it was at least a functioning institutional reality. Tocqueville wrote to Senior, "With us for the moment at least all things seem completely restored to their normal state," and confidently forecast that if his country could preserve her peace and institutions for two decades "even in their present imperfect state," her freedom might come to rest on a firm basis. He regarded any antiliberal manifestations in France as transitory and "contrary to all the permanent instincts of the country." [27] France had dramatically and conclusively given birth to a new and permanent social and political condition. Even in the midst of slowly growing pessimism by 1840, Tocqueville continued to believe that a new age of general stability had arrived, and that society in France had already achieved its final form, at least in so far as great intellectual and political revolutions were concerned. The only chapter of the last part of the *Démocratie* which he permitted to appear as a separate article was an analysis of why great revolutions would become more infrequent.[28]

The Revolution was therefore in one sense a finished work, and the French aristocracy had forever lost its privileged position in the nation. The spirit of equality was now "the soul of France," [29] but Tocqueville was equally convinced that the French Revolution had arisen from a France already more democratic and more centralized than any other nation in Europe. Its basic results arose from a point of departure several centuries old. Its violence Tocqueville assigned principally to the failure of a single class—the French nobility. It was this failure which occupied the largest part of the article for Mill's review.

Writing for an English audience and deeply impressed with the slow development of democracy in England, Tocqueville naturally

[27] Letters of Jan. 27, 1836, and Jan. 11, 1837, *Correspondence and Conversations,* I, 15–18. See also Tocqueville to Mill, Feb. 10, 1836, and June 24, 1837, *Oeuvres* (M): *Corr. angl.,* I.

[28] Tocqueville, "Des révolutions dans les sociétés nouvelles," *Revue des deux mondes,* ser. 4, vol. XXII (April 1840), 322–334. This appeared as a chapter in the *Démocratie,* "Pourquoi les grandes révolutions deviendront rares." See also *Ecrits politiques,* I, 206.

[29] *Oeuvres* (M): *Corr. angl.,* I, 321, "Notes de Tocqueville sur le livre, *La France sociale, politique et littéraire* par Henry Bulwer."

contrasted the alienation of the French aristocracy with the continuing success of its English counterpart. Just as the Irish aristocracy had never ceased to be foreign, the French aristocracy also "stood in the midst of the people as strangers favored by the prince, rather than as leaders and chiefs." [30] The artfulness of the English aristocracy consisted precisely in the fact that it had identified itself with popular demands. Tocqueville also propounded his ideas on the two great props of aristocratic leadership in England, decentralization and wealth.

For Tocqueville, the most significant development in French history in the light of his English and Irish experience was the loss of function which had progressively severed the French aristocracy from both leadership and power. Fortunately for the aristocracies that still existed, Tocqueville noted with obvious reference to England, the power that sought to destroy them knew little of their secret, the local influence of a thousand invisible ties that connected them with the people. The first and almost unnoticed political loss of the French nobility had been its most fatal one. Upon the withdrawal from participation in local administration the separation from an organic place in the body politic was certain. The French nobles preserved the features of inequality, such as civil and economic exemptions, which made them hated, and allowed themselves to be relieved of political functions which would have made them necessary accessories and leaders of any political movement.

Tocqueville also contrasted the French nobility's loss of social and economic preponderance with the condition of their English counterparts. While in England customs concerning entail and primogeniture went beyond the demands of the law, in France no laws concerning entail could prevent the breakup of estates whose owners were in competition with fluid commercial wealth they could not hope to equal and in which they declined to participate. Although Tocqueville conceived of the loosely defined English ruling class as containing many of the most enlightened men in

[30] Tocqueville, "Political and Social Condition of France," 144.

England, it was primarily the nature of the English aristocracy as
an aristocracy of wealth that he stressed in accounting for its continued dominance in society. He felt that the rich among the
French nobility, even "in default of political power might by their
wealth have acquired some influence over the people [but] volun-
tarily withdrew themselves from them." [31]

In spite of the fact that the nobility of the old regime was already,
in an economic sense, a partially democratic body containing very
rich and very poor individuals, hatred of inequality was much
more virulent in France than in England. Tocqueville sought to
explain this fact on the basis of the exclusive, irritating, and permanent character of French inequality. The English brand of inequality, which made positions of power depend as much upon
accessible wealth as any other factor, actually made inequality more
highly valued. As the pursuit of wealth had absorbed the imagination of the English, it became a self-sustaining prop of society,
reinforcing the original principle of inequality. "In this manner
the very vices of the institution sometimes constitute its strength."
The condition of a rapidly expanding economy, combined with
the existence of tremendous individual fortunes, tended to make
the aristocracy more brilliant and more valuable. The idea of the
imaginary grandeur which even the poorest had the remote possibility of reaching fortified the aristocratic principle. "Increase the
greatness of the object to be attained and you may without fear
diminish the probabilities of obtaining it." [32]

The methods of accumulation of wealth also differed in England.
Industry became the natural outlet for the acquisitive instinct and
land hunger was deflected. Land was only an object of luxury and
ambition, not of speculation. Tocqueville partially accepted the
point of view of the English economists who insisted that immense
landed domains were not merely a remnant of feudalism, but could
be found at both extremes of civilization—"first when men are in
a state of semi-barbarism, and do not prize, indeed do not know,

[31] "Political and Social Condition of France," 142.
[32] "Political and Social Condition of France," 150.

any other kind of wealth; and lastly when they have become highly civilized, and have discovered a thousand other means of enriching themselves." [33]

England's immunity to the *esprit littéraire,* which in France had led to the victory of the enlightenment over the old regime, was also explained in terms of the psychological relation between wealth and prestige: "In a nation where wealth is the sole, or even the principal foundation of aristocracy, money, which in all societies is the means of pleasure, confers power also. Endowed with these two advantages, it succeeds in attracting towards itself the whole imagination of man . . . In such a country literature is little cultivated, and literary merit therefore scarcely attracts the attention of the public." [34] While the English imagination was being siphoned into the pursuit of wealth, the Frenchman of talent gained recognition but not equality in the salons of the nobility. The literary world slowly turned against the very concept of aristocracy. Intellectually, as well as politically and economically, the old French ruling class had surrendered its primacy long before 1789.

Tocqueville's article reflected one ambiguity, arising from the voyage of 1835, which did not appear critical for his analysis. The economic and social condition of the English and French aristocracies seemed as sharply divergent as their political characteristics. Equal weight was assigned to the acquisitive instinct, economic prosperity, and the spirit of local leadership as inhibitors of class alienation. Tocqueville had yet to confront a situation where he would have to revaluate the effects of the first two in the absence of the third.

Although Tocqueville's trip to England in 1835 caused him to alter his view of the English aristocracy and to give it a place apart in his sociological and historical framework, it had not caused him to alter his conception of aristocracy as an ideal type. Of both England and Ireland he wrote, "It would not be just to judge

---

[33] "Political and Social Condition of France," 154.
[34] "Political and Social Condition of France," 151.

aristocracy theoretically by either of these two peoples. They constitute exceptions." For any complete evaluation, "it would be necessary to seek out the virtues and vices most natural to aristocracy." [35] The second half of the *Démocratie* (1840), where this passage was fully amplified, abided by this conclusion. As with his treatment of democracy, Tocqueville sought no specific country as his aristocratic model. In dealing with certain characteristics of American society, such as its intellectual propensities or its national pride, England was cited as the aristocratic counterpart to American society. On the development of local government and on the sources of American literature, the English aristocracy received its due. But England was almost always used as background for specifically American, rather than democratic, propensities. Regarding the characteristics defined as more ideally aristocratic, the Continental, or more specifically the French, nobility were the obvious models. In its engrossment with commerce and industry the English aristocracy, much as America's decentralization, was now recognized as exceptional. Furthermore, many of the essential qualities assigned by the *Démocratie* to an aristocratic social state were totally inapplicable or least applicable to England. The sense of caste, of exclusiveness, of belief in a permanent social hierarchy, so central to the *Démocratie*'s discussion of aristocratic habits and feelings, were antithetical to Tocqueville's observations of English society. From the incommunicability between classes separated by "high immobile barriers" from the rest of the nation, to the rigidity of marital customs and the preciousness of aristocratic poetic style, the Continent was the more obvious source of his statements. In describing the features of the modern egalitarian society, Tocqueville had been careful not to link his outline to any specific example. He felt that its true dimensions, while predictable, were not yet present in any contemporary community. While there was no similar impediment to his analysis of aristocracy, Tocqueville probably preserved a parallel anonymity in this case both for stylistic and methodological reasons.

[35] *Oeuvres* (M): *Voyages Angleterre*, 134 and note a.

Tocqueville had as yet made no thorough investigation of medieval or even early modern societies. In any event, the English model admittedly fitted least well into his system. It was a hybrid of aristocracy and democracy, of middle-class materialism and rigorous religious morality, of political reform and landed entrenchment. The aristocratic and democratic elements had not interfered with the growth of national wealth at home and power abroad, and communications between classes appeared real and effective. Even cultural life throve on the interaction, for "when liberty reigns in an aristocracy the upper classes are ceaselessly obliged to avail themselves of the lower and thereby they draw together." [36] The taste for movement and fame, for energy and habitual enterprise, could not fail to render such a society both more vigorous and more creative. Tocqueville's analysis of social customs and ideas might show that aristocratic man and democratic man were like two distinct orders of humanity, but it was no longer asserted that, in reality, the mixture was basically untenable.

With a pattern peculiar to itself, England seemed to contain so many elements of both social conditions that none could say whether it had not already crossed the invisible boundary. The *Démocratie* of 1840 attempted only once to point to a new chink in the armor of the English aristocracy. Tocqueville could not withhold a parting thrust at the smug landed gentry, who looked with disdain on the small farms of France. He no longer looked for the partition of the land in England, but Nassau Senior himself, in a conversation with Beaumont in October 1836, may have started a new chain of thought in their minds. Senior proposed that though it had been created with the consent of the landed interest, the new poor-law administration was sapping their influence over the rural population. The aristocracy was bartering its position for a mess of pottage and some tax relief.[37] Senior's suggestion was reinforced by Beaumont's personal observation in 1837 that the

[36] *Oeuvres* (M): *Démocratie*, II, 63n.
[37] Yale Mss(B) C.X.5: *L'Irlande*, notes, Conversation with Senior, Paris, Oct. 27, 1836.

justices of the peace were abandoning the meetings of the local poor-law guardians to the lesser farmers and retail tradesmen. Thus three years later the *Démocratie* warned: "I have often heard great English landowners congratulate themselves that nowadays they draw much more income from their estates than their fathers could. Perhaps they have good reason to rejoice, but certainly they do not realize what they are glad of. They believe they are making a clear gain and they are only making an exchange. It is their influence that they are yielding for hard cash; and what they gain in money, they are soon to lose in power." [38]

Yet Tocqueville could not bring himself to assert that England's aristocracy had in fact lost its touch. As he read over the final chapter of his great work, he wrote in his notes, "There is only one aristocracy which knows how to defend itself, that of England. All the others are general staffs without armies." [39]

[38] II, 195–196. See also Beaumont, *L'Irlande,* II, 383n, and Webb, *English Poor Law History, Part II,* I, 229.

[39] Yale Mss(T) C.V.k: copy of notes for the *Démocratie* of 1840, paq. 7, cahier 1, p. 4 (March 1840).

VII ❖ The Industrial Revolution

EARLY in 1837 Tocqueville was ready to enter politics in earnest. His Norman neighbors were not quite so ready. Suspicions about his legitimist family connections could not be dissipated overnight and his opponents did nothing to stifle them. After suffering his first and only defeat at the polls in an attempt to capture a seat in the Chamber of Deputies that November, he settled back and concentrated on finishing the *Démocratie*. Success came finally in the elections of March 1839.[1] Beaumont, of course, joined him in the Chamber as soon as he could, in 1840.

As Tocqueville moved from the writing table to the hustings his hopes were high. The intellectual world had responded with tremendous approval to the *Démocratie*'s attempt at "a new science of politics for a new world." The realm of action now seemed equally in need of a "new kind of liberal." By regaining the lost leadership of his ancestors and by maintaining a self-imposed standard of excellence within the new rules of democratic competition, he felt he could best help France to pass through the final stress of transition and to breathe life into her new political institutions.

Tocqueville saw two great blocs of Frenchmen who had to be reconciled, "those who had made democracy an ideal" without considering the preconditions of morality, belief, and enlightenment necessary for its success, and those for whom the word

---

[1] On Tocqueville's campaigns see Marcel, *Essai politique,* 293ff, and Sister Mary Lawlor, *Alexis de Tocqueville in the Chamber of Deputies* (Washington, D.C., 1959), 17ff.

"democracy" was a synonym for upheaval and atheism, who could not see that, whatever its limitations, it could be made consistent with order and morality. Into this delicate balance of old and new, religion and politics, aristocracy and democracy, came the problems of the industrial revolution, shattering not only Tocqueville's categories of political antagonism, but the constitutional process as well. The fall of the Bourbons had marked, whatever his personal feelings, the triumph of his political principles. The onslaught of economic man, whether bourgeois or proletarian, meant a restatement of French social conflicts in terms which his great political vision seemed unable to reconcile. His new science of politics wavered uncertainly before *this* new world.

While still in America, Tocqueville had reflected that there might be an important link between political liberty and economic prosperity, but perhaps because of the obviously unique conditions, he made little attempt to investigate the economic development of the country. His tours of England seem to have stimulated him to more serious thought. In 1835 he had been immensely impressed by the nonrevolutionary character of its dynamic business class. The interaction of certain commercial practices with political customs might therefore help form the basis for the political education of a people like the French, whose experience in all kinds of associational activity was far inferior to that of the Anglo-American world. Thus the primary glory of England's commercial revolution was, for Tocqueville, not its prodigious wealth, but its significance as an index of human activity. The English middle class became for him "an immense *Démocratie*" which combined the passion for wealth, for liberty, and for religion in a way which both produced "those marvels of industry which astonish the world," while it assured him that "the heart of man is vaster than one supposes." [2] It was characteristic of Tocqueville that he assigned much more importance to political and moral qualities than to the development

[2] Yale Mss(T) C.V.g: copy of rough drafts for the *Démocratie* of 1840, paq. 9, cahier 1, p. 171.

of technical skills, capital, or communications, and believed that liberty was the true source of all other benefits. Montesquieu, he recalled, had said that the commercial spirit naturally endowed men with the spirit of liberty. Tocqueville insisted on a reversal of causality. In his final notes in England he tried to relate the two qualities of its society which had most deeply impressed him, liberty and commerce:

To be free one must be able to invent and persevere in a difficult enterprise, to be able to act on one's own; to live free, one must become accustomed to an existence full of agitation, movement and peril . . . When I see the force given to the human spirit in England by political life, when I see the Englishman sure of the aid of his laws, relying on himself and seeing no obstacle but the limits of his own powers, acting without constraint . . . animated by the idea that he can do everything . . . seeking the best everywhere; when I see him thus, I am in no hurry to observe whether nature has carved out ports around him, and given him coal and iron. The cause of his commercial prosperity is not there: it is within himself.[3]

He was convinced that England was industrially the prototype of the world. Perhaps his conception of the relation of its economic system to political life was also the dominant factor in his acquiescence to the competitive assumptions of the age. In the *Démocratie* of 1840, he could not point to a single "commercial and manufacturing people" from the Tyrians to the English who might be identified as an unfree people.[4]

The journey of 1835 also made Tocqueville and Beaumont feel that they had been derelict in their duty toward economic theory. Although they had long since begun a joint study of the writings of Jean Baptiste Say,[5] both Frenchmen found it convenient to rely

[3] *Oeuvres* (M): *Voyages Angleterre,* 91. For the integration of this idea into the *Démocratie* see Yale Mss(T) C.V.a: copy of notes for the *Démocratie* of 1840, paq. 8, p. 47, and *Oeuvres* (M): *Démocratie,* II, 146.

[4] *Oeuvres* (M): *Démocratie,* II, 146; see also Yale Mss(T) C.V.g: copy of rough drafts for the *Démocratie* of 1840, paq. 9, cahier 1, pp. 159–160.

[5] See Tocqueville to Beaumont, Dec. 2, 1828, Yale Mss(T) A.III. It was probably Say's *Cours complet d'économie politique pratique* (Paris, 1828–29).

on the authority of men like Nassau Senior to acquaint them with
the subtleties of political economy. Senior provided Tocqueville
with his *Outline of the Science of Political Economy;* Tocqueville
considered Senior the thinker most capable of supplementing his
own thought in the interpretation of economic problems.[6]

While the question of government intervention in economic development represented only a small part of Senior's interest, it
became for Tocqueville and Beaumont the major problem that
political economy had to solve. Senior, who was not a blind advocate of laissez-faire, on this issue agreed with the classical school in
England that in general governments usually did more harm than
good by tampering with the economic structure. Being more concerned with the political dangers of a growing concentration of
power than the process of capitalism itself, Tocqueville and Beaumont therefore welcomed an attitude which appeared most firmly
established in England: that the chief business of government was
not to establish industry but only to dissipate the political causes
that prevented industry from prospering. Not only did private industry in England perform all economic tasks more quickly and
cheaply than the state, but the correlation between the industrial
activity of private associations and political liberty seemed decisive
reasons for restricting government regulation of industry. Both
Beaumont in the Chamber and Tocqueville in the Academy advised against extending the sphere of state penetration into industry. "I am of those," concluded Tocqueville in an address in 1846,
"who think that among us the State has already extended the
sphere of its action beyond measure, that it interferes too much in
details . . . simultaneously expanding and enervating . . ."[7]

Tocqueville, however, wavered from this theoretical position of
noninterference even in principle. Discussing a law concerning joint
stock companies in 1838, Tocqueville described his great fear that in

---

[6] Tocqueville to Senior, Jan. 11, 1837, *Oeuvres* (B), VI. The *Outline* appeared in
1836.

[7] *Oeuvres* (B), IX, 78, "Rapport à l'Académie des sciences morales et politiques
(1846): *Du monopole des sels par la féodalité financière* par M. Raymond Thomassy";
see also Beaumont, *L'Irlande,* II, 120.

a century given to the extension of governmental power over the direction of industry, each new law would give it further possession of the most private and intimate phases of human life. On the other hand the *Démocratie* of 1840 recognized that the great capitalistic enterprises, with their vast accumulations of men and wealth, were exposed to sudden shifts of fortune which posed a threat to the lives of their workers and the stability of society. It seemed reasonable that "they should not be allowed to retain as much independence of the government as an individual might be allowed." [8] He realized that the problem required an entire book to itself rather than a paragraph in the *Démocratie*, but he never came to grips with it in a detailed analysis.[9] If even in theory Tocqueville found himself constantly hesitating between conflicting demands, his record in the Chamber of Deputies was even more revealing. He did not make a single major speech on economic issues during the July Monarchy. It was Beaumont who assumed the burden of working out a policy on railroad legislation, tariffs, and the regulation of child labor and working conditions.

The question of French railroad construction brought out this ambiguity most clearly. Tocqueville and Beaumont were in complete agreement on the question, but it was Beaumont who gave voice to it in the Chamber, while Tocqueville confined himself to supporting amendments and making an extensive report for his departmental *conseil-général* in la Manche. The main problem in France was whether the railroads should be built with some degree of state initiative and support. As a matter of theoretical preference both Tocqueville and Beaumont supported the cause of private enterprise "adopted in a general and absolute manner by the English," [10] and Tocqueville at first voted against government subven-

---

[8] *Oeuvres* (M): *Démocratie*, II, 318. See also Tocqueville to Royer-Collard, *Oeuvres* (B), VII.

[9] See Yale Mss(T) C.V.g: copy of rough drafts for the *Démocratie* of 1840, paq. 9, cahier 1, p. 4. Compare with his efforts devoted to the Algerian question, *Ecrits politiques*, I, 129–440.

[10] See Edmond L'Hommedé, *Un Département français sous la monarchie de juillet: le conseil-général de la Manche et Alexis de Tocqueville* (Paris, 1933), app.

tion of the railroad system. Even after the Chamber had decided on a policy of subsidies, he felt that it would have been more economical for France to have followed the English pattern. Beaumont, too, in all his parliamentary speeches from 1840 on, insisted that in countries where the state created the railroad system, it had been badly conceived.

Yet for a variety of reasons, both Tocqueville and Beaumont found themselves not only accepting but advocating state intervention, to build the railroads. Beaumont, as the reporter of the investigating commission on railroads in 1840, found that the "spirit of association" had momentarily faltered (due to the failure of some of the railroad companies) and had to be restored. Secondly, in the tense atmosphere which followed the Eastern crisis of 1840, both Prussia and England appeared to be potential military rivals. Beaumont noted with alarm that both across the Channel and on the Rhine great railway systems were giving foreign powers an advantage in military transportation which France could not tolerate.[11] Since incidents involving British vessels were endemic off the Norman coast, and since the farmers of la Manche feared the loss of the Paris market to better-serviced areas, Tocqueville found himself under considerable pressure to show special interest in a strategic Paris-to-Cherbourg line. Beaumont took up the fight in the Chamber for this also, since his friend was always reluctant to speak for local interests.

Tocqueville was also involved in a similar conflict of interest with regard to the issue of free trade. During his second English voyage the problem of removing protective barriers had been raised in his mind. Confronted with the immense prosperity of English trade and the way English economists explained its theoretical foundations, its progressive abolition of customs and tariffs ap-

---

22, p. 299, "Rapport au conseil-général de la Manche par sa commission spéciale sur un projet de chemin de fer de Paris à Cherbourg." An extract of this report also appeared in the *Journal d'agriculture pratique,* VIII (February 1845), 378–382.

[11] See *Moniteur,* June 3, 1840, p. 1276, and June 11, 1840, p. 1380; and *Oeuvres* (B), IX, "Notice sur Cherbourg," 191–194.

peared to prove that the trade prohibitions of the protectionist French policy were retarding the French rate of growth. Again, however, political considerations made his participation in the French free-trade movement minimal. Tocqueville confined himself to ordering *The Economist,* the organ of free trade in England, for the library of the Chamber. While wishing to introduce free trade with precautions and "infinite gradations," he once more refused to go beyond voting for specific measures, not once speaking at length in support of any.[12] The heavy protectionist sentiment in his local constituency may also have contributed to his hesitancy.

Tocqueville proved to be a very ineffectual ally of the liberal school of economics in France. The *Journal des économistes* complained that his parliamentary reports stopped the moment they reached the economics of an issue. He not only hesitated at points on which they were most confident, but came to diametrically opposite conclusions as to the direction of French economic development. Thus the "optimistic" school of economists, led by theorists such as Frederic Bastiat and Charles Dunoyer, could believe in the inevitable decentralization of the state because the processes of individualistic economic production would prove themselves so much more efficient than those under government control. "Providence," affirmed Dunoyer, "wanted to accumulate the powers of government in order to abolish them."[13] From the logic of economic efficiency the true and unavoidable tendencies of governments would be toward the reduction of its functions to the repression of violence and the protection of property. Tocqueville, approaching French history from the process of the administrative accumulation of power, could not accept these predictions.

Toward the end of the 1830's it became increasingly evident to him that the industrial revolution was taking a dangerous turn on the Continent. The later chapters of the *Démocratie* were symp-

[12] See Tocqueville, *Journeys to England,* 110–111, and Tocqueville to Lord Radnor, Nov. 5, 1843, *Oeuvres* (B), VI.

[13] Charles Dunoyer, "Du système de la centralisation, de sa nature, de son influence, de ses limites et des réductions utiles qu'il est destiné à subir," *Journal des économistes,* I (1842), 389.

tomatic of this realization. While England continued its economic expansion relatively free of public control or subsidies, on the Continent, where the ruler's incentive was habitual, the government tended to become the chief entrepreneur for new projects requiring immense outlays of capital. As the means of production increased, innumerable private associations did not crop up in France as they had in England to integrate them into the social structure. On the railroad question both French politicians and capitalists expected government initiative and support.[14] Industry, far from encouraging the spirit of association, was only strengthening the administrative spirit by calling into the service of the government "a vast number of engineers, architects, mechanics, and handicraftsmen."[15] Whatever the relation between a growing business class and social stability, if political habits did not precede the acquisitive instinct or maintain their autonomy from it, commerce might help to subvert liberty.

The English pattern had been reversed, and private economic attitudes flowed into public life, destroying the public realm. Tocqueville saw the culmination of this process in the Guizot ministry, which rested upon a passive middle class whose preponderant influence was, in turn, explicitly recognized and accepted as the general interest of the country. "More and more each one of us seems to retire into himself," he warned the Chamber of Deputies in 1842, "each province, each department, each arrondissement, each commune, sees nothing in political life except an opportunity to satisfy private interests . . . and considers political life only as a thing which is foreign to him."[16] In Tocqueville's anguished estimation, a new, apolitical commercial aristocracy was in danger of

---

[14] When Adolphe Thiers, eminent historian and parliamentarian, told Tocqueville in 1837 that all great public works in France would have to be made at the expense of the state and its agents, Tocqueville commented, "Not to be forgotten when I speak of the ultracentralizing tendencies of our day" (Yale Mss(T) C.V.d: copy of notes for the *Démocratie* of 1840, p. 30).

[15] *Oeuvres* (M): *Démocratie*, II, 317.

[16] *Moniteur*, Jan. 18, 1842, p. 107.

being formed—as exclusive, vicious, incapable, and unworthy of governing the country as that of the old regime. The ambitions of the French bourgeoisie, engrossed in reproducing the material abundance of their English counterparts, sealed Tocqueville's incipient conviction that the English combination of liberty, social stability, and economic progress depended on the political spirit which underlay it. This may account for his reluctance in the *Démocratie* to cite the English middle classes as an example of the new prevalence of the commercial ethic or to equate them with the middle class in France.[17]

The second volume of the *Démocratie,* published in 1840, represented the height of Tocqueville's theoretical concern with the apathy of the middle class. Utter political stagnancy, bureaucratization, and self-centered materialism were the keynotes of the new democratic world. But just as he put the final touches on the portrait of the mass age, a new disruptive element appeared on the political scene—the French working class.

For most of the upper classes the "social question" was something entirely different in the first decade of the July Monarchy from what it became in the second.[18] Tocqueville's own interest in the problem of social agitation among the lower classes extended back to the wake of the July Revolution, when the Paris workers' dissatisfaction with its results attracted his attention. But his early concern was prompted more by a humanitarian impulse than by a fear of their revolutionary potential. Tocqueville and Beaumont's

---

[17] The virtual absence of the English middle classes in the *Démocratie*'s description of the commercial propensities of the new age caused some surprise and criticism across the Channel. Ironically, Mill, in his review, pointed to Birmingham as a complete social and moral equivalent of America. Tocqueville felt, however, that the English middle classes did not jibe as well with the American as did the French for certain purposes; see *Oeuvres* (M): *Corr. angl.,* I, 320–321.

[18] See Pierre Quentin-Bauchart, *La Crise sociale de 1848: Les Origines de la Révolution* (Paris, 1920), and Armand Cuvillier, *Hommes et idéologies de 1840* (Paris, 1956), 87ff.

study of the penitentiary system of 1833 was partly rooted in a desire to contribute to the amelioration of the working class, who, they declared, "are in want of labor and bread; and whose corruption, beginning in misery, is completed in prison." [19]

Tocqueville, however, was soon drawn into attempting to probe deeper. His first extended investigation and fundamental statement on the causes of poverty appears to have been occasioned by a combination of his English experience and a French problem. England was the only country, in Tocqueville's range of travel, that had attempted a national and systematic program to provide for its indigent population. The first trip to England, in 1833, gave him some idea of the functioning of the unreformed poor law. Before going to England in 1835 he was requested by the academic society of Cherbourg to give a paper on the problem of public relief. Aided by documents on the English Poor Law Amendment Act from Nassau Senior, Tocqueville formulated his ideas in a *Mémoire sur le paupérisme* (1835). Although it was written before the journey of 1835, his basic ideas on governmental action to alleviate poverty were already essentially formed.

Tocqueville opened the *Mémoire* with a paradox. The countries which appeared to be most backward had the smallest indigent populations, and among the most opulent peoples a part of the population was obliged to live from public charity. England was, in Tocqueville's estimation, the pioneer representative of that combination of wealth and penury which all modern societies were tending to develop. "Traverse the English countryside," he continued, "and you will believe yourself transported into the Eden of modern civilization. Magnificently kept roads, new and clean houses, fat herds . . . farmers full of strength and life, more dazzling riches than anywhere else in the world, and a simple competency more embellished and more sought after than elsewhere." [20]

---

[19] *Système pénitentiaire,* 1, and see 308–313 for Tocqueville's first views on poor laws.

[20] Tocqueville, "Mémoire sur le paupérisme," 294. A supplementary memoir, though promised to the Academy, never appeared.

Yet up to a sixth of the population in England lived off public funds.

His explanation was simple. Out of the stable agricultural society of the Middle Ages had arisen a commercial and industrial society stimulated by technological improvements and the demand for greater comforts. The general effect had been a gradual rise in the condition of the masses, a general prosperity which would afford the great majority of mankind a slow and gradual increase in well-being. Tocqueville considered this one of the general laws of modern communities and an economic parallel to the rise of democracy. His general expectations were thus a projection of the optimistic economic expansion of early nineteenth-century England and France in the framework of the prevailing economic system of England. The majority of mankind would enjoy increasing ease and comfort, society would become more nearly perfected, comfortable, and stable.

However, as was shown by the English example, this trend would be accompanied by another tendency. A growing minority of indigents who would be exposed to the full insecurity of the free-market economy was the price of general prosperity and progress. This was also an irreversible law of modern societies. Tocqueville, at this point, even considered the unfortunate few "as having received from God the special and dangerous mission of providing for the material well-being of the rest of society by its risks and perils . . . The industrial class, which secures the possessions and pleasures of the greatest number, is exposed to miseries that would be almost unknown if this class did not exist." [21]

In addition to real physical deprivation, Tocqueville also observed as a result of his English experience the development of new psychological desires that were creating a revolution of expectations simultaneously with the increase of material goods. While the poor in England might appear almost rich to a Frenchman, their dynamic environment also made them unable to bear what would be very tolerable for a French or Spanish counterpart. "In

[21] "Mémoire sur le paupérisme," 308–309.

England the standard of living for which a man can hope is higher than in any other country in the world. This facilitates the extension of pauperism in that kingdom." [22]

Tocqueville did not make any detailed statistical correlation between English economic growth and the pauper population. He merely combined the observations of his first voyage to England with Senior's poor-law reports and some of the central ideas in the recently published *Economie politique chrétienne,* by Alban de Villeneuve-Bargemont.[23] There was no discussion of historical changes in the modes of production and distribution except in a brief paragraph that mentioned the change from an economy based chiefly on agriculture to one increasingly based on a multitude of nonagricultural pursuits. The analysis of the *Mémoire* rested upon the assumption that the insecurity of a wage-earning class would remain a minority problem against the background of a society of independent property owners with varying degrees of wealth but with a minimum of economic independence.

The condition of the poor was not central to Tocqueville's thought in the 1830's. He took for granted the existence of physical deprivation, economic dependency, and political impotence. Poverty was a political problem only to the extent that it impinged on his prognosis of the evolution of mankind toward a basically middle-class "equality of conditions." His experience before 1835 had convinced him that those who were not taxpayers were probably incapable of intelligent political activity and would be denied the vote in every society. While preparing the first part of the *Démocratie,* Tocqueville wrote: "Even in the United States the poor who pay no taxes obey laws to which they have neither directly nor

[22] "Mémoire sur le paupérisme," 311–312.

[23] Tocqueville relied on his own trip of 1833, Blackstone's *Commentaries,* the *Poor Law Enquiry* of 1833, the *Report from . . . Commissioners for Inquiring into . . . the Poor Laws* (London, 1834), and the text of the Poor Law Amendment Act of August 14, 1834, provided by Senior. For the European context of the problem, he used Villeneuve-Bargemont's *Economie politique chrétienne, ou recherches sur la nature et les causes du paupérisme en France et en Europe,* 3 vols. (Paris, 1834). This was a seminal work in French and social Catholicism.

indirectly consented. How could this come about if the right to participate in the affairs of government is a right inherent in the nature of man?"[24] If the published work did not include this curt dismissal of the political rights of the most unfortunate economic class, it is still apparent that poverty, unlike liberty, had no personal or universal significance for its author. He considered the small landed proprietor as the most stable and the most typical citizen of the new democratic era.

Even when Tocqueville came to deal with the economic effects of democracy in the second part of his work on America, his conclusions, drawn from a wider social perspective were still generally optimistic. Save in the realm of large-scale mass production, whose degrading effects he had observed in Manchester, Tocqueville believed that labor was enhanced by the growth of democracy. Not only did it achieve a new sense of dignity and honor, but a lessening of the distance between the worker and employer appeared to be the logical implication of the general tendency toward equality. Tocqueville's notes for his chapter on wages contained the following comment: "Democracy has a general and permanent tendency to bring master and worker nearer to each other, and to increasingly equalize their profits . . . This is the general rule, but in some parts of industry such as it is presently constituted the contrary is observed . . . This is an exceptional case (*fait exceptionnel*) but very formidable, more formidable in that it is exceptional."[25]

Since even in England it appeared that most industries would be divided among small entrepreneurs, and since political cohesion was not a characteristic of this class, it would be easier for the workers to press for their rights against them. Social mobility, legal and political equality, and educational opportunity would mitigate the dangers of a new industrial serfdom. There were no longer

---

[24] Yale Mss(T) C.V.h: copy of notes for the *Démocratie* of 1835, paq. 3, cahier 5, p. 6. The *Démocratie* referred to America as the one nation where, with "universal suffrage," the principle of popular sovereignty had attained "all the practical development of which the imagination can conceive" (*Oeuvres* (M), *Démocratie*, I, 56).

[25] Yale Mss(T) C.V.f: copy of notes for the *Démocratie* of 1840, paq. 4, cahier 1, p. 41.

"races of the poor." The diversity of Birmingham rather than the polarity of Manchester would seem to have been a more influential experience in this case, infusing Tocqueville with its image of innumerable gradations of wealth and flexible class lines. When the second volume of the *Démocratie* was completed in 1840, Tocqueville still felt that amidst all the confused and unpredictable characteristics of the new age the security of property, the leveling of wealth, and the softening of extremes of poverty were the clearest and most permanent results of social development of which he could be certain.[26]

There still remained the nagging problem of how to deal with the indigent minority. In the *Mémoire* of 1835, the only conceivable remedies were alternative forms of relief. The latter part of the *Mémoire* was an examination of public and private charity. Tocqueville agreed with Senior that the most constant source of human degradation, in England at least, was due to the misguided benevolence of the aristocracy under the old poor law. If there was nothing more attractive at first glance than the idea of public charity, the practice belied the principle. England, he declared, was the only country in Europe which had provided its poor with a legal right to charity, and reaped a whirlwind of paupers. "Any measure which establishes legal charity on a permanent basis and gives it an administrative form, thereby creates an idle class living at the expense of the other classes . . . Such a law is a deadly germ, deposited in the midst of the laws, [and] . . . if the present generation escapes its influence, it will devour the well-being of generations to come." [27]

Here Tocqueville took issue with the report and the act of 1834, which had reaffirmed the principle of public charity while attempting to draw a sharp line around the indigent, who alone were to be "within the province of the law." [28] To Senior, the reform was aimed at elevating the position of the able-bodied laborer above

---

[26] See *Oeuvres* (M): *Démocratie*, II, 158, 197, 259, 336–337. For a parallel in Beaumont, see *L'Irlande*, I, 197.

[27] Tocqueville, *Mémoire sur le paupérisme*, 324.

[28] *Report from . . . Commissioners for Inquiring into . . . the Poor Laws*, 227.

the able-bodied pauper and maintaining the independence of the first while providing new incentive for the second.[29] Reflecting Villeneuve's profound suspicion of English public relief, Tocqueville doubted whether the crucial distinction between indigence and poverty could be maintained with any degree of rigor while a general right to relief existed.

Tocqueville also insisted that the very principle of the right to relief depraved men. The whole idea of rights, which usually placed men upon an equal plane by removing any idea of begging or gratitude from certain political demands, became warped when applied to an unlimited economic claim to relief, since it legalized inferiority. A fatal relation was created between the magistrates and their wards that deprived them both of the virtues of citizens, giving rise on the one hand to habits of submission and on the other to arbitrary powers. The chief reason for Tocqueville's rejection of the right to relief for the able-bodied was thus political.

There was still another problem of human misery to be considered, and, in the spirit of the report on the Poor Law Amendment Act, Tocqueville recognized not only the utility but also the necessity of public charity applied to the inevitable hazards of infancy, old age, sickness, and insanity. But the entire sequence of circumstantial misfortunes was separated from economic poverty.

---

[29] There is an interesting parallel between the workhouse system created by the Poor Law Amendment Act of 1834 and the penitentiary system which Tocqueville and Beaumont were attempting to introduce into France. Both arose from an impulse toward moral reformation which was penetrating the whole Atlantic community. Like the workhouse, the penitentiary was designed to act vigorously and systematically to produce a regeneration in the inmate, enabling him to achieve economic independence and orderly reintegration into society. Rigorous rules, moral guidance, long periods of silence, isolation from contamination, and a work ethic for the inmates; strict economy in construction and administration; these were the common methods for reforming both able-bodied paupers and criminals. In both pauperism and criminality the majority of reformers saw an epidemic to be checked and a vice to be discouraged, but treatment began only within the workhouse, the prison, and the reformatory. Tocqueville's enthusiasm for the system of isolation is surprising in one who felt so deeply that it is not good to be alone, but it must be seen in the context of the early nineteenth century, when the ordinary prison was little more than a compulsory association for the perfection of criminals.

All "regular and permanent charity" would inevitably deprave the people, reduce the wealthy to poverty, dry up sources of savings, stop the accumulation of capital, and culminate in "a violent revolution in the State." [30] The *Mémoire* of 1835 was Tocqueville's firmest stand against direct and continuous aid for the relief of destitution. In this matter he saw no need to adopt a practice which many English political economists were trying so hard to reduce to the minimum without explicitly denying the right to assistance outright. Tocqueville realized even in the *Mémoire* that private charity, with its relatively unorganized response to a complex society, could no longer furnish a sufficient answer to human suffering on a mass scale. Over the next decade the wider ramifications of the problem of poverty took on a new urgency.

In the Chamber of Deputies after 1839, the attitude of Tocqueville and Beaumont toward social legislation did not differ markedly from that of the middle classes in either England or France, who placed their chief hope in the progressive improvement of the workers through self-discipline and self-reliance. In effect Tocqueville and Beaumont's efforts took two paths. The first was to advocate "indirect" government aid to the workers through subsidized savings banks, hospitals, mutual charity associations, and easy credit institutions. Tocqueville believed that in the absence of a poor law the incentive for such institutions would be even greater in France than in England.[31] The second was to support education for workers' children, limited electoral reform, and minor changes in the tax structure. Beaumont was by far the more active of the two in this area, while Tocqueville played a passive role until the eve of the February Revolution.

Even slight deviations from the laissez-faire principle brought Beaumont into conflict with the representatives of the orthodox school in the Academy such as Blanqui, Passy, and Dunoyer. With a keener political sense than his adversaries, Beaumont proclaimed that some intervention by the government for the well-being of

---

[30] Tocqueville, "Mémoire sur le paupérisme," 341.
[31] *Annuaire des cinq départements de la Normandie,* VIII (1842), 329–330.

the poor was a duty in some cases. He warned that it was "because one does not do for the laboring classes what the simplest and wisest theories recommend that vague and mad theories arise."[32]

This reference to "vague and mad theories" was made in 1845. It revealed a growing awareness on Beaumont's part that social problems were being discussed in a wider context than that employed in Tocqueville's *Mémoire* of a decade before. Fine distinctions between direct and indirect government intervention seemed like scholastic hair-splitting to a group of thinkers who denied some of the basic assumptions of the academic economists—above all the value of the unrestricted labor market and unlimited private property. But in order for Tocqueville and Beaumont to respond to these "vague and mad theories" more was needed than their formulation. Tocqueville was fundamentally suspicious of "utopian" historical predictions and experiments in social organization.[33] The only thing vaguely resembling recognition of socialist tendencies in the *Démocratie* of 1840, apart from an indirect reference to the Saint-Simonians, was his fear that the state might take over large spheres of economic life in the course of administrative expansion. He and Beaumont reacted slowly to the growing influence of socialist theories among the working classes in France. Just as in England, a limited range of social contacts delayed their appreciation of the depth and scope of proletarian protest. As late as 1843 Tocqueville was unfamiliar with the basic arguments and main works dealing with the "right to work," and requested Arthur de Gobineau, then collaborating with him on a study for the Academy, to provide him with information on them. Four years later he had read at least enough of the writings of Owen, Saint-Simon, Fourier, Louis Blanc, and some of the socialist novelists to begin a short refutation of their theories.

[32] "Discussion . . . sur . . . l'organisation du travail," *Séances et travaux de l'Académie des sciences morales et politiques: Compte rendu,* VIII (1848), 193.
[33] See *Oeuvres* (M): *Ecrits politiques,* I, 249–251; [Milnes], "Alexis de Tocqueville," 525.

During the last years of the July Monarchy Tocqueville and Beaumont advocated the creation of legal aid for the poor, introduced amendments to abolish marriage taxes for the indigent, and condemned the inefficiency of the French insurance institutions for the poor as compared with their English counterparts. Tocqueville became a charter member of the *Annales de la charité* (1845), and the Société d'économie charitable (1847). These were pioneer ventures of the conservative branch of the social Catholic movement (though it included some democrats and non-Catholics) led by Armand de Melun, a disciple of Villeneuve-Bargemont. Beaumont took part in a congress on penitentiary reform in September 1847 at Brussels. From it emerged a charity international, the Société internationale de la charité, which proved to be as short-lived as Marx and Engels' Democratic Association, also in process of formation at Brussels and London. In the Chamber of Deputies Beaumont attacked the Guizot ministry for having waited for almost eight years to launch an inquiry into the social problem, and he became a leading figure in the banquet campaign of 1847. Tocqueville, fearful of the government's inaction, but equally fearful of the consequences of a direct appeal to the masses against the *pays légal,* declined to follow Beaumont into the streets.

Although they saw the seriousness of the crisis more acutely than most of their contemporaries, their response was entirely pragmatic. They emphasized the inevitable economic inequality in all human societies, and recommended only minor reforms which had already been proven effective in other countries. England became their chief source of political and financial legislation. At the end of 1847 Tocqueville prepared to advocate a major reform of the budget. It was to consist of a complete reorganization of the tax system, redistributing the assessment in favor of the poor. Working-class agitation was assuming threatening proportions. "What would be more in accordance with this mood than a financial reform, whose result would be to more equitably modify the distribution of public expenses among the different classes of the nation?" Tocqueville asked his colleague Jules Dufaure in July of 1847. He volunteered to introduce the reform, for his party, showing what the English had done for thirty years in the same respect.[34]

He was convinced of the explosiveness of the situation but still believed that revolution could be avoided by timely and mild reforms. Writing to Senior in the summer of 1847, he held that the French economic structure would "continue to rest on its present foundation because even if some wanted to place society on another one, they would not know how to go about it." [35] He adhered to the basic premise of the *Mémoire sur le paupérisme,* that the existing system was inseparable from a civilized social order and economic progress. The ideological condition of France was more disturbing because of its general revolutionary potential than because of the program of any socialist group. Even when he felt an uprising to be impending Tocqueville would offer nothing beyond electoral and fiscal reform, "to assure the poor all the *legal* equality and all the well-being compatible with the individual right to property and the inequality of conditions which flows from it." [36]

It was the Revolution of 1848 which forced Tocqueville to revise his belief that the "given" bourgeois economy was one of the few definitive consequences of the democratic evolution of modern society. The "vague and mad theories" had crystallized in an irreversible event. Instead of being at the end of a great social revolution, he found himself once more in a continuing revolutionary cycle which appeared to have no visible terminus and no immutable limits. He realized that his cautious measures would have come nowhere near satisfying the working classes. Even a poor law would not have had time to effect a quick pacification of the social unrest. "It was not want," he told Senior, "but ideas, that brought about this great upheaval, fantastic ideas on the relations between labor

[34] See letter of July 29, 1847, *Oeuvres* (B), VI; *Moniteur,* June 19, 1846, p. 1849, amendment introduced by Beaumont and Tocqueville among others; *ibid.,* May 22, 1847, p. 1267; *Annales de la charité,* I (1845), 67; *ibid.,* III (1847), 155, 325–328, 529–604.
[35] Letter of August 25, 1847, *Oeuvres* (B), VII.
[36] *Oeuvres* (B), IX, 519.

and capital, exaggerated theories on the role which the social power could play in the relations of worker and employer, ultracentralist doctrines, which had come to persuade the multitude that it depended on the state not only to save them from misery, but to afford them comfort and well-being." [37] Here was the "terrible originality" of the new upheaval. Socialism became the essential issue of the February Revolution. In 1848, Tocqueville wanted more than anything else to confine the revolution to its political achievement. In his election campaign, in the debates of the drafting committee of the new constitution, and in the new legislature his method was to uphold the image of the revolution as the fulfillment of 1789. He summed up his position in the Constituent Assembly on September 12, 1848. Speaking against the proposed constitutional clause guaranteeing "the right to work," he declared that the February Revolution had been primarily due to the failure of the July Monarchy to achieve the genuine political participation of all classes. [38] All power, influence, and activity had been locked in the bosom of a single class, and unlike the English or Americans, the French people could take no real part in public affairs. The only question now was whether France would cure her political ills, or abolish liberty altogether by a socialist program.

Tocqueville did not examine socialist systems individually but pointed to those common points which he felt to be their essence. The first was their energetic, continued and immoderate appeal to the material passions of man, the second was their attack on property as the origin of all the world's evils. But the worst trait of socialism was its profound defiance of liberty, of human reason. In socialism he saw only the logical culmination of an omnipotent centralizing urge combined with a contempt for man as individual and citizen. It was "a new form of servitude."

Concerning the problem of economic deprivation, Tocqueville, in his "right to work" speech would agree only that the State could

---

[37] Letter of April 10, 1848, *Oeuvres* (B), VI. For a detailed discussion of Tocqueville's reaction to 1848, see Gargan, *Alexis de Tocqueville,* 55ff.

[38] *Oeuvres* (B), IX, 536–552.

help those "who, after having exhausted all their resources, would be reduced to misery if the State did not extend its hand to them."[39] The alternative offered by Tocqueville in opposition to the "right to work" was largely a recapitulation of the position taken by Beaumont in the debates of the constitutional drafting committee four months before. Beaumont, taking the lead in the discussion of this clause, had acknowledged that the workers had rights which had previously been ignored or neglected. These were essentially the ones demanded or conceded by Tocqueville and Beaumont before the Revolution of 1848: freedom of work and association, free education and the encouragement of worker's credit institutions, savings banks, and mutual insurance companies. There was one new item—a very "English" right to relief. Beaumont had insisted that the "right to work" clause was misleadingly worded since it really only intended, and should only guarantee, the "right to subsistence."[40] The attempt to substitute a right to existence for the right to work indicated a shift in Tocqueville and Beaumont's public policy in the wake of the February Revolution. They could not help reflecting that England had maintained the right to relief in spite of its potential abuses without forfeiting its industrial and commercial prosperity or being afflicted by the class war which imperiled the social structure of the Continent. In effect Tocqueville was now willing to accept general public relief as a political lubricant rather than as an agent of alienation.[41] Whatever the destinies of France in other respects, it would have to have a poor law on the English model.

In one respect the "right to work" speech remained at the point fixed by the *Mémoire sur le paupérisme*. Tocqueville insisted that there was nothing in the French Revolution which made the state "put itself in the place of individual foresight, of the economy or

[39] *Oeuvres* (B), IX, 551–552.

[40] Yale Mss(B) D.IV.b: "Comité de Constitution," paq. "Droit au travail."

[41] See Yale Mss(B) D.I.b: Beaumont to Tocqueville (copy), Sept. 16, 1848, and conversation with Senior, Feb. 4, 1851, *Correspondence and Conversations*, I, 204. See also Senior, *Journals Kept in France and in Italy from 1848 to 1852*, ed. M. C. M. Simpson (London, 1871), I, 276–277.

honesty of the individual, nothing which authorized the state to interpose itself in the midst of industry." [42] With the right to work as a principle of economic organization, the state would inevitably become either the only employer by fulfilling its engagements, or the organizer of industry, regulating profits, wages, production, and consumption.

It was Tocqueville's economic rather than political judgments which captured attention. Beaumont, newly appointed special ambassador to England, informed Tocqueville of the acclaim his speech had received in London. He immediately predicted that the distinction between the right to work and the right to relief would appeal to those English economists who had come to acknowledge some beneficial influence of the poor law in England but were hostile to the socialist elements of the February and June uprisings. Although John Stuart Mill rejected Tocqueville's distinction, Nassau Senior quoted Tocqueville's speech in his own lectures on economics and in the *Edinburgh Review*.[43]

Harriet Grote was inspired by the speech to complete a polemic which showed how completely the overriding political principles of Tocqueville became submerged in the economic aspects of his speech. Her pamphlet, *The Case of the Poor against the Rich,* argued against any attempt to interfere with property rights for the sake of abolishing poverty as self-defeating. "All the remedial suggestions we have heard may be resolved ultimately into an interference with the law of property, more or less plausibly veiled." [44] Every complaint against a fundamental principle of civil society had to be treated as an attack upon society itself.

---

[42] *Oeuvres* (B), IX, 551–552.

[43] See Senior, *Industrial Efficiency and Social Economy,* 297; see also Senior, "Lamartine's *Histoire de la Révolution de 1848,*" *Edinburgh Review,* XCI (January 1850), 271–272. Mill insisted that the "right to work" was the poor law of Elizabeth made more efficient by concentrating on the whole labor market, not individuals, in his essay "Vindication of the French Revolution of February 1848, in Reply to Lord Brougham and Others," in *Dissertations and Discussions* (New York, 1882), III, 55. Mill, however, quoted Tocqueville's analysis of the causes of the February Revolution at great length in this essay.

[44] London, February 1850, p. 17.

Tocqueville, in response to the pamphlet, agreed that he too could not conceive of men living outside "those primordial laws." But he reminded her that they were living in an era of basic transition. Property might also be an institution relative to its historical setting. "Who can therefore affirm that one form of society is necessary and that another cannot exist?"[45] This statement was not merely the result of his sense of historical change, but came out of his sensitivity to the shadow cast by socialism in 1848, which Tocqueville projected beyond its crushing defeat in the June days. He buried his doubts in his *Souvenirs:* "The more I study the former condition of the world and see the world of our own day . . . the more I am tempted to believe that what we call necessary institutions are often no more than institutions to which we have grown accustomed."[46]

Thus property was never allowed the honor of absolute devotion that Tocqueville gave to liberty. But outside of his *Souvenirs,* in all his public utterances he remained tied to the principle of private property. "The duty of honest men," he concluded in his letter to Harriet Grote, "is nonetheless to defend the only one [society] that they understand, even to die for it, until a better one has been shown."

Liberty and private property were seen to be intimately related, not simply because of any postulated absolute, but because those nations where the idea of private property was most respected also contained the greatest sum of political activity. In the spirited defense of property in which both Tocqueville and Beaumont became engaged, the Anglo-American world emerged as the sphere where liberty and property were most eminently protected. In his final work, the *Ancien Régime,* Tocqueville saw the chief difficulty of France in resolving the problems of the industrial revolution as the same one which had robbed their free institutions of life—a lack of appreciation of political activity. Freedom was now judged by Tocqueville to be independent of any particular economic doc-

[45] Tocqueville to Mrs. Grote, July 24, 1850, *Oeuvres* (B), VI.
[46] Page 84.

trine and had to be ultimately desired as a good in itself. In England he saw a nation which, however powerful materially, had never sacrificed its political ideals to its material improvement. Summarizing his basic attitude toward the course of French history, he alluded to nations that had grown weary of freedom "in the midst of their prosperity; they allow it to be snatched without resistance from their hands, lest they should sacrifice by any effort the very well-being which they owe to it." [47]

In the 1850's, as in the 1830's, private property and economic independence were still, for Tocqueville, a precondition of genuine political activity on the part of the citizen. This independence provided a self-sufficient sphere of human life which was both beyond the power of the state to improve effectively, and which could only deprive the citizen if state control were attempted. However, economic dependence was already a fact for a great number of Frenchmen and the proportion was continually increasing. There could be no question of maintaining liberty of action in a segment of the nation already economically subservient to others, as individuals, over whom they had no effective checks. The logic of their condition might imply the necessary formation of new types of associations and new theories of the relation of property to political activity if political action itself were to continue to have a place in the modern world. The wage-earning class could not be citizens in the restricted sense which made property owning the economic and psychological prerequisite of political activity. Tocqueville was therefore evading a real political problem. Even if the nonpropertied class had remained a minority, and even if the most blatant forms of poverty and dehumanization were, as he rightly predicted, exceptional and temporary in the Western world, this class would remain forever excluded from the realm of political action. Its members were condemned to permanent dependence either on the will of their employers or on a state whose every effort at protection would entail more subservience to the administrative apparatus. The only path between the horns of this dilemma appeared to be

[47] *Oeuvres* (M): *Ancien Régime*, I, 217.

new forms of association for both political and economic activity, and in neither did Tocqueville prepare to step beyond most of his liberal contemporaries.

It was John Stuart Mill, more sympathetic to socialism and more continuously concerned about working class conditions, who used Tocqueville's idea of the importance of association in the political realm as an answer to the social and economic problems of the working class. He suggested voluntary association as the only way to preserve the initiative of the individual workers while improving the position and conditions of the membership as a whole. Otherwise he foresaw recourse only to an omnipotent administrative state industry or the totally undependable conditions of individual employer control. And over a century after Mill and Tocqueville, the *Démocratie*'s seminal ideas on the importance of voluntary associations were extensively quoted in a study of union democracy in America.[48]

One of the chief difficulties in Tocqueville's defense of private property, which he regarded as a basic prerequisite not only of civilization but of an effective citizenry, was his failure to investigate the changes in the idea of property itself. The "right of property," which Tocqueville had described in his "Mémoire sur le paupérisme" as the first step in civilization, was not identical with the rights of acquisition that emerged with the development of capitalistic economic theory. He made no clear distinction between the classical concept of property as the chief precondition for full-fledged citizenship and arguments for the unrestricted accumulation of wealth. His partiality for a landed peasantry as the backbone of a democratic social system indicated his clear inclination toward the older view with its roots in classical political thought. He sensed the corrosive effects of the acquisitive concept fostered by the growth of commerce and industry, but he also accepted both aspects of the idea of property as necessarily connected and de-

---

[48] See Mueller, *John Stuart Mill*, 166–167, 205, and S. M. Lipset and others, *Union Democracy: The Internal Politics of the International Typographers Union* (Glencoe, Ill., 1956), 74–77, 105.

fended the independence of the capitalist because he feared for the independence of the citizen. For Tocqueville the varieties of socialism were merely intractable movements toward a centralized, monolithic society.

In a sense England may have acted as a limiting influence on this aspect of Tocqueville's thought. The almost religious sanctity of private property in the same society that possessed the most effective polity in Europe struck him as the best empirical example of a necessary link between property and liberty. England in the 1850's, even more than two decades earlier, might well demonstrate to a contemporary a causal connection between liberty and property. Tocqueville and Beaumont, then, kept largely within the limits of their original economic assumptions, both for their analysis of the movement of the industrial revolution and for the solution of its obvious problems. Tocqueville always remained most profound when treating the political implications of socioeconomic processes within the upper and middle classes. The world of the working class in France as in England remained largely unexplored by him. Although the *Démocratie* asserted that there was no longer a separate race of the poor, when the workers and their spokesmen burst rudely into his life in 1848, Tocqueville viewed them as alien and unpalatable beings. He perceived the power of the egalitarian impulse directed against the contemporary economic system, but he could not empathize with yearnings and hatreds born of experiences which he had never shared. His moral vantage point was fundamentally and narrowly that of the proprietary class to which he belonged.

During the final years of his life Tocqueville, as a member of the Société d'économie charitable, maintained his contacts with the socially conscious minority among the upper classes. He participated in the attempt to revive the "charity international" during the universal exposition of 1855 in Paris.[49] However, with the waning of working-class agitation after 1849 Tocqueville's interest in socialist theories lapsed. In his *Ancien Régime* (1856) socialism was pejora-

[49] See J.-B. Duroselle, *Les Débuts du catholicisme social en France (1822–1870)* (Paris, 1951), 618.

tively identified as an heir of the bureaucratic spirit of prerevolutionary France, but the sting of its imminence and of its terrible originality was missing. Tocqueville also showed great interest in the peasantry and the machinery of poor relief in the eighteenth century, but his concern there was mainly historical. A decade after the Revolution of 1848 Beaumont reminded him that despite the surface tranquillity, the French proletariat was still imbued with socialist passions and that they should be reading Louis Blanc's writings as carefully as they studied those of their fellow liberals.[50]

The social problem faded from Tocqueville's writings after 1851 in the face of a more immediate political issue. Under the dictatorship of Louis Napoleon, Tocqueville returned to the problem of liberty with an assurance and passionate conviction which he could never manifest elsewhere. With the removal of even the forms of political life to which they had both devoted their lives to preserving, Tocqueville and Beaumont returned to bedrock convictions. And, in the context of the failure of liberalism after 1848 throughout the Continent, England settled into her final position in Tocqueville's imagination.

[50] Beaumont to Tocqueville, Feb. 5, 1858, Yale Mss(B) D.I.b, paq. 11, cahier 9, pp. 38-39 (copy).

VIII ❖ *Tocqueville versus England*

ON NOVEMBER 30, 1840, Alexis de Tocqueville rose before the Chamber of Deputies to indict England and Russia for conspiracy to keep France from taking her rightful place in the Middle East and to demand revenge for her greatest humiliation since Waterloo. "Do you believe that a nation that wants to remain great can be witness to such a spectacle without taking part in it? Do you believe that we are to let two peoples of Europe seize this immense inheritance with impunity? I will tell my country with firmness, with conviction—rather than suffer this, let there be war!" [1]

If Tocqueville's activity on behalf of domestic reform before 1848 was a confused attempt to forestall an eruption from below, his efforts in foreign affairs were an even more desperate bid to halt the petrification of the middle-class *pays légal*. Until overshadowed by the social question, foreign-policy debates were the main occasions for his polemic speeches. Anglo-French relations became the testing ground for the oracle of the democratic era. If a new science of politics was needed for a new world, then an emerging democratic society demanded a new diplomacy. The supremacy of popular parliaments, the atmosphere of open debate, and the necessity of continually appealing to public opinion would change the methods and the aims of international relations.

---

[1] *Moniteur,* Dec. 1, 1840, p. 2349. Sister Mary Lawlor, in her study of *Alexis de Tocqueville in the Chamber of Deputies,* provides a thorough account of Tocqueville's speeches on the Eastern question and the right of search in their historical context, but does not mention Tocqueville's last major speech in the Chamber on foreign policy in 1845.

Comparing the preponderant influence of England in world affairs with the relative insignificance of America, Tocqueville, in the *Démocratie* of 1835, concluded "that almost all the peoples that have influenced the world . . . have been directed by strong aristocracies." [2] He warned his readers that if they desired elevated thoughts, a scorn of well-being, and a spirit of honorable devotedness to pervade a society, and if they wished to encourage a love of glory, they had better not expect these to come easily to a democratic society. A democracy promised more for the general prosperity and security of its members than for their heroic potentialities. The amelioration of manners and the compassion that equality fostered would combine with the calculating quest for the acquisition of wealth to quell the "violent and poetic" emotions which characterized the military spirit. "I believe," declared Tocqueville in 1840, "that it may be accepted as a general and permanent rule that among civilized peoples warlike passions will become rarer and milder as conditions become more equal." [3]

But as a basis for action the problem was only posed rather than being solved. Was the "internal peace and prosperity" principle a wholly beneficial tendency, or was a degree of power and glory still to be hoped for? Tocqueville was ready to consider all appeals that might check the inveterate individualism of a new age, and of France in particular. Among the notes for the *Démocratie* of 1840 appeared the reminder on the subject of public apathy: "Here, everything I can say on association, aristocratic persons, liberty, great passions . . ." [4] Thus the second part of the *Démocratie* proposed that the rulers of democratic societies would be wise to involve the people in dangerous undertakings in order to provide a field for action, and that war "almost always elevates the thoughts of a people and raises its heart." [5]

[2] *Oeuvres* (M): *Démocratie,* I, 240.

[3] *Démocratie,* II, 270.

[4] Yale Mss(T) C.V.k, paq. 7, cahier 1, 74 (Tocqueville's ellipsis).

[5] *Oeuvres* (M): *Démocratie,* II, 274. But for his earlier reservations see Yale Mss(T) C.V.c: notes for the *Démocratie* of 1840, paq. 5, cahier 1, pp. 14–15.

Tocqueville was given ample opportunity to bring these ideas before the French public when, on the heels of the completion of the *Démocratie* and his election to the Chamber of Deputies, France became deeply embroiled in a flare-up of the Eastern question. For the new deputy it was a classic example of the action of a democratic nation in foreign affairs. Significantly, the chief rival of France was England. The clash of expanding spheres of influence came to a head in the conflicting claims to Syria by the Ottoman sultan and his defiant vassal in Egypt, Mohammed Ali, who was supported by the French. Tocqueville refused to regard the Eastern crisis as the result of a complicated series of maneuvers which had converted Anglo-French cooperation into a temporary antagonism. Mohammed Ali, the machinations of Lord Palmerston in England, of Soult and Thiers in France, and the tight infighting of the various European diplomatic corps all seemed secondary to a greater consideration. France needed to do something "beyond itself," less to meet the demands of the particular situation than to combat the tendency of its citizens to retire into a narrow and sterile egotism. Thus the Eastern crisis was the occasion for, rather than the cause of, Tocqueville's appeal for a bold foreign policy.

On July 2, 1839, in his first speech before the Chamber, the new deputy from Valognes revealed his point of departure, the necessity of appealing to the nationalism of a new democratic age. A strong policy depended not on the unity of a government but on the opinions of the country. "France," he declared, "formerly so strong, so great . . . sharing in all great enterprises, no longer concerns itself with anything." The belief that the government was afraid to act would be fatal to the entire regime if it ever "took root in the heart of this proud and excitable nation." [6]

In the months following Tocqueville's initial speech, the Syrian affair became more critical. Palmerston was determined to show the French government that they were not in a position to pursue a policy in Syria despite England's opposition. He made direct overtures to the Russian government, undercutting the basic French diplomatic assumption of Anglo-Russian rivalry. The Anglo-

[6] *Moniteur*, July 3, 1839, p. 1195.

French "liberal coalition" of the 1830's vanished before an agreement between Russia and England for the settlement of the Eastern question favorable to the sultan. Maintaining that France had broken her commitments to the other powers to a joint European settlement, Palmerston effected her complete isolation by arranging a secret settlement between England, Russia, Prussia, and Austria on July 15, 1840.

When, shortly thereafter, the treaty was revealed to France, the reaction was explosive. Even the more moderate of the French journals appeared to accept war as the probable outcome of the situation. Tocqueville was not displeased by this turn of events. At the time of the diplomatic earthquake, he observed that he had never seen a country where "the primary symptom of public life, which is the frequent contact of men with each other," was less apparent than in his own.[7] He welcomed an occasion when France could unite her patriotic sentiments around a cause which would be a legitimate reaction to an insult, as well as an assertion of France's position in the European concert. "You know what a taste I have for great events and how bored I am in our little democratic and bourgeois *pot-au-feu*," he wrote to Beaumont.[8]

Tocqueville, like later French statesmen, displayed a curious ambiguity about maintaining national pride without recklessly throwing France into an impossible situation. War against all of Europe would inevitably lead to French defeat. He warned Beaumont that this fact should never be forgotten, but should also never be revealed to the nation. The problem was to maintain a conception of France at home and abroad without actually bringing the crisis to a point where war was inevitable.

The accession of the Guizot ministry under the shadow of French capitulation to Palmerston in the Eastern crisis and "in defiance of the national sentiment" occasioned Tocqueville's entrance into the ranks of the opposition. His participation in the general policy

[7] Tocqueville to Royer-Collard, Aug. 15, 1840, in Léon d'Estresse de Lanzac de Laborie, "L'Amitié de Tocqueville et de Royer-Collard," *Revue des deux mondes,* 7th per., LVIII (1930), 903.

[8] Letter of Aug. 9, 1840, *Oeuvres* (B), VII.

debate of the Address to the Throne on November 30, 1840, was the most belligerent moment of his parliamentary career. In three sweeping generalizations Tocqueville angrily condemned all the governments of Europe, including his own, for attempting to make France forget her past and mortgage her future. The first charge was that France had been deeply humiliated by the great powers. It had to take a stand which would save face vis-à-vis Europe— even at the risk of war. The second was that France was being excluded by England and Russia from participation in one of the great innovations in nineteenth-century politics—the expansion of Europe. The third was that the new Guizot ministry, by identifying the patriotic spirit with revolution was allowing the revolutionaries, whom Tocqueville bitterly opposed, to retain a monopoly on the greatest source of civic unity left to the French nation.

As in his earlier speech in 1839 Tocqueville had begun with a discussion of the issue at hand, the French reaction to diplomatic stratagems in the Near East. But here the more generalized basis of his recommendations and the underscoring of the close link between foreign policy and internal policy became more insistent. Syria was, as Beaumont had suggested in the press, only the beginning of an unprecedented drama.[9] Egypt and the Ottoman Empire occupied a small place in the larger picture that Tocqueville sought to place before his audience:

What is happening in Egypt and Syria is only part of an immense picture, only the beginning of an immense scene. Do you know what is happening in the Orient? An entire world is being transformed; from the banks of the Indus to the Black Sea, in all that immense space, societies are crumbling, religions are being weakened, nationalities are disappearing, all the [old] lights are going out, the old Asiatic world is vanishing, and in its place the European world is rising. Europe in our times does not attack Asia only through a corner, as did Europe in the time of the crusades: She attacks . . . from all sides, puncturing, enveloping, subduing.[10]

[9] See Beaumont, *De la politique extérieure de la France au 29 Octobre 1840* (Paris,
[10] *Moniteur,* Dec. 1, 1840, p. 2349. 1840).

Tocqueville drew a picture of eastern societies disintegrating and disappearing under the impact of European expansion, firmly convinced that France must insist on a role in the new order, not only because of her civilizing capacities but because he automatically assumed that grandeur in the modern world demanded this participation.

What disturbed him most was not the consequences of action outside Europe but the psychological implications of France's withdrawal from the sphere of glorious deeds. He was as much obsessed with the decline of France in the eyes of Europe and in her own eyes as with actual accomplishments in the non-European world. The political philosopher in him could not believe that his country's difficulties were anything less than the superficial expression of a more deep-seated antagonism. His search for the underlying social conditions beneath events led him to eternalize the diplomatic isolation of July 15.

France was in a state of hidden hostility with the older powers of Europe, not because of her actions in the East, nor even because the Revolution of 1830 had cracked the edifice of the Restoration. The source of the enmity, according to the analyst of democracy, was "the ensemble of laws, of customs, of ideas, of sentiments that our fifty years of revolution have created and that we all wish to support, whatever Prince occupies the throne." With this image he also conjured up the memory of the revolutionary era before the Chamber as the chief deterrent to a European offensive against France. The world knew that if France had diminished in material strength "she has retained that extraordinary power which finds in particular moments an unequaled energy." [11] Tocqueville feared that the memory of these impetuous and proud moments in which all Europe had been defied might be irreparably damaged and his country would lose a psychological advantage which had partially compensated for her relative military decline.

However, when he conjured up the specter of France as the potent catalyst of democracy in Europe, he appeared to be tying himself to

[11] *Moniteur,* Dec. 1, 1840, p. 2349.

the revolutionary spirit at home. This was precisely what had forced Guizot and the Doctrinaire liberals to rally round Louis Philippe and suspend their hostility to his interference in the machinery of constitutional government a few months before. He castigated the Guizot majority for accusing all who opposed total French appeasement of being "agents of discord" and advocates of a propaganda war in the manner of 1793. In an attempt to convince the Chamber that the nation could wage a great war without causing an internal revolution, Tocqueville insisted that linking the two was not only contrary to an energetic foreign policy but would ultimately force the country to run the risk of the very revolutions that it wished to avoid. Conceding that there was "a small society of barbarians" always ready to use any moment to seize the reigns of government, he refused to allow the revolutionaries to usurp the banner of patriotism. Wounded and aroused, national honor was "the only link among all the broken ties which lie scattered on the surface of this country, the only one perhaps which is whole and strong." [12]

Therefore Tocqueville's vague suggestions for immediate action derived from a desire to do something more for a psychological effect than for concrete ends. His advice was as general as the framework in which he placed French foreign policy. The remedy for the tarnished image of France, thrust contemptuously from the European concert, was to demand concessions as the price of peace. The government had to declare "certain consequences of the treaty of July 15 intolerable, which we will not submit to without making war." He left it entirely up to the Chamber to pick out the offensive items. The stance of defiance was what was important: "A government which cannot make war is a detestable government." [13]

Every personal opportunity outside the Chamber was used to drive home the seriousness of the affair. In a welcoming note to a new acquaintance, Richard Monckton Milnes (a Member of Parliament and later Lord Houghton), Tocqueville gravely wrote that he would make his visit to Paris useful and agreeable because the only

[12] *Moniteur,* Dec. 1, 1840, p. 2350.
[13] *Moniteur,* Dec. 1, 1840, p. 2349.

remaining chance of peace between England and France was to get to understand each other. Henry Reeve, who was making prodigious efforts to act as an intermediary for a negotiated settlement, was so alarmed by his friend's stand that Tocqueville's correspondence, which emphasized the possibility of revolution and war in Europe, was passed on to Lord Lansdowne, who read it to the cabinet. Lord Melborne "attached great importance to it," though it did not sway Palmerston.[14]

Tocqueville's other English friends were equally dismayed by the arguments of the political philosopher turned fire eater. Nassau Senior cited Tocqueville's war speech in an article in the *Edinburgh Review* to show how easily the militarist streak in the French national character could appear in her "wisest" and "most moderate statesmen." In his direct correspondence Senior confined himself to underlining the weak point in Tocqueville's speech and the attempt to inflate the issue so many degrees beyond the case in hand. No matter how masterly the analysis of the importance of national images was in foreign policy, to make France's whole future hinge on an act of general defiance to all Europe where the issue was not a matter of immediate survival was tantamount to standing a pyramid on its head.[15]

John Stuart Mill also found Tocqueville's position untenable and incomprehensible and severely criticized his friend's contribution to the war fever. Mill was inclined to judge Palmerston's methods severely, but he thought France's position was also dictated primarily by the devious maneuverings of her leaders. Mill would have hung Palmerston and Thiers together, but he did not know which of the two could be considered more responsible for the situation. He clearly saw that Tocqueville regarded the breach in Anglo-French

[14] Charles C. F. Greville, *The Greville Memoirs, 1814–1860*, 8 vols. (London, 1938), V, 343, note by Reeve. See also Pope-Hennessy, *Monckton Milnes: The Years of Promise*, 139. Both Monckton Milnes and George Grote attacked Palmerston's policy in Parliament for endangering the peace of Europe; see *Hansard's Parliamentary Debates*, ser. 3, vol. 56: Jan. 26, 1841, pp. 50–59, 78–83.

[15] "France, America and Britain," reprinted in *Historical and Philosophical Essays*, and Senior to Tocqueville, Feb. 27, 1841, *Correspondence and Conversations*, I, 23.

understanding as an opportunity as much as a misfortune. He may have also sensed that Tocqueville was as envious of the success of his "aristocratic" neighbor as he was indignant over its acts. A democratic social condition apparently did not alter imperial ambitions.

Tocqueville replied that he was sorry to witness the split between England and France, but he considered the action of England as the cause of legitimate French resentment and again insisted that national pride was the greatest sentiment which remained to France. "I need not tell you, my dear Mill, that if it be important to keep up in a nation, especially in a nation as versatile as ours, the feeling that leads to great actions, the people must not be taught to submit quietly to being treated with indifference." [16]

Mill was profoundly disappointed by Tocqueville's rebuttal. He did not regard the direction of French sentiment as a proper antidote to the enervating effects of modern democracies, and maintained that it was necessary to instruct a nation that its image did not depend on noisy saber rattling. What constituted national glory and national esteem for the English liberal was not the "low and grovelling aims" of French foreign policy but "the love of liberty, of progress, even of material prosperity." Mill implicitly rejected Tocqueville's desire to keep alive the more heroic virtues of an aristocratic and warlike foreign policy and could not understand the "defiance of foreigners" that lay at the heart of the French sentiment against July 15. In the name of civilization, he admonished Tocqueville, "France and posterity have the right to expect from such men as you better ideas of national glory and importance." [17] He detected not pride but angry weakness in the popular will that Tocqueville chose to exalt.

It was obvious in this exchange that Tocqueville and Mill were basically concerned with different things. Mill was afflicted by the degree to which an eastern squabble had affected the peace of Europe. Tocqueville, while he had not yet made it his keynote in the Chamber, was really concerned with the French political spirit and its possible decline. Particular action in the Near East was

[16] Letter of Dec. 18, 1840, *Oeuvres* (M): *Corr. angl.,* I.
[17] Mill to Tocqueville, Aug. 9, 1842, *Corr. angl.,* I.

obviously subordinated to France's position in Europe and even her European status to her domestic problems.

For a time after his war speech of 1840, Tocqueville still cited the state of public opinion toward England against Guizot's efforts to reinstate an Anglo-French accord. Any permanent union between the two nations, however appealing in principle, was no more than "a beautiful dream." [18] As the war scare passed, however, humor and discretion replaced rancor. Tocqueville was soon being good-naturedly lampooned in Charles Buller and Monckton Milnes' political parodies as the voice of outraged democratic nationalism, and the French patriot kept to himself his notes on "how the English in India could be destroyed." [19] But even Palmerston's departure and the resumption of the entente cordiale under the impetus of Lord Aberdeen and Guizot did not alter the basic situation for Tocqueville. France was no longer isolated, but it seemed to have gained little prestige or independence in the renewal of ties. It was symptomatic that the cause of France's weakness lay as much in hidden hostilities within as in her relations with the outside world. From the very outset of his parliamentary activity Tocqueville had been convinced that the principle cause of France's internal enervation lay "not in a multitude of secondary incidents . . . but in the political habits of the nation." [20] This fundamental theme was now woven into the analysis of foreign affairs as well.

Beaumont, often Tocqueville's alter ego in the Chamber, drew upon the method of his studies of America and Ireland, and looked for the "radical vice" in the Guizot system. He found it "in the existence of a ministry which is not following our institutions." Only by substituting private interests for political sentiments and deftly abusing all the resources of administrative centralization and public money in elections, had it retained power. [21] Tocqueville seconded this description of the relation between a weak foreign policy and

[18] *Moniteur,* Jan. 28, 1843, p. 163.
[19] See E. M. Wrong, *Charles Buller and Responsible Government* (Oxford, 1926), 44, and *Oeuvres* (M): *Ecrits politiques,* I, 481.
[20] Tocqueville to J. J. Ampère, January 1842, *Oeuvres* (B), VII.
[21] *Moniteur,* Jan. 27, 1843, p. 151.

the domestic situation. The point of departure of the Guizot ministry, he observed, was the lack of confidence of the country. Operating contrary to the spirit and the institutions of 1830, and upheld by
a majority without program or aims, the *pays légal* was becoming
a closed corporation which bargained away its political control to
Guizot and the king for economic and administrative privileges and
a tacit agreement to embalm the status quo.[22]

Tocqueville's call for great acts in foreign affairs imperceptibly
gave way to vehement pleas for the salvation of political action at
home. In 1840, Tocqueville believed that a bold foreign policy could
revive the political spirit of the country. By March 1843 he asserted
that the basic impetus had to come from within the French body
politic. This, he wrote to Reeve, was his "new policy," one which he
retained to the end of the July Monarchy. Every speech on Anglo-
French relations henceforth became a harangue on "the decline of
France's institutions and the progressive debasement of the parliamentary power."

On the occasion of the Address to the Throne in 1845 Tocqueville
and Beaumont made a final joint effort to persuade the Chamber to
sever the entente as a preliminary to the destruction of the Guizot
ministry. Beaumont, speaking first, restated the chief objection to the
English alliance. It was the French government which concerned
him, not England, which had "never been greater or more powerful
than at this moment . . . As you are weak," he declared to the
ministry, "as you are hostile to the country . . . you seek strength
elsewhere—[in] London. That is the secret of the close English
alliance."[23] Following Beaumont, Tocqueville declared that the
"weak and undignified conduct" of the Guizot ministry disturbed
him much more than the existence or absence of an alliance between
the two countries. Tocqueville brought every argument he could
muster against what he considered the basic and pernicious principle
of both the Guizot ministry and the Thiers faction of the opposition,
that "the alliance with England is one of the absolute necessities of

[22] *Moniteur,* Mar. 2, 1843, pp. 349–350.
[23] *Moniteur,* Jan. 20, 1845, p. 123.

our political situation [and] the central point of your conduct." [24]

True to his usual pattern Tocqueville proceeded to place the question in an institutional and sociological framework. At this point, and precisely to sever England from France, he emphasized the aristocratic-democratic dichotomy at the expense of their analogous parliamentary institutions. The partisans of the English alliance held that France was the natural friend of England because both countries desired the extension of free institutions. Tocqueville declared that this was not the case. At a more fundamental level there was an even greater divergence. Parliamentary forms of government did not prevent frequent clashes throughout the world. Tocqueville, almost wishfully, declared that France was a logical and inevitable protectress of liberal institutions such as England could never be. England's constitution derived from an aristocratic and particular historical development and its institutions incurred "neither friends nor enemies." France represented a different sort of liberty—logically, necessarily, and universally applicable to all men. Here Tocqueville's adherence to the democratic principle emerged not as a matter of resignation to the inevitable but as a firm belief in the potential strength of a society founded upon that principle. "What is France in the world? What is its role? What is it if not the heart and head of democracy, of that new condition which can be praised or cursed but which must be acknowledged because it is in the nature of things? That is what France represents." [25]

Tocqueville then turned to England: "What does England represent? The old aristocracy, the old institutions of Europe, the old world." Tocqueville embraced without reservations the concept of "aristocratic" England to drive home to the Chamber the need for a decisive change in France's image of herself. Instead of a cause for intimate union, he presented a "deep antagonism which does not reveal itself superficially, but which exists beneath institutions." [26]

[24] *Moniteur,* Jan. 20, 1845, p. 125.

[25] *Moniteur,* Jan. 20, 1845, p. 125. See also *Ecrits politiques,* I, 124–126.

[26] *Moniteur,* Jan. 20, 1845, p. 125. Tocqueville went to some pains to acquire from his English friends accurate material for his attack on the entente. See Tocqueville to Reeve, Jan. 4, 1845, *Oeuvres* (M): *Corr. angl.,* I.

To this sweeping social antagonism Tocqueville added the spice of competitive material interests. Wherever France took a step forward in commercial expansion she would have to antagonize England. Once again a careful distinction was drawn between transitory collisions and the inevitable conflicts arising from a more deepseated rivalry. It was important to place the cause of conflict outside the realm of particular ministries and to prove that it did not matter whether Palmerston or Aberdeen directed the British Foreign Office.

Since the English were not committed by their institutions to foster one particular form of government throughout the world, England could follow her commercial interests all the more closely in foreign affairs. Moreover, she was bound by her economic situation to a continual growth which could brook no voluntary concession to other nations in matters of trade. Her supremacy was not a matter of choice, but one of necessity. Tocqueville thus disowned any connection with "perfidious Albion" propaganda: "Think of the singular and unique condition of England, unique in its greatness, unique in its perils; think of a nation which has gathered into its hands the whole trade of the world . . . and which in order to live, is obliged to maintain this extraordinary and abnormal state." [27]

The same "abnormality" which had once served Tocqueville as a possible key to revolution in England now became his primary economic argument against the possibility of a permanent Anglo-French alliance. All the energies, skills, and intelligence across the Channel were already wagered on industrialization. Two thirds of the English population was engaged in trade and industry. With her workers mobilized and concentrated, but as yet unrevolutionary, this aristocratic and dynamic nation saw in commerce the only guarantee of its existence.

To be a permanent ally of such a people one would have to renounce everything. While Tocqueville admitted the inevitable predominance of England, France would get less than nothing if she did not re-establish her position as an independent power. If the separation between England and France rested on profound differ-

[27] *Moniteur*, Jan. 20, 1845, p. 125.

ences in the principles and material developments of the two societies, there could be only one reason for a continued alliance on the part of a French government—fear not of revolutionaries, but of the French people. "You want the English alliance!" he thundered at the ministerial bench:

In fact, it is necessary for you—but why?—because the government that you give France renders it indispensable. It is clear that if you didn't have this intimate, continuous, and complete alliance with England, you would be obliged to count on yourselves sometimes, and often on the nation; you would be obliged to identify yourselves with the spirit of the nation . . . If you did not have this absolute security, which permits you to sleep in England's arms, you would be obliged to activate the nation, to lead it in such a way that it could, if necessary, sustain a struggle . . . you would be obliged to reawaken, to reanimate, to uphold her patriotism . . . But you want to spare yourself all these things; for this the intimate alliance with England is indispensable.[28]

The really surprising fact about this speech, with all its beating of the ideological and economic drums for a departure from the entente, was the mist in which it concealed the basic and overwhelming reasons for such an understanding by every nonrevolutionary constitutional French government in a hostile Europe. Tocqueville strained his own convictions to no avail, and his arguments were to evaporate as soon as they were exposed to the drafts of the February Revolution and ministerial responsibility. At the moment this lay too far in the future to dampen the comfort of speaking boldly and decisively in loud opposition to the overwhelming tide of belief in the English alliance.

The great theme of national prestige and democratic sentiments which Tocqueville had offered to his colleagues in the Chamber of Deputies in 1839 and 1840 dominated the speech of 1845 as well, but it also revealed the shift in his concerns. France's global destiny, though less aggressively stated, was still one of Tocqueville's fundamental interests. But with much greater emphasis and urgency, he reiterated France's role as the democracy par excellence in Europe.

[28] *Moniteur,* Jan. 20, 1845, p. 126.

The antagonism of revolutionary France and reactionary Europe, vividly etched in 1840, was now transformed into a milder dichotomy between aristocratic, though liberal, England, and democratic France. But he was no longer content simply to refer to the democratic instincts or the democratic social structure as the necessary basis of French national power. France's message and heritage were also the universally applicable liberalism of her institutions. The aristocrat who had broken with his past was being forced by the rise of new revolutionary currents to define more precisely the democratic emblem to which he had openly given his allegiance. In seeking to free France from the English embrace by destroying the "analogy of institutions" he acted under the assumption that a France, cut loose from the entente, would be forced into its true posture of democratic liberalism.

In his speech against the alliance in 1845 Tocqueville seemed to be talking only to himself and his friends. The government ignored him, the Chamber ignored him, and the London press ignored him.[29] Within a year, however, Tocqueville's dream of a break with England seemed to come true, with shocking results. While the leaders of the parliamentary opposition moved from the Chamber to the reform banquets, Guizot began overtures of his own to the bulwarks of the Restoration. Estrangement from England, accelerated by the return of Palmerston in 1846, was the ominous signal for the realignment. To his disgust Tocqueville saw his country supporting Metternich in Italy and Switzerland against both revolution and reform.

"Will we therefore see only the shameful sides of the entente cordiale?" he raged at the Guizot ministry for its failure to protest the extradition of political refugees from Tuscany to the papal states. "Will we be allied only when it is a question of diminishing us in the world, and when there is a question of honor and humanity will alliance be a vain word?" He commented bitterly that the entente cordiale which he had fought because it prevented France from taking effective action abroad was timidly abandoned when liberal

[29] *The Times*, Jan. 23, 1845, p. 4, dismissed the whole debate as a fight of shadows.

action was possible. "Our government, instead of joining its voice to that of England . . . instead of uniting its influence with the salutory, and unfortunately futile, influence of England, united its influence to that of Austria." [30]

Tocqueville helplessly watched the reversal of roles which France was undergoing, and his correspondence with his English friends, which had been continuous throughout his opposition to the entente cordiale, now began to reveal lines of political agreement in matters of foreign affairs as well as economic and social policy. George Grote, writing against the Guizot-Metternich policy in Switzerland, confided to him, "You are almost the only Frenchman to whom I would venture to write so frankly and copiously about Guizot, for I know well that, generally speaking, condemnation of him by an Englishman is a sure way of procuring support for him." [31]

Tocqueville had in fact become so imbued with the idea that the Guizot ministry was fatal to France that by the time Guizot finally achieved one real, if temporary, diplomatic victory over England in the Spanish Marriages affair, Tocqueville again found himself in opposition to almost all French public opinion because he refused to support the government. While he was satisfied with the French victory on the particular question, he would not, like many of his colleagues in the opposition, support the ministry. He again broadened the particular question of the marriages into one of lack of confidence in the basic policy of a government that had corrupted the political spirit of the nation.[32]

These final bickerings over foreign policy were soon submerged in the rising tide of revolutionary agitation. Tocqueville's rigid opposition to Guizot, in spite of the ephemeral success against England, was the truest gauge of his realization that the paramount problem of France no longer lay in questions of external glory but

[30] *Moniteur,* June 16, 1846, p. 1811.

[31] George Grote, *Seven Letters concerning the Politics of Switzerland pending the Outbreak of the Civil War in 1847,* ed. H. G. [Harriet Grote] (London, 1876), 170.

[32] *Moniteur,* Feb. 2, 1847, p. 204. Tocqueville was not displeased that France had for once managed to get satisfaction for the English humiliation in the Eastern affair. He later felt that the incident had ultimately weakened the regime.

in a renewed revolutionary condition. He had abandoned arguments based on the necessity of imperial expansion and the saving uplift of bellicose passions in favor of a complete reliance on the influence of constitutional liberty on foreign public opinion. It again became important for him to be able to speak to foreigners of "the two great free nations of Europe—those which I know the best . . . where questions are decided only after discussion before the country and obedience is rendered to public opinion alone—France and England." [33]

On January 27, 1848, Tocqueville delivered his final speech to the Chamber, predicting, with an accuracy which surprised even him, the imminence of revolution. More than power was now at stake.

France, amidst the noisy thunder of her first revolution, gave the world principles which have since been the regenerative basis of all modern societies. That was its glory, the most precious part of itself. Well, gentlemen, it is these principles which our conduct is hurting . . . Europe is beginning to wonder if we were right or wrong; it is wondering if, as we have so often repeated, we are leading human societies toward a more happy and prosperous future or toward more misery and ruin. That, gentlemen, is what pains me most in the spectacle we are presenting to the world. It harms not only us, but our principles; it harms our cause, it harms that intellectual fatherland, which, as a Frenchman, I hold greater than the physical and material country which surrounds us. [34]

Once more the government shrugged. Less than a month later, on February 24, 1848, the ministry and the monarchy were gone. Tocqueville felt vindicated that the foreign policy of France and its weak dependence upon foreign alignments had arisen from a mutual lack of confidence between the French government and its people, a deficiency which produced more damaging results than the humiliation of 1840.

---

[33] Tocqueville to Charles Sumner, Aug. 6, 1847, Harvard College Library, Charles Sumner Mss, Am 1.4, "Letters Received," 130, Foreign, no. 72.

[34] *Oeuvres* (M): *Démocratie,* II, 371, "Discours prononcé à la Chambre des Deputés le 27 janvier 1848, dans la discussion du projet d'adresse en réponse au discours de la couronne."

During eight years in the Chamber he had moved slowly from a position in which France's subservience to England was the focus of his parliamentary speeches to a point where it was regarded as a relatively minor symptom of a deadly internal disease. In 1842 Tocqueville could still say to his electorate at Valognes that it was principally because of its foreign policy that he was opposing the cabinet. By 1848, the foreign policy of the Guizot ministry was irrelevant.

In his *Souvenirs* Tocqueville was willing to admit that he had perhaps attacked the foreign policy of the July Monarchy too forcefully.[35] This conclusion, however, was not merely a token of contemplative hindsight that the Guizot ministry's entente cordiale could have been one of its better policies had it been effectively implemented. It arose from the ironic fact that when Tocqueville became the foreign minister of France for a moment in 1849 the English alliance became the cornerstone of his own foreign policy. Not only did he seek complete accord with England on every major action during his brief tenure in power, but the English press and Parliament were courted as assiduously as their French counterparts.

After 1848 it was no longer a question for Tocqueville of stirring the people to renewed action, but of salvaging institutions which in 1840 had been taken as accomplished facts.

[35] Page 38.

IX ❖ England versus Despotism

IN THE summer of 1851, working desperately and futilely for a modification of the constitution which would save it from destruction by Louis Napoleon, Tocqueville wrote to Arthur de Gobineau concerning his report for the Assembly's committee of revision: "The effect produced in France has satisfied me on the whole, and what has come from abroad, above all from England, has satisfied me still more."[1] He also chose this moment to recall to Nassau Senior a thought which he had expressed in 1835, describing England as intellectually his second country.[2] This pledge of intellectual allegiance was more than an attempt to remove the skeptical reserve in which his English friend held the entire scheme of revision. It was a foreshadowing of the fact that within a few months Tocqueville was to transfer his hopes for the future of political liberty across the Channel.

Decisive events in France gave England's place in the scheme of liberty new meaning. These were the Revolution of 1848 and Napoleon's destruction of the Second Republic. However skeptical Tocqueville had been of the parallels drawn between 1688 and 1830, until shortly before the end of the July Monarchy he thought the analogy valid in one respect, that for both nations it represented the end of a long period of upheaval in political life. For the petty passions which he regarded as dominating the political life of the

[1] Letter of Aug. 6, 1851, *Oeuvres* (M): *Corr. Gobineau*. See also *Oeuvres* (B), IX, "Rapport fait à l'Assemblée législative au nom de la Commission chargée d'examiner les propositions relatives à la revision de la Constitution . . . (8 juillet 1851)," 574–606.

[2] Letter of July 27, 1851, *Oeuvres* (B), VII.

July Monarchy he and Beaumont found consolation in the fact that England had successfully passed through a similar phase in constitutional development. What alarmed both was that while England showed great vigor immediately after 1688, France appeared weakened rather than strengthened by the settlement of 1830.

Vague historical parallels could not survive the shock of the February Revolution. Shortly after that event Tocqueville made his final comparison of pre-1848 England and France. The two nations had differed less in social structure than in political spirit. France had failed to tap the real secret of her neighbor's strength and independence. They were wrong to take England for an example, he told the Second Republic's Constituent Assembly, but "even in aristocratic England the people partook, if not directly, then at least extensively, in public affairs. If it did not vote itself, and it often did, it made its voice heard, it made its will known to those who governed; there was mutual understanding. And here? No resemblance . . . all of political life was enclosed in the limits of a single narrow class; and below that, nothing!" [3]

Once and for all, Tocqueville was convinced of the disparate paths which England and France were pursuing. The stability of the English system in the face of the Continental explosion caused Tocqueville to lash out bitterly against those who had been hypnotized by the fallacious analogy. His reaction was a bitter denunciation of the "school of 1688," and extended to all the "metaphysical historians" who attempted to fix French history in a pattern completely bound by precedents, and fatalistically accepted events on which they might otherwise have had a decisive influence. "Sometimes," he complained to Senior, "we draw from our own history; sometimes from yours. Sometimes we use the precedent as an example, sometimes as a warning. But as the circumstances under which we apply it always differ materially from those under which it took place, it almost always misleads us." [4]

Both political expediency and historical disillusionment appeared

[3] *Oeuvres* (B), IX, 548, "Sur la question du Droit au Travail."
[4] Conversation of May 17, 1851, *Correspondence and Conversations*, I, 255.

to make further citations of the English example unpalatable. It was America which furnished the bulk of Tocqueville's examples in his campaign speeches and his debates on the constitution in the Assembly in 1848. Both he and Beaumont stressed their studies of America as qualifications for statesmanship in the new republican government. In his campaign speeches Tocqueville was not above pulling the lion's tail by rousing the anti-British prejudices of his Norman constituency.[5] The example of the United States, however, was far more useful in counteracting the socialist attack on the rights of property within the provisional government[6] and on the committee for the constitution. Odilon Barrot complained that the committee was so haunted by antiroyalist sentiment in Paris that it rejected many institutions, whatever their utility, for the simple reason that they had a monarchic taint or origin. Under these circumstances it is not surprising that Tocqueville, in the committee debates, went out of his way to deny the continuity of the English tradition in American institutions, such as the bicameral legislature, which he wished to see adopted in France.[7]

With the withering of the revolutionary impulse after the June days of 1848, Tocqueville and Beaumont discovered new threats to constitutional government in the hostility of the royalist parties and the designs of the prince-president.

Parallel to the whole evolution of Tocqueville's policy under the impetus of the antiliberal tendencies from both the left and the right, the former "antagonism" of aristocratic English and democratic French societies now paled into insignificance. In foreign

---

[5] See *Journal de Cherbourg: Organe des veux et des intérêts du peuple,* March 23, 1848.

[6] Tocqueville, *Adresse au citoyens de Valognes,* March 19, 1848, in *Assemblée constituante, élections, la Manche* 1848: "For me the Republic is above all, the rule of the rights of each guaranteed by the will of all; it is profound respect for all kinds of legitimate property. I have not forgotten that I have seen a vast republic, the United States, thus attain the highest degree of prosperity."

[7] Archives Nationales, C 918, Procés-verbaux du Comité de Constitution de 1848, séances des 25–27 mai. Beaumont deserted the bicameral minority in the final committee vote, bowing to "public opinion," one of the few instances in which he voted in opposition to Tocqueville. See also Barrot, *Mémoires posthumes,* II, 320ff.

policy as well as in historical perspective, the analogy of liberal institutions began to override all differences separating the two societies. As France under the Barrot ministries attempted to join the conservative camp of the European system without losing its "liberal image," England almost naturally became the chief ally of the liberal republicans, including Tocqueville. During his brief term as foreign minister (June–October 1849), English cooperation or acquiescence was sought on almost every diplomatic maneuver. With growing reaction throughout the Continent, England's immunity from both revolution and reaction brought her back even more forcefully into Tocqueville's perspective. Well before the *coup d'état* of December 2, 1851, England had become, in his estimation, the great source and example of political wisdom and moderation.[8] On the day of the *coup,* Tocqueville and Beaumont were among the 230 deputies who assembled at the *mairie* of the tenth arrondissement in Paris and pronounced the president deposed. The invasion of the meeting by army troops and the subsequent arrest and detention of the legislators announced the end of their political careers.

Appropriately, this last parliamentary act of Tocqueville's in the French political arena was followed by an effort to stir public opinion in England. Palmerston had characterized Tocqueville's entire efforts at revision as "scatterbrained," and although Palmerston's overhasty recognition of the *coup* resulted in his dismissal from the cabinet, the English press appeared more concerned with their impetuous foreign minister's lack of tact than with the violent destruction of the French constitution.[9]

One important London newspaper, *The Times,* suddenly became aroused. This seems to have been due largely to an account of the *coup* written by Tocqueville, smuggled out of France by Harriet Grote and published through the efforts of Henry Reeve. It appeared anonymously in *The Times* on December 11, 1851. Tocque-

---

[8] Conversation of Jan. 25, 1851, *Correspondence and Conversations,* I, 180.
[9] See Greville, *Memoirs,* VI, 315–320, Dec. 23–27, 1851, and Franklin C. Palm, *England and Napoleon III: A Study of the Rise of a Utopian Dictator* (Durham, N.C., 1948), viii–ix.

ville, in genuine shock at English apathy, presented a vivid sketch of both background and events denying the president's charges of legislative and socialist conspiracy. He concluded with a description of the destruction of the opposition press and the summary arrests. "Force overturning law, trampling on the liberty of the press and of the person, deriding the popular will . . . such is the result of this *coup d'état*." Tocqueville made a final appeal to the English people to condemn the "military saturnalia" of December 2, and called upon the English as the jury of last resort of liberty in the world to reject the official account of the advent of the new regime. "If England were to acquit the oppressor, the oppressed would have no other resource but God." [10]

Tocqueville's account created a momentary flurry, but English public opinion in general remained unruffled, content that order had been restored in France after four years of indecision. The English government took the official position "that it was not for England to point out to such a country as France what institutions would suit her best"—as long as it was not a socialist republic.[11] Tocqueville insisted that continuous moral condemnation and public pressure was England's limited but imperative duty. Any display of support for the Bonapartist regime was to be a great source of vexation for Tocqueville during the remaining years of his life, and the beginning of a continual struggle against it was prefigured in his letter to *The Times*.

To his bitter regret he found that many who had condemned him for taking the oath to Louis Philippe in the name of the Charter were

[10] Tocqueville's letter proved to be as irritating in some quarters as it was welcomed in others. Lord Clarendon wrote to George Cornewall Lewis on December 13: "*The Times* is doing a vast deal of harm upon French affairs; but Reeve's virtuous indignation is not to be controlled; so, in order that he may please Guizot and the Grotesque [Harriet Grote] and her dear Alexis (as she calls Tocqueville) a bad feeling is to be created between the two countries" (Sir Herbert Maxwell, *The Life and Letters of George William Frederick, Fourth Earl of Clarendon*, London, 1913, I, 330).

[11] Lord Granville to Lord Normanby, the British ambassador at Paris, Jan. 26, 1852, Public Records Office, Foreign Office (Gifts and Deposits), 29, 215, quoted in Palm, *England and Napoleon III*, 102.

willing to support the new ruler. Tocqueville found the arguments in support of Louis Napoleon beyond his comprehension, and condemned the "insane fear of socialism" as a bogus rationalization. "It is not a question of supporting Louis Napoleon, it is said, but of reaffirming authority, morality, religion. These are the words of philosophers—not of statesmen. It is not a question of what one wants, but of what one does." [12] As long as the exaggerated fear of socialism lasted he could foresee no action by the upper classes against the regime, and the lower classes appeared as satisfied with the dictatorial establishment as with the republic that had crushed them.

Neither Tocqueville nor Beaumont ever abandoned the idea of returning to political life if the regime should be liberalized, and Beaumont was to make one final unsuccessful attempt to re-enter the legislature after Tocqueville's death. Years of waiting, however, began to produce a sense of moral and political isolation in Tocqueville. The political indifference of the majority of his fellow citizens made him feel shut out of the intellectual commonwealth of his age.[13] It is not surprising that the volume of his correspondence with his English friends and his interest in English affairs increased in proportion to his lack of interest in the inner workings of Napoleon's court. For Tocqueville it meant the opportunity of influencing English opinion in behalf of the cause of constitutionalism in France and of censuring any deviation on the part of his chosen people from the fulfillment of their liberal mission. Until Henry Reeve left *The Times* in 1855, he was able to continue to influence mildly its editorial policy toward Louis Napoleon, and when he took over the direction of the *Edinburgh Review,* in 1855, Tocqueville asked for the inclusion of reviews and articles which would bolster the morale of liberal thinkers in France. The French liberal came in turn to depend upon this Whig quarterly as his chief source of information on England.

Through his personal dealings and correspondence with the

[12] Quoted in Redier, *Comme disait M. de Tocqueville,* 229.
[13] Tocqueville to Mme. Swetchine, Oct. 20, 1856, *Oeuvres* (B), VI.

Grotes, Lewises, Seniors, and Monckton Milnes, Tocqueville was frequently able to spread his opinions to wide circles of English political life. His efforts in arousing British opinion consisted in part in convincing his friends that they were not immune from Continental influences and that the existence of despotism in Europe was a threat to English liberty. It was his hardest and least successful task. He constantly met reminders of the English immunity to 1848 in rebuttals to his own warnings, and his realization that English indifference constituted a prop to the French regime often made him more vehement than precise. He was forever warning of the potential Napoleonic threat to England, and insisted above all that Britain would increasingly have to come to grips with Continental ideas, methods of government, and political alliances.

Tocqueville, however, was primarily concerned with the immediate effect of English opinion and government actions with regard to the emperor. He had the bitter satisfaction of pointing out to Monckton Milnes that for the first time in decades an English government seemed to fear and flatter a French one. Harriet Grote devoted innumerable pages to explaining that *The Times*'s cordiality toward Louis Napoleon on the occasion of his marriage had no political implications.[14] Every friendly move of the English government toward the "destroyer of French liberty" was "sacrificing honorable opinions and tastes, without a motive." [15] Nassau Senior's article "The Continent in 1854" was especially annoying, since it linked continuance of the Anglo-French alliance to the existence of the imperial government. He feared that England might become the bulwark of the French government, even after it had ceased to be popular at home, and that a repetition of the situation under the July Monarchy would ensue. National vanity of the worst kind would be bolstered by any unnecessary friendli-

---

[14] Harriet Grote to Tocqueville, Feb. 13, 1853, Lady Eastlake, *Mrs. Grote,* 121–130. See also James Pope-Hennessy, *Monckton Milnes: The Flight of Youth, 1851–1885* (London, 1951), 20–21.

[15] Tocqueville to Senior, March 25, 1852, and Feb. 15, 1855, *Correspondence and Conversations,* II, 25–26, 92–94.

ness on the part of England toward France. The only permanent friends of England, Tocqueville vehemently insisted to Senior, were the friends of her constitution, not the imperialists. The inevitable fall of the Napoleonic regime made it imperative for the English to strengthen the feeble roots of political liberty.[16]

Only in the case of the Crimean War did Tocqueville concede a legitimate instance of an English alliance with Napoleonic France for the sake of a struggle against the archetype of despotism. Out of the chaos of war aims, Tocqueville, true to character, selected the broadest ideological conflict. Twenty years before the opening of hostilities, the first part of the *Démocratie* had concluded with a prediction that the world's future belonged to two great nations, Russia and America. The two nations were depicted as representing two great points of departure: Russia, the sword, centralization, and the principle of despotism; America, the principle of peaceful expansion and self-government. These two polar principles were now represented by the protagonists of the Crimean War. The gathering of armies on the Black Sea was a continuation of the great struggle between the English and Slavic peoples for the domination of the world.[17]

Tocqueville suggested to Beaumont shortly before the outbreak of hostilities that Russia could be thought of as an America without liberty or intelligence, a land of absolute uniformity, in short "a frightful mutation of democracy." [18] Beaumont adopted this idea as his theme in an article written early in 1854 on Russia and the United States.[19] Expanding Tocqueville's thesis in an atmosphere engendered by the Crimean conflict, he depicted the two nations

---

[16] Senior, "The Continent in 1854," *North British Review,* XLIV (February 1855), 336, and conversation of May 28, 1855, *Correspondence and Conversations,* II, 104–107.

[17] See Tocqueville to Henry Reeve, March 26, 1853, *Oeuvres* (M): *Corr. angl.,* I. For the background of Tocqueville's ideas regarding Russia and America, see Bernhard Fabian, *Alexis de Tocquevilles Amerikabild* (Heidelberg, 1957), 8off.

[18] Letter of Nov. 3, 1853, *Oeuvres* (B), VI.

[19] Beaumont, "La Russie et les Etats-Unis sous le rapport économique," *Revue des deux mondes,* ser. 2, vol. V (1854), 1163–83.

for the French public as the embodiments of liberty and despotism.

Tocqueville's original thesis was enlarged to incorporate an attack on the socialist principles of the Revolution of 1848. Beaumont was already thoroughly imbued with the idea that there was an intimate link between the centralized absolutism of the old regime and modern socialism. It was an easy step to the extension of this theory to Russian society too, in view of its traditions of communal landholding and its bureaucratic state. Russia was made the supreme example of the distrust of all individual initiative and rights. It was the barbaric prototype of all centralized control of economic and political activity. Thus when Beaumont challenged the modern world to choose between American liberty and Russian despotism, the choice was also one between socialism and private property. The leveling flatness of Russian life, reflected in the endless expanse of her unbroken steppe, was offered as the terrible alternative to the Anglo-American principles of self-government, individual initiative, decentralization, the infinite variety of political and economic activity, and the dignity of man. Beaumont and Tocqueville, with their new and intense concern for the reintroduction of political liberty in France, now insisted that the really distinguishing principle of American society was not equality, but liberty, and that England and America represented only two aspects of the same ideal. The American nation thus became fused with the larger Anglo-American community of constitutionalism.

It is no wonder that, with this interpretation of the Crimean War, Tocqueville complained that the French did not understand the larger aspects of the conflict, and insisted that England enter the struggle against the Russians with clear-cut ideological commitments. "Peoples, like individuals," he insisted to Reeve, "who have any self-respect pledge themselves as to their future conduct by their past. You have been for a great number of years the champions of liberty: you have embraced its cause when it was strong; I think it would be a lessening of yourselves to abandon it when it is weak." [20] Tocqueville was greatly concerned that the alliance should not blur the similarities between French and Russian des-

[20] Letter of March 26, 1853, *Oeuvres* (M): *Corr. angl.,* I.

potism. The English, in the estimate of their French champion, not only had to win, but had to appear as the primary agents of the victory lest their moral force be lost with their prestige. He became dismayed at the inefficiency and failures of the British army compared with the French, and shuddered at the possible feedback of those failures upon the English constitution at home and the impression England made abroad. At one point during the struggle he advised one of his English friends that a mass army had become a necessity in England; not since he was a child had he heard such contempt heaped upon English military power.

If Tocqueville was fearful about the English conduct of the war, he was even more fearful of the possible failure on the part of the allies to defeat Russia decisively and to push her far back from her western frontier. "I am convinced," he warned Senior, "that Russia cannot be stopped in a permanent manner except by the creation beside it of powers borne from the hate that it inspires . . . in other words, by the restoration of the Kingdom of Poland and of a living Turkey." [21] Thus he regarded the outcome of the Peace of Paris as a terrible conjunction of all that it was most imperative to avoid: a territorially intact Russia, an England whose military reputation had been tarnished, and an imperial France whose overwhelming contribution to the allied victory was undeniable. External military glory now reinforced internal class fears. The Napoleonic regime was at the apogee of its strength, with no visible cloud on the horizon.

Tocqueville's concern with England's internal development was also one of the great interests of his final years. There had been a kind of detachment in the analysis of England's future by both Tocqueville and Beaumont in the 1830's which disappeared after the *coup d'état*. Tocqueville brooded like a mother hen over every turn of events which might make the English constitution appear like a machine getting out of order. When George Cornewall Lewis, who in February 1855 became Chancellor of the Exchequer, requested an analysis of the French civil service examination system as a background for a proposed English reform, Tocqueville's

[21] Letter of Sept. 19, 1855, *Oeuvres* (B), VII.

reply was not so much a description as a warning to Lewis against the entire leveling principle of uniformity in examinations for advancement in the public service as incompatible with England's constitution. "I am not English," he concluded after this lengthy bit of advice, "but I am a man, and that gives me the right to preoccupy myself with England, whose fate exerts so much influence on that of humanity." [22] Warning signals were delivered to his English correspondents year after year on every occasion when the party system was too fluid, when the organization of the army came under fire, or when any reform agitation appeared to threaten the balance of 1832.

In his concern for the continuance of the British aristocracy, however, he was dominated by the idea that under this system England had retained her liberty. One of the entries in Senior's journal recorded Tocqueville as saying that while England preserved her aristocracy she would preserve her freedom, and with the destruction of the aristocracy freedom would also disappear. Tocqueville, checking over the account of the conversation, added a note to the journal: "This also goes farther than my idea. I think the maintenance in England of aristocratic institutions very desirable. But I am far from saying that their abolition would necessarily lead to despotism, especially if their power were diminished gradually and without the shock of a revolution." [23] His defense of the mid-Victorian constitutional equilibrium stood in revealing contrast to his more open acceptance of the democratic revolution in England in 1835. He probably now felt that it would be the height of folly to tamper too much with the last outpost of liberty in Europe. He never attempted to transform his admiration for the English aristocracy into a program for the revival of a privileged political or social group in France. For Tocqueville the old regime had been tried, judged, and buried forever.

The last and greatest threat to the English reputation which Tocqueville lived to witness was the Indian Mutiny of 1857.

[22] Letter of Nov. 18, 1855, *Oeuvres* (B), VII.
[23] Conversations of Feb. 22–23, 1854, *Correspondence and Conversations,* II, 69n.

Tocqueville was no novice on British rule in India. During his first years in the Chamber of Deputies he had made an extended survey of the literature on the subject and had even planned a major work on that "great, unique subject, poorly understood even among the majority of the English." [24] He had, in fact, completed a preliminary study in 1843, but abandoned the effort under the distractions of domestic political demands. The Mutiny called forth a flurry of advisory letters to English friends as the full scope of the uprising became known.

Tocqueville did not regard the revolt as a mass movement awakened by any national or democratic impulse, but the last reflex of the princely governments, who were making a final effort against the centralizing and leveling effect of the century-old British expansion in India. He believed that if the Hindu masses were really in a revolutionary condition, the uprising would end in the ejection of the English from India, no matter how preponderant the military superiority of the Europeans. It was the "spirit of exclusion" which had done so much damage in Ireland, the self-imposed separation and isolation of the conquerors, which had called forth a "revolt of barbarism against pride." [25] He strongly advised against any attempt at large-scale colonization by Europeans, which would only aggravate the existing resentment. The westernizing of India was to be the task of government action and not of individuals. He optimistically predicted a new direction for English Indian policy as a result of its re-entry into the full glare of British political life. To Beaumont he wrote, "the whole strength of the English is in themselves, in their practical perspicacity, in their energy to correct, repair, to make up the deficiency of institutional vices, and the effect of discordant facts." [26]

[24] Tocqueville to Reeve, Nov. 14, 1843, *Oeuvres* (M): *Corr. angl.,* I; see also *Oeuvres* (M): *Ecrits politiques,* I, 441–550. He also advised Beaumont to take up the project.

[25] Tocqueville to Reeve, Jan. 30, 1858, *Corr. angl.,* I.

[26] Letter of Aug. 17, 1857, *Oeuvres* (B), VII. For Tocqueville's frequent recourse to English examples in his writings on French colonial policy see *Ecrits politiques,* I, *passim.*

Another aspect of the uprising in India was more disturbing to Tocqueville—the European reaction to it. While admitting that the British in India had not completely fulfilled their civilizing mission, Tocqueville identified the maintenance of British rule with the cause of civilization. He bitterly resented any Continental expressions of satisfaction with British difficulties. In this connection there also remained the problem of an attitude of many English liberals toward India which might threaten an important aspect of English prestige, namely, the compatibility of liberty with continued political eminence and power. Even during the period when he was most hostile to the conduct of British foreign affairs, Tocqueville admired the "feeling of greatness and power" which the domination of India had given the entire English people.[27] He therefore reacted vehemently to the vein of liberal opinion which contended that the whole venture in India was a misfortune and that England would be better off without this imperial headache.

In October 1857, Tocqueville protested to Lady Theresa Lewis, the wife of George Cornewall Lewis, against even the idea of abandoning India. Tocqueville conceded that even if it cost more than it brought in, even if England's domestic situation might be simpler without the complications of imperial domination, its loss would lower the position of England in the world. It would be the abandonment of a commitment not only to India but to what British rule there symbolized to Europe:

There has never been anything under the sun as extraordinary as the conquest, and above all the government of India by the English, anything which from every corner of the globe more attracts the imagination of man to that small island of whose very name the Greeks were unaware. Do you believe, madame, that a people can, after having filled this immense place in the imagination of the human species, withdraw from it with impunity? I do not believe it. I think that the English are obeying an instinct not only heroic, but just, in wishing to retain India at any price since they possess it. I add that I am perfectly certain that they will conserve it, although, perhaps, in less favorable conditions.[28]

[27] *Oeuvres* (M): *Ecrits politiques,* I, 478.
[28] Letter of Oct. 18, 1857, *Oeuvres* (B), VI.

Tocqueville's previous anxieties concerning France's reputation abroad were now bestowed on England.

England not only represented the most potent political system in the world, but also furnished examples of the combination of theory and practice which was his own ideal. He and Beaumont were especially impressed with George Cornewall Lewis, who found time both to direct the finances of England and to produce substantial historical and political essays. Speaking before the French Academy in 1853, Beaumont cited his English friend as the embodiment of the English philosopher-politician who obtained his knowledge of statecraft on the hustings as well as from a profound knowledge of ancient Athens and Rome.[29] In a similar manner Tocqueville contrasted English and German political thought. Coming to the latter late in life, he saw it as representative of a type of abstract detachment from the world which he could not comprehend, and toward which he felt an instinctive dislike. He felt that the Germans, for all their thoroughness and gravity, being almost exclusively men of the study, always amazed one with their lack of real knowledge of human action. The English writers not only presented learned arguments, "but what can always be used in governing this world."[30] The interdependence of knowledge about and action among men never seemed more conclusively proven. It was one of the basic assumptions of his last work.

While assuming the role of conscience of the guardians of liberty in England, Tocqueville struggled against the atmosphere of political exhaustion which permeated France. No spark went untended. He hailed Montalembert's eulogy of contemporary English politics, *De l'avenir politique de l'Angleterre* (1856), as a perfect description of his own sentiments.[31] It read, indeed, like a sequel to the *Ancien Régime*. He asked Reeve to review Duvergier de

[29] "Rapport sur l'ouvrage de M. G. Cornewall Lewis . . . *Essay on the Influence of Authority in Matters of Opinion*," *Séances et travaux de l'Académie des sciences morales et politiques: Compte rendu*, XXIII (1853), 219–220.

[30] Tocqueville to Beaumont, March 23, 1858, *Oeuvres* (B), VII. George Grote's *History of Greece* was the work cited on this occasion.

[31] Tocqueville to C. F. R. Montalembert, July 10, 1856, *Oeuvres* (B), VII.

Hauranne's *L'Histoire du gouvernement parlementaire en France*
in the *Edinburgh Review*. Tocqueville and Beaumont observed to
their dismay, however, that the younger generation could no longer
be lured by descriptions of political activity and the battle cry of
liberty, but turned increasingly to business and purely cultural
pursuits. The French liberals had to face the contention that
aesthetic opportunity and economic prosperity were perhaps the
compensation France might receive for abandoning her ill-fated
experiment in parliamentary government.

In the 1830's Tocqueville and Beaumont had given a good deal
of weight to the arguments that continuous and universal political
activity had a deadening effect on standards of cultural excellence.
Now discarding many of their former concessions, Tocqueville
contended that "almost all the masterworks of the human spirit
have been produced in centuries of liberty . . . Absolute governments inherited only the forms of the activity of mind and of the
freedom of imagination that free institutions had created," a façade
which disappeared when their true tendencies became apparent.[32]
Tocqueville explained the ages of Augustus, the Medicis, and
Louis XIV as the heirs of more virile political ages, as were the
artistic and intellectual achievements of the first Napoleonic regime.

The attempt to correlate intellectual achievement and political
liberty was extended into the area of economic activity. This was
not an academic question, for if one could maintain that the intellectual atmosphere of the Second Empire was at least partially
stifled by the existence of imperial censorship, it appeared that
France could prosper without political liberty. If Britain basked
in the golden age of her world economic primacy, France in the
first decade of the Empire was making startling and very visible
progress in industry and finance.

Beaumont's last report to the Academy of Moral and Political
Sciences, shortly after Tocqueville's death, dramatically showed
how much their emphasis had shifted. Beaumont reviewed the

---

[32] *Oeuvres* (M): *Ancien Régime*, II, 345.

development of Ireland since the appearance of his work in a manner especially geared to cover the sore spot in England's political and economic achievements. In 1839 his point of departure in *L'Irlande* had been the primary injustice of a foreign and unassimilated aristocracy and the consequent inevitability of the rise of democracy against the British constitution. He now showed the British system vigorously at work, risking the destruction of the religious and political base of the aristocracy in Ireland, not under the pressure of an overwhelming democratic movement, but moved by a sense of injustice arising equally from within all political parties. Beaumont also raised the problem of the occurrence of the horrible famine of the forties and of the continuing poverty in Ireland under free institutions, while his own countrymen, "seeing a nation formerly free, prospering under despotism, imagine that it owes its good fortune to the advent of tyranny." [33] The answer was a replica of Tocqueville's on the problem of cultural creativity. Beaumont admitted that a nation which had recently descended from a condition of political freedom to one of despotism might, as in its intellectual life, live off the capital of vitality acquired during its years of liberty. Ireland, on the other hand, while still far from having received the economic rewards of its free institutions, was nevertheless assured of its future wealth and prosperity.

Less strident but equally significant was Tocqueville's emphasis on the successes of English society in every field when he published his study on France before the Revolution. Since the *Ancien Régime*'s chapter on the economic background of the Revolution argued that economic progress, not retrogression, was the rule in the decades before 1789, he parried the possible conclusion that autocratic France had done materially as well as constitutional England. Tocqueville took special pains to point out that the government was already too decrepit to be despotic in the last years of the old regime, and that only France's era of constitutional gov-

[33] "Notice sur l'état présent de l'Irlande, 1862–1863," *Séances et travaux de l'Académie des sciences morales et politiques: Compte rendu,* LXV (1863), 391–392.

ernment could compare with these years in peace and prosperity. This chapter also contained Tocqueville's lengthiest praise of the constitution, the society, and the economy of England.

While Tocqueville was attempting to rally the disheartened liberals and revive the apathetic and prosperous upper classes, he also plunged into a struggle against the "metaphysical historians" among his own friends who posed the hypothesis that French society was in full decadence and incapable of the free political life to which Tocqueville sought to return.

Under the initial impact of the Revolution of 1848, Tocqueville had moments of deep pessimism as to the stability of the very fundamentals of European civilization.[34] In the light of the stable social situation which was maintained throughout the years of uncertainty which preceded and followed the *coup,* however, he became convinced that French society was not as fundamentally diseased as her political institutions, and felt that any correlation between the nineteenth century and previous periods of decline were false. An ardent belief in the basic health of European society in general, and French society in particular, enabled him to remain within the sphere of political solutions and to advocate the reviving of political virtues rather than yielding to a rejection of the world in the manner of a St. Augustine. "We are asleep," he wrote to J. J. Ampère, who, like many others, was struck by the analogy of turbulent France with imperial Rome, "your Romans were dead." [35] His essential optimism was based not upon a rejection of the implication of historical analogies or comparative statistics but upon the ability of human effort to resolve a redeemable situation. His reaction to crises, even in moments of deepest doubt, was to cling more firmly to the primarily political virtues: "vigor, courage, knowledge, *l'esprit de conduite.*" [36]

When the human capacity for decisive action itself was chal-

---

[34] Tocqueville, *Souvenirs,* 74–75, 83–84.

[35] Letter of May 12, 1857, *Oeuvres* (B), VI.

[36] Tocqueville to Eugene Stoffels, July 21, 1848, *Oeuvres* (B), V. See also Tocqueville to Gobineau, Nov. 17, 1853, *Oeuvres* (M): *Corr. Gobineau.*

lenged, Tocqueville brought out the full armory of his basic belief in man's capacity for freedom. This challenge was explicitly thrown to Tocqueville by the racial theories of his protégé and friend Arthur de Gobineau, whose famous *Essai sur l'inégalité des races humaines* appeared in 1853. The work resulted in an exchange of letters between the two which became so heated that the discussion was dropped unresolved for the sake of the friendship. Gobineau's essay combined two elements to which both Tocqueville and Beaumont violently objected, a theory of racial determinism and a prognostication of decadence and decline. Among the most irritating of Gobineau's ideas was the fact that he regarded France as no longer capable of a free government because of the debasement of her Germanic element. Tocqueville's total rejection of Gobineau's theories was restricted to private correspondence, while Beaumont, as in their parliamentary years, assumed the task of giving voice to their condemnation of racial determination in his article on Russia and America.[37]

While Tocqueville's basic disagreement with Gobineau stemmed from his belief that "human societies, like individuals, are worthwhile only in the enjoyment of liberty," and his confidence in human potential and divine justice, he challenged the evidence in Gobineau's essay as well. Again he called upon the Anglo-American world. He confidently predicted that the essay would get little notice in England or America, except in the South, and that only in Germany, a country which because of its political inexperience was not overly concerned with the practical consequences of ideas, might it capture a large audience. England became his favorite example against the claims of the decadence of the century and Europe. "I am sure," he wrote to Gobineau, "that Julius Caesar, if he had had the time, would have gladly written a book to prove that the savages which he had met on the island of Great Britain were not at all of the same human race as the Romans, and that while the latter were destined by nature to dominate the world, the others

---

[37] See Beaumont, "La Russie et les Etats-Unis," 1182, and Tocqueville to Gobineau, Feb. 19, 1854, *Corr. Gobineau.*

were to vegetate in a corner."[38] This was one reason that Tocqueville placed so much importance on the British retention of India. English industrial and colonial expansion were symbols of the tremendous vitality of European civilization.

Tocqueville's single-minded struggle against what he detested in interpretations of the past and the present extended into the very fabric of his personal life. Once again he instinctively drew close to England. Despite his withdrawal to private life he refused to follow the example of his class and relinquish his influence in his old constituency. Like an English squire, or his ideal of one, he made weekly rounds to the poor and kept up innumerable contacts with the local peasantry, perhaps with the day of his return to politics in mind. He made inquiries about English agricultural techniques and received livestock from across the Channel. The frequent English guests at his chateau were struck by the round of daily occupations and intellectual gatherings, "as fully appreciated and enjoyed as they could be in any part of England."[39] No wonder that one admirer saw in him the model of an English gentleman—independent "in thought and purse," a "landowner, member of parliament, a scholar."[40]

The Anglophilia of Tocqueville's later years was but the outward sign of a continuous fusion of personal existence and political ideals. Just as the image of England ran through his daily life, it ran through every page of his *Ancien Régime* of 1856; as his culminating comparison between England and France it requires a chapter to itself. But it was more to Tocqueville than a restatement of ideals or a brilliant synthesis of French society before the Revolution.

---

[38] Letter of Nov. 17, 1853, *Corr. Gobineau.* Tocqueville became especially sensitive to any deterministic acquiescence in the Napoleonic regime, especially if it occurred in the writings of Englishmen. He protested when Sir James Stephen explained English liberty "principally by the German blood which flows in its veins" (Tocqueville to Stephen, Feb. 14, 1858, *Oeuvres* (B), VI).

[39] [Milnes], "Alexis de Tocqueville," 542.

[40] Charles E. Smith, ed., *Journals and Correspondence of Lady Eastlake* (London, 1895), II, 268–269.

It meant a partial return to the world. As the *Démocratie* of 1835 spectacularly launched its author on his public career, the *Ancien Régime* paved the way for a fitting final act. With a book so patently hostile to the emperor, Tocqueville could hope for good reviews in Paris, but no repetition of the public ovation which had greeted the *Démocratie*. But what France could not allow England gave him—the last triumph of his life.

History, which he had condemned for so many false and bitter analogies, now happily repeated itself in June and July of 1857. Once again the book preceded the man, with Reeve as translator. Once again the verdict in England was unanimous—much more so than in France. Once more, English society permitted itself a rare outburst of enthusiasm on his arrival. The most exclusive clubs and salons bid for his presence. Although he did not participate directly in the parliamentary process again, his statements before the committee on bribery at elections in 1835 were recalled by the Chancellor of the Exchequer during a debate on the ballot on June 30, 1857. The Downing Street receptions of Lady Theresa Lewis gave Tocqueville ample opportunity to meet the political world again. He was treated as a returning fellow countryman. Most of his old friends were now at the peak of their careers. To the old circle were added Lords Clarendon, Stanhope, Stanley, and Aberdeen, as well as the young Walter Bagehot, Sir Edmund Head, Sir William Stirling-Maxwell, and Sir Charles Lyell—a substantial but far from complete tally.

At the formidable London breakfasts, which then served as miniature public forums, Tocqueville was always the center of attention. Although he spoke English well enough, the language of conversation switched to French when he entered the room. Even the ebullient Thomas Babington Macaulay broke off his triumphant flood of words to speak a hard and unwieldy French. The effects of years of virtual political and social isolation dropped from Tocqueville like an outworn shroud. For once his public personality was equal to his ambition and he seemed magnetic, lucid, and graceful. Toward the end of the visit a breakfast lingered for hours "because we remembered that it is Tocqueville's last day." George Ticknor, an American onlooker, noted that in the consensus of London society Tocqueville was "decidedly the lion of the season." [41] The visit reached its climax when, through Lord Clarendon, Tocqueville met with Prince Albert. The prince had been deeply impressed by the *Ancien Régime* and rendered its author the incomparable service of praising it before the French emperor despite its scarcely concealed contempt for Bonapartist methods. [42]

The British Government would not let him depart without a final and official token of esteem. Because there was no regular packet service between England and Cherbourg, Sir Charles Wood, the First Lord of the Admiralty, ordered a vessel put at Tocqueville's disposal. Thus the citizens of Cherbourg were mystified when, on a day late in July 1857, the paddlewheel steamer *Sprightly* entered the harbor, rendered the customary salute, deposited a single passenger and his belongings, and departed immediately. Any observer of the scene might have shrewdly surmised, as did one local newspaper, that a special emissary of the emperor had returned from a secret mission to England.

There was a final touch to the return voyage which must have pleased the political man in Tocqueville. In Paris both the liberals and the government took cognizance of a visit that had become a public ovation and a means of return usually reserved for a prince. [43] When, from the perspective of his Norman estate, Tocqueville reviewed his unexpected reception in England after an absence of more than two decades, his reaction was in character. "I met," he wrote to a friend, "such a flattering reception in that country that I must, in good faith, attribute it as much to the principles which

[41] *Life, Letters and Journals of George Ticknor,* 10th ed. (Boston, 1880), II, 366.

[42] See Sir Theodore Martin, *The Life of His Royal Highness, the Prince Consort* (London, 1880), IV, 109, Aug. 11, 1857. For Tocqueville's flattering opinion of Albert and the latter's rejoinder, see *Oeuvres* (M): *Corr. angl.,* I, 353–354. Tocqueville was truly surprised at the warmth of the invitation: "Lord Clarendon told me that Prince Albert absolutely had to see me" (Yale Mss(T) C.I.b: Tocqueville to his wife [London], "samedi matin").

[43] See [Milnes], "Alexis de Tocqueville," 541, and a copy of a letter of Beaumont to Tocqueville, Aug. 2, 1857 in Yale Mss(B) D.I.b, paq. 11, cahier 9, p. 3.

I maintain as to myself, and have been able legitimately to rejoice in that." [44]

Even the magnitude of English approval could no longer lure an aging politician into a cheerful mood about France, but on the level of political faith it could hardly fail to touch him. His contacts were largely with the same class of men whom he had met two decades before, and the feeling of continuity could only be enhanced. English society surprised him by being so consistent with its old pattern. It appeared that if England had changed it was in reverse—that she was now even less agitated by revolutionary passions than in 1835. It was not, however, the order but the activity and the unity of the English political scene which dominated his accounts of the trip. The incredible variety of English local life might eventually be curtailed, but Tocqueville still confidently predicted at most a very slow and almost insensible evolution in this direction. "It is the greatest spectacle in the world, though all of it is not great," he wrote. "One encounters, above all, things unknown in the rest of Europe—things which consoled me." [45]

For the first time in twenty years he felt himself outside the class warfare which had torn the French constitutional system apart. The entire body of vocal and educated men in England agreed on the necessity of a free society. Tocqueville found himself more envious of that mutual understanding which seemed to elude France than of England's economic supremacy. He also found an accord between political liberty and religion which appeared impossible in France. Shortly after his return to France, he confided to Beaumont that all the results of his observations, historical research, and travels had combined "to give the opinions of our youth the character of an absolute conviction. For me, it is self-evident that liberty is the necessary condition, without which there has never been a truly great and virile nation." [46]

Tocqueville's last journey, in a sense the last public act of his life, was a confirmation to him of the stark contrast between England and France which he had propounded in the *Ancien Régime* the year before. He was never more concerned with the present than when he turned to his nation's point of departure. In the *Ancien Régime,* France and Europe were confronted by England at both ends of their continuing revolution.

X ❖ England and France in the Mirror of History

L'ANCIEN RÉGIME ET LA RÉVOLUTION, which appeared in 1856, was Tocqueville's final comparison between England and France. It was only the first part of a study which was to have surveyed the entire revolutionary era, culminating with the First Empire. As Louis Napoleon clasped the image of his uncle across the corpse of parliamentary government, the era of Napoleon I was to be shown as the last link of a chain going far back into prerevolutionary France. Until his health gave out in 1858, Tocqueville continued to work on the larger design and bequeathed a few more chapters and some immensely suggestive notes to posterity.

His motives for undertaking the investigation were clear. As early as December 1850 he had toyed with the idea of writing a work on the French Revolution and Napoleon. The *coup d'état* added new force to the idea.[1] In April 1853, speaking in the Academy of Moral and Political Sciences, the only platform remaining open to him, Tocqueville declared that political science formed "around every society a kind of intellectual atmosphere in which both governed and governors move, and from which they draw, often without realizing it, the principles of their conduct."[2] As ever, the scientific and political potential of theoretical analysis were joined. At the same time Tocqueville did not overestimate the im-

---

[1] For the biographical background of the *Ancien Régime,* see André Jardin's introduction to the second volume of the Mayer edition, and Herr, *Tocqueville and the Old Regime.* Herr gives the best summary to date of the reception and long-range impact of the work in France.

[2] *Oeuvres* (B), IX, 123, "Discours prononcé à la séance publique annuelle de l'Académie des sciences morales et politiques."

mediate effects of any theoretical effort no matter how effectively it might depict the problems of a nation's political habits. He believed that his country had entered an era in which the uneducated classes, those still least susceptible to immediate influence by political philosophy, were the real center of social power and social change. "Nevertheless," he wrote just after the *Ancien Régime* appeared, "as mass movements, even the most vulgar, are born in ideas and often in very metaphysical and abstract ideas . . . it is always useful to throw these ideas into circulation, in the hope that if they are just they will eventually be transformed into passions and facts." [3]

While Tocqueville's views were enlarged and modified by the four years of research into the archival materials of prerevolutionary France, the principal theses of the work had been enumerated twenty years before in an article in the *London and Westminster Review,* "Political and Social Condition of France," in 1836. The over-all picture of the prerevolutionary origins of bureaucratic centralization, of the alienation of classes, and of the basic continuity of French political and administrative development had appeared in 1836. But the changed political situation in the France of 1856 refracted the total view of the *Ancien Régime.*[4] It gave a tone to the work which appeared no more strikingly than in the picture of England.

The article of 1836 had viewed the French Revolution as a completed revolution in the sense that its basic egalitarian principle seemed to have been certified by the Revolution of 1830 and the democratic social state established in its broad outlines.[5] The *Ancien Régime* was written in full consciousness that European society, and French society in particular, was in the midst of social and political upheavals with no end in sight. The Revolution could no longer be viewed simply as a historical catalytic agent which

---

[3] Tocqueville to Odilon Barrot, July 18, 1856, *Oeuvres* (B), VII.

[4] *Oeuvres* (M): *Ancien Régime,* I, 73.

[5] *Ancien Régime,* I, 33–34, 65–66, "Etat social et politique de la France avant et depuis 1789" (1836).

had disappeared after establishing a new social order. It now appeared to be a dangerous and virulent germ, capable of multiplying itself indefinitely—the really "new phenomenon of the Revolution." Tocqueville was deeply conscious of this "virus of a new and unknown kind" without being able to diagnose it. He could find no precedent for the "immoderate, radical, audacious, half-mad but powerful character" of its leaders in the social agitation of the past.[6] The race of revolutionaries hovered around the edges of his study without ever finding a proper setting. This continuity of the spirit of revolution which attached to no single institution or system of ideas and could be satisfied by no particular reform infused the *Ancien Régime* with a lack of finality foreign to the earlier essay.[7]

The second change of outlook from 1836 was the new relation which Tocqueville assigned to the roles of liberty and equality as the underlying sentiments of the French Revolution. In the aftermath of the July Revolution constitutionalism had appeared as legitimate a result of the French Revolution as the abolition of feudal dues or the redistribution of economic and social power in the class structure. Believing that French society had inherited a spirit of liberty as strong, if more irregular, than its neighbor across the Channel, the French aristocrat had been very tolerant toward the lack of effective political institutions in the old regime. Written for an English audience, the essay in the *Westminster Review* had amplified the sporadic flouting of governmental authority by the proud nobility of prerevolutionary France and carefully underlined the distinction between servility and loyalty, between a personal obedience which was given almost on sufferance and the degrading obedience produced by fear or force. Tocqueville, far from separating this spirit from that of political liberty, pictured freedom as growing within the Frenchman in proportion

---

[6] Tocqueville to Louis de Kergorlay, May 16, 1858, *Oeuvres* (B), V. See also Charles de Rémusat, "De l'esprit de réaction: Royer-Collard et Tocqueville," *Revue des deux mondes,* 2nd per., vol. XXXV (1861), 805.

[7] See *Oeuvres* (M): *Ancien Régime,* II, 228, 337; and I, 208.

to the degree of his exclusion from the constitutional framework. "Liberty was disappearing from institutions and maintaining itself more than ever in manners. It seemed dearer to individuals in proportion to the lessening of their security." [8]

The article had gone even further, stating that this spirit of independence was the source of the modern idea of liberty which developed in the eighteenth century; that is, by a singular transformation, personal liberty had changed its character. The "taste which the French had always had for independence became a reasoned and systematic opinion which, extending from person to person ended by absorbing the royal power itself." [9] Tocqueville's causal description and his moral evaluation could not have been more clear. He could easily conclude in 1836 that the French had conceived of the democratic idea of liberty more quickly and precisely than any other nation.

In the perspective of 1856 nothing so completely changed in Tocqueville's assessment of social facts as his rejection of the primacy of France in the genesis of liberty. It was not only that the French of the old regime desired social reforms before liberty, but the tie between anarchic private and corporate rights was rigorously severed from the growth of a public spirit. The privileges of the various corporate bodies might have sporadically prevented abuses of authority, but these principles were now seen as "the prejudices, the false ideas which most stood in the way of the establishment of orderly and salutary liberty." [10] It was no longer merely a question of a simple transformation of the old private sentiments into new public ones, but an entirely new order of customs which were basically antagonistic to the jealous defense of private and exclusive privileges.

Independence was still more than servility, but it was not liberty, nor even the germ of liberty. Tocqueville still regretted that the pride of the old nobility, which might have served its country well,

---

[8] *Ancien Régime,* I, 60, "Etat social" (1836).

[9] *Ancien Régime,* I, 63.

[10] *Ancien Régime,* I, 169.

was gone. He still insisted that nonservile obedience to a king was a lesser degradation than obedience to an illegitimate despot, but significantly, Tocqueville in 1856 showed himself less apologetic for the politically bankrupt nobility of the old regime, even after the democratic and socialist upheavals of 1848, than before. The failure of political liberty in the 1850's had made him much less sympathetic to its absence in the 1750's. The *Ancien Régime* emphasized the limits of pride in oneself. The old intermittent and irregular liberty was "always contracted within class limits," always tied to the exclusive and divisive ideas of exception and privilege, and "almost never went so far as to ensure to all citizens the most natural and necessary guarantees."

Instead of the spirit of independence leading to political liberty, Tocqueville now concluded that it had led to precisely the opposite effect.[11] Having prepared the French to rebel against despotism, "it rendered them perhaps less ready than any other people to replace it by the free and peaceful rule of laws."[12] By comparison with England, the enlightened classes of France (including the bourgeoisie), far from having been too oppressed, were too often free to do what pleased them at the expense of the people. A highborn Frenchman of the eighteenth century had more opportunity to resist the government than his English counterpart. Never had Tocqueville so bluntly and so severely divided the public from the private virtues, rights of classes from rights of citizens, factors of integration from factors of alienation, as when he concluded: "So wrong is it to confound independence with liberty. There is nothing less independent than a free citizen."[13]

---

[11] In the article of 1836, when reference is made to French liberty in the eighteenth century, it is modified by the adjectives "instinctive," "irregular," "passionate," "exalted," ["]lively," and "deep-rooted." In the *Ancien Régime*, "irregular" still keeps its place but otherwise a new stock of modifiers is used: "strange," "contracted," "diminished" (*réduite*), "deformed," "unruly and unhealthy" (*déréglée et malsaine*). It was still fruitful only in the private realm—in the production of vigorous personalities and original minds.

[12] *Ancien Régime*, I, 177.

[13] *Ancien Régime*, I, 302.

The backward glance seemed to prove that French society was a study in political pathology. England of the 1850's was also projected back into the eighteenth century; her stability and vitality became the primary features of the image which emerged in the pages of the *Ancien Régime*. The European, rather than the French, revolution was seen by Tocqueville to have been operative in England centuries before the events of 1789; English society had been effectively adjusting to the modern world well in advance of the Declaration of the Rights of Man. Even when treating of the revolutionary decade and the Napoleonic era, Tocqueville's notes indicated his constant idea of England as the successful antagonist to the proselytizing ideology of revolution. His projected chapter on the wars of the Revolution was to have been concluded by a vivid description of England's stubborn resistance. That opposition was possible only because England possessed an ideological weapon capable of appeal against the French Revolution: "A great spectacle, liberty alone capable of fighting against the Revolution." [14]

The *Ancien Régime,* as a reflection of its author's general purpose, bore a striking resemblance to the *Démocratie.* Just as in 1840 he had been interested in showing how far men's inclinations and ideas were affected by the equality of conditions, in 1856 he wished to perform a parallel task treating the presence or absence of regular political activity in a society. His starting point was personal but his appeal was to a reflection upon results which could be arrived at independently of his concern with the preservation of liberty. Without attempting to lay claim to providing an all-inclusive chain of causality he located a single phenomenon of French history which, when isolated, appeared to make a decisive difference in the development of its institutions, its ideas, and the general patterns of its actions. In the *Démocratie,* however, Tocqueville sought to free his study from any specific society in order to create a type. The *Ancien Régime* was not an analysis of a particular example of a condition common to all Europe, of an aristocracy in decline, or a

[14] *Ancien Régime,* II, 247, "La Révolution débordant en Europe. Conquêtes. Leurs causes."

predemocratic social condition approaching its moment of birth. It represented a shift from a static picture of the old regime, based on a generalized "aristocratic principle," to historical comparisons of the diverse political and social developments of France, England, and Germany.

Looking at the European revolution, Tocqueville was struck by two important facts: the unity of its point of departure in the medieval society of the twelfth and thirteenth centuries, and the partial divergence of the English development from the mainstream of European history. A posthumously published chapter on the French Revolution universalized the English experience of twenty years before: "The societies of the Middle Ages were really only aristocratic bodies, which contained only (and therein, in part, lay their greatness) small fragments of democracy." [15] In his family papers Tocqueville found evidence of close contact with the lower classes among his own ancestors as far back as three centuries before the Revolution.

Against the background of this medieval European polity French and German history emerged as a detailed study in the death of political activity in comparison with the vigorous continuity of English free institutions. Tocqueville underscored the progressive decline and devitalization of the older combination of political assemblies and the social hierarchy of classes on the Continent. He was now convinced that England was as far from the relatively static hierarchic structure of the medieval polity as were the Continental societies. She was seen to have become a modern nation even earlier than the rest of the Continent because of the vigor of her political institutions and was more responsive to shifts in social, economic, and ideological pressures, though less inclined to generalize changes in the spirit of her laws by changes in form. "In England," observed Tocqueville,

where it could be said at first sight that the old constitution of Europe is still in full vigor, the same [transformation] occurred. If one wants

[15] *Ancien Régime,* II, 124. See also 148–149.

to forget the old names and pass over the forms, one will find the feudal system essentially abolished as early as the seventeenth century: all classes freely intermingled, an eclipsed nobility, an open aristocracy, wealth leading to power, equality before the law, and equal taxes, a free press, public debates—all new principles of which the middle ages was unaware . . . England of the seventeenth century is already a completely modern nation, which only preserved, as if embalmed, some of the relics of the Middle Ages.[16]

In this view of England as the harbinger of the modern age, Tocqueville implied his judgment of the true meaning of the French Revolution, the abolition of political and social privilege, and the creation of institutional organs for political activity. England thus stood as an example to France of the proper limits of the revolutionary impulse, an impulse which stopped short of dictatorship, antireligious sentiments, and attacks on individual rights, especially property rights. The primacy of the political aspect of the French Revolution was thus an expression not only of an analytical conclusion but of a deep-seated desire to convince the reader that this aspect had also been the first and best part of the revolutionary upheaval.[17]

Tocqueville's most original conclusions on the nature of French society in the seventeenth and eighteenth centuries had come from his investigations of the administrative archives. In employing these documents he had merely followed his own earlier insight that France's administrative matrix had exerted a much more powerful influence upon her ideas, acts, and habits than had her political institutions.[18] For the easiest access to the French character he had advised foreigners to study French civil and administrative law. The continuity of French society before and after the Revolution was a central thesis of the *Ancien Régime*. Thus it was not surprising that he began the discussion of French society not with an investigation

---

[16] *Ancien Régime*, I, 94.

[17] *Ancien Régime*, I, 95.

[18] *Oeuvres* (B), IX, 60ff, "Rapport fait à l'Académie des sciences morales et politiques (1846), sur le livre de M. Macarel, intitulé *Cours de droit administratif.*"

of the Enlightenment but of administrative organization. This was, in fact, an organizational and stylistic counterpart to his conviction that both the feudal hierarchy and its political institutions had become husks whose power had been drained into the centralized bureaucracy. The atrophy of political life had resulted in the proportionate growth of bureaucratic power and the habits of secrecy, irresponsibility, and submission, which became the dominant traits of French public life.[19] The monarchs of France and their agents emerged as the terrible simplifiers of the old regime. There was no balancing of administrative efficiency against political liability as in the *Démocratie* of 1835. The historical achievement of the Bourbons in unifying France was buried beneath the failure of parliamentary government in nineteenth-century France. Here the image of England played a decisive role. At least one nation had bound together liberty and unity without a system of centralized administration. In the 1850's she seemed as immune to Continental administrative practice as to Continental politics.

The spirits of government in England and France were vividly contrasted in a note on their colonies in North America entitled "How it is in Canada that the centralization of the Old Regime can best be judged." [20] Tocqueville always assumed that in a colony the constitutional barnacles of the mother country were quickly discarded. Algeria was, he told Senior, "a louse under a microscope," [21] and the continuity of the impulse toward administrative centralization could best be seen in eighteenth-century Canada or nineteenth-century Algeria.

What in 1832 had been a study of the comparative success or failure of colonial regimes now became an epitome of the habits

---

[19] *Ancien Régime*, I, 108–109.

[20] *Ancien Régime*, I, 286–287.

[21] Conversation of March 3, 1855, *Correspondence and Conversations*, II, 103. He substituted the more polite "object" for "louse" in the *Ancien Régime*. Lord Elgin, governor-general of Canada from 1846 to 1854, told Tocqueville of his own surprise when the French Canadians at first resisted all attempts to give them control of their own administration. See Claude Marie Raudot, "L'Administration locale en France et en Angleterre," *Le Correspondant*, LVIII (February 1863), 304.

of the mother country. "When I want to discover the spirit and vices of the government of Louis XIV, I must go to Canada." [22] There was a note of bitterness in the *Ancien Régime,* aroused by an acute awareness on Tocqueville's part that he was no longer discussing a colony lost three generations before his time but a legacy of "the petty, artificial methods and the small devices of tyranny" which had come unscathed down to the Second Empire. Canada and Algeria were strung together on the endless chain of bureaucratic tyranny, "preponderating, acting, regulating, controlling, wanting to foresee everything, to undertake everything." It was a machine forever and uselessly active, "always more aware of the interests of the administered than he is himself." [23]

The United States, conversely, was considered to be the direct extension of the English ideal of decentralization without any mention of a new point of departure: "The administration proper does little in England, and individuals do a great deal; in America administration interferes in nothing and individuals in association do everything." [24] In both colonies democratic tendencies were operative, but the French society had fused them with the imported principles of absolutism while the British had combined them with liberty. In the *Ancien Régime,* Tocqueville viewed the English victory in the New World as a triumph of liberty. The linking of England and America was completed by the inclusion of America among the "English provinces." [25]

The continuity, stability, and wisdom of English political principles and performance claimed Tocqueville's entire attention. Seventeenth century and revolutionary England, the first "completely modern nation," was depicted as having acquired new institutions "little by little" and with consummate art. More significantly, the *Ancien Régime* never really dealt with what was the most dramatic and violent political rupture in the Anglo-American world—the American Revolution. Despite the fact that Tocqueville's reputation,

[22] *Ancien Régime,* I, 286.
[23] *Ancien Régime,* I, 287.
[24] *Ancien Régime,* I, 287.
[25] I, 287.

interests, and methods pointed toward a comparative analysis of the genesis of revolutions, the *Ancien Régime* stopped at a general distinction between the French Revolution, with its more extensive ideological and international ramifications, and those which had preceded it. Only once was the Revolution in France briefly measured against another. The English Revolution of 1640 was cited to demonstrate the relatively limited legal and social disruptions caused by entire revolutionary cycles when compared to the collapse of the French administrative system in 1787–88. This was as close as Tocqueville came to an anatomy of revolution, at least before death intervened.[26]

In the *Westminster Review* article of 1836 Tocqueville had only dealt with the decline of local government in terms of the divorce of the French nobility from local government. Now he carefully traced the destruction of political life through the provincial assemblies, municipal governments, and parish meetings. Tocqueville was struck in his investigation of the intendants' records by the existence of parochial government throughout feudal Europe. He entirely discarded the theory, expressed in the *Démocratie* of 1835, that the significant features of American local institutions were unique adjustments to New World conditions. In the microcosm of parish government in England and France the story of disparate political development repeated itself. In France the parish, cut loose from the seigniory, had been crushed in the embrace of the central government to a point where Turgot could describe it as "a collection of silent dwellings, and equally silent dwellers." [27]

The enslavement of the parish in France contained for Tocqueville all the significance of the frustration of his own goals for French local government. "In both America and France," he observed, "we see general assemblies of the inhabitants meeting periodically to elect magistrates and to regulate public affairs. They resemble each other, in fact as a living body resembles a corpse." [28] Beaumont in

[26] See *Ancien Régime*, I, 242, as well as Tocqueville's notes, II, 188, 334–335. In a note for the sequel to the *Ancien Régime* Tocqueville considered using revolutionary America as another example of a limited political change (*ibid.*, II, 337).

[27] *Ancien Régime*, I, 121.

[28] *Ancien Régime*, I, 120.

L'Irlande had contrasted the "feudal-Norman county" in the English constitution with the "democratic-Saxon" parish. The former had predominated in the Irish political system and the latter in America, while both enjoyed peaceful coexistence in separate spheres of the English constitution.[29] Tocqueville now modified this conclusion, declaring that the republican element, clearly illustrated in communal vitality, formed "the foundation of the English constitution and English habits."[30] Thus the flowering of local government in America flowed from the essential principle of the English polity. Transported at a single stroke far from the feudal remnants of Europe, "the rural parish of the Middle Ages became the New England township." In almost the same terms that Beaumont had used to describe parish and municipal government in Ireland Tocqueville traced the corruption and enervation of political life in France through cities, villages, and corporate bodies of every kind.

This shift of emphasis concerning the fundamental element in the British constitution from a principle with class connotations to one implying participation, action, and responsibility of men in an essentially political context was symptomatic. Tocqueville was, in fact, altering his entire terminology to conform to certain features of the English polity. Thus England's class structure and even her economic prosperity would be necessarily subordinated in his analysis to her sense of community. The *Ancien Régime* continually alluded to England's "more varied and more energetic," activity. Tocqueville's only regret was that the ultimate historical strength of British institutions had not been as apparent to France in 1750 as they were a century later. "England itself, poorly known in any event, had not yet furnished the striking arguments in favor of liberty that it has since done. Free institutions produced internal and unseen effects

[29] *L'Irlande*, I, 295, 398.

[30] *Ancien Régime*, I, 287. J. Toulmin Smith, eulogist of the English parish, quoted the *Ancien Régime* at length in *The Parish: Its Obligations and Powers, Its Officers and Duties* (London, 1857), 7. Almost a century later V. D. Lipman's *Local Government Areas, 1834–1945* (Oxford, 1949), opened with a quotation from Tocqueville on the spirit of local government.

which were hidden to foreigners; their fecundity and their greatness were not yet manifest." [31]

Tocqueville was prepared to argue for the effectiveness of the apparently haphazard English legislation and administration of both the eighteenth and nineteenth centuries. He asked his contemporaries to consider that administrative procedures in England had remained more complex and irregular than those of France, yet "the imperfection of special organs is irrelevant because its vital spirit is so strong." [32] Tocqueville devoted one of his longest notes to elucidating this "vital spirit." He outlined the chaotic jumble of customary law amid regional diversity in England. But comparing this "monstrous machine" with the French judicial organization of 1856, he insisted that there was no country in Europe in "which, even in Blackstone's time, the great ends of justice were more fully attained than in England; not one where every man, of whatever rank, and whether his suit was against a private individual or the sovereign, was more certain of being heard, and more assured of finding in the court ample guarantees for the defense of his fortune, his liberty, and his life." [33] The protection of the individual against arbitrary procedures appeared infinitely more important in the contemporary context than the secondary vices of a judicial system.

Against the background of the twofold English ramparts of local government and judicial guarantees Tocqueville outlined for his contemporaries the growth of the Intendancy, creeping in among older authorities; one by one he catalogued the corruption of the classes of France. The administrators themselves had none of the true features of a ruling class. Trained to rule in silence, they also obeyed or disobeyed in silence; when confronted by a shift in regimes, they merely acted as efficient tools, not as a group with a vested interest in the retention of their political power.[34] The silent,

[31] II, 372.
[32] *Ancien Régime*, I, 222, 308–310.
[33] *Ancien Régime*, I, 309.
[34] *Ancien Régime*, I, 243. For a case previously studied by Tocqueville see *Oeuvres* (B), IX, 1–23.

continuous flow of decisions caused the French to regard government as a providential agent.

In the 1830's Tocqueville had viewed the creation of a small peasant landholding class as a prerequisite for those habits of independence necessary to a free democratic society. In the *Ancien Régime,* the dependence upon government appeared to be as much a habit for the landholder as for other subjects. Any natural propensity against bureaucratic tutelage was more than negated by the ever widening circle of the administrative reflex. As in the case of the bourgeoisie of the July Monarchy, economic arrangements followed political habits. Even the farmers, lamented Tocqueville, looked to the intendant to improve agriculture by a system of inspection and honorary awards. "Medals and Inspectors! Would such an approach ever enter the head of a Suffolk farmer!" [35]

Contemptuously he traced this habit of subservience into the ranks of the bourgeoisie, who were subsequently called upon to take control of French political life and who twice surrendered it abjectly to the Bonapartes. Rather than seeing the spirit of liberty as growing out of the self-reliance of business, Tocqueville pointed out that the habit of administrative obedience and administrative thinking encouraged the development of dependence on central government and concluded that no group in France had been ready to act intelligently in 1789. The central government had succeeded too well in stifling almost every public body that bore the dangerous marks of associative action for a purpose not directed by the administrative hierarchy.

And what, after all, had been gained by the sacrifice of power to leviathan? Tocqueville's concluding remark on the unsystematic machinery of government in England was a challenge: "Is there, however, a single country in Europe where public credit is greater, private property more extensive, more sure, and more diversified, or society more stable or opulent?" [36]

Tocqueville was probably right in claiming that the English were

[35] I, 136.
[36] *Ancien Régime,* I, 222.

better protected from arbitrary procedures than the French both in 1756 and 1856. He overplayed the unsystematic decentralization of English public administration, however. If England was socially more stable than France or Germany, if despite widespread suspicion of government interference England in the 1850's did more for the pauper, the criminal, the tenement dweller, and the child laborer than did the contemporary Prussian and French bureaucracies, it was not just the courts, or the "vital spirit" of local government, which deserved credit for the achievement.[37] It was unfortunate that Tocqueville did not follow the administrative development of England very closely after 1835. The iron chain of centralization, despotism, and revolution which he drew from the French experience might have been less rigidly presented if he had observed the growth of central control in England. In dealing with the protection and health of the less favored portion of society, the central government with its standards and inspectorates had already substantially replaced private initiative and local autonomy. Despite widespread suspicion of governmental interference, the spirit of Victorian compromise was at work in the problem of centralization as well.

Tocqueville had formerly placed great emphasis on England's stability arising from her total involvement with the acquisition of wealth. The economic factor faded in the *Ancien Régime,* as did considerations of institutional deficiencies, in the bright glare of English political activity. "Common interests," declared Tocqueville, "had closely knit together the various social classes in England, but they differed widely in habits and ideas; for political liberty, which enjoys that admirable power of creating among all citizens necessary relations and mutual ties of dependence, does not always make them similar; it is unitary rule which in the long run always has the inevitable effect of making men at once identical and indifferent to each other's fate." [38]

In the timely formation of new political ties lay the only solution

[37] Roberts, *Victorian Origins of the British Welfare State,* 324–326.
[38] I, 146.

which might have spared the old regime the violence of a necessary destruction. None of the "detestable institutions" and privileges among an increasingly homogeneous people "could have lasted twenty years if it had been possible to discuss them." [39] Tocqueville conceived of the Revolution as inevitable from that moment that public opinion again became a force in France in reaction to the abolition of the parlements in 1771. Political reawakening combined with political inexperience to produce the collapse of Bourbon absolutism.

The isolation of classes was illustrated mainly through a discussion of the political disintegration of the French nobility, the hereditary remnant of a once powerful political and social order, whose privileges were to become the first target of the French Revolution. A comparison between the upper classes in France and England led Tocqueville far from the concept of the "aristocracy of wealth," which had been a crucial element in his article of 1836 and in the second part of the *Démocratie*. The term did not even appear in the *Ancien Régime*. But more than ever he regarded her unique aristocracy as the true point of departure and the most important development in English history. He had made efforts, through correspondence with Senior and readings of Blackstone and Macaulay, to trace this revolutionary change to its origin. He never felt it satisfactorily accounted for by contemporary English histories, and though its precise beginnings eluded him, his instincts were sound.[40] He was certain that it was a key to the peculiarities of England's laws and her political spirit, never fully recognized even by Montesquieu.

To illustrate his hypothesis, Tocqueville returned in the *Ancien Régime* to the linguistic evidence of the word "gentleman." It was already impossible to translate the word literally when Molière wrote in *Tartuffe*, "Et tel que l'on voit, il est bon gentilhomme." In

[39] *Ancien Régime,* I, 289.

[40] See Tocqueville to Senior, July 2, 1853, *Oeuvres* (B), VI, and Tocqueville to Beaumont, Dec. 21, 1856, *ibid.,* VII. See also Marc Bloch, *La Société féodale: Les Classes et le gouvernement des hommes* (Paris, 1940), 73–77.

1833 Tocqueville's comparison between the two words had been a contrast between two concepts of class delineation; now it was linked to the historical divergence of the two nations. The title of gentleman was not only accorded to all Englishmen of good education but "in each century it applied to groups a little lower on the social scale." [41] Finally, America again revealed the culmination of English class solvency in the indiscriminate designation of all citizens as gentlemen. The very opposite trend had occurred in the development of French society. While the leveling processes had become more of a reality in the institutions of the nation and in the distribution of economic power, the privileges and consciousness of class had increased. The term *gentilhomme,* confronted by the reality of 1789 and unable to adapt to a new era, had dropped from common usage.

In France and the rest of Europe the feudal system had led to a creation of castes; in England alone had a real aristocracy developed. The older nobility and the "people" engaged in the same occupations, entered the same professions, and, what was always ultimate proof for Tocqueville, intermarried. He again placed an important emphasis not on the ease of entry into the ranks of the titled aristocracy, which had been available also to Frenchmen, but the vague boundaries of the English upper classes. Although Tocqueville had recognized the factor of indefiniteness as early as 1833, in 1836 he had defined the French nobility as an aristocratic body because it had one of the three elements which at that time seemed an inherent part of the principle of aristocracy—birth. The English aristocracy on the other hand had been accorded a large portion of the three essential elements—birth, wealth, knowledge—with wealth as its predominant characteristic. In 1856 Tocqueville returned to a political definition of aristocracy. The French nobility, by forming a hereditary caste, defined in an extrapolitical sense, was therefore not an aristocracy, nor even a part of one. [42]

If Tocqueville was unaware that by 1760 the Intendancy was a

---

[41] *Ancien Régime,* I, 148.
[42] Compare *Ancien Régime,* I, 45, "Etat social" (1836), and I, 244.

preserve of the nobility, he knew that it was harder for a *roturier*, or non-noble, to become an officer under Louis XVI than under Louis XIV. He concluded that this marked a gain for the nobility as individuals and members of an isolated social group, not a return to political leadership. The rigidity of class boundaries, extending far down into the ranks of the third estate, psychologically negated whatever legal mobility there was.[43] If the term "aristocracy" was not abandoned completely in referring to the second estate in France, it was only used when Tocqueville wished to point to some fine quality of the nobility which went beyond concern with its own rights. The following sentence is typical: "One senses, while reading its [the nobility's] *cahiers,* in the midst of its prejudices and beyond them, the spirit and some of the great qualities of aristocracy. It must always be regretted that instead of bringing this nobility under the rule of law, they were destroyed and uprooted."

The English aristocracy not only retained the leadership of the nation but kept its position through participation in living political institutions. Political freedom was cited as the a priori necessity for the slow development of the English constitution. Tocqueville had formerly conceived of the cause of slow change and lack of general ideas as arising from the habits formed by the complexities of an "aristocratic" frame of mind tending toward individuality. He now saw this patchwork mentality as flowing not from the principle of inequality but from continuous political participation. Nothing comprehensive (in revolutionary terms) could be effected under a state of things like that of England, where there was ample opportunity for individual grievances to be heard "or a local or class interest to obtain redress."[44]

Thus the destruction of political life and class division were now

---

[43] See *Ancien Régime,* I, 150–151, and II, 360: "Inequality growing in institutions and customs in proportion as it decreases in fact (all this, *idée mère*)." On the third estate, Tocqueville had read Augustin Thierry's *Essai sur l'histoire du tiers-etat* (Paris, 1853). See A. Augustin-Thierry, *Augustin Thierry (1795–1856) d'après sa correspondance et ses papiers de famille* (Paris, 1922), 259.

[44] *Correspondence and Conversations,* II, 49, "Extract from Mrs. Grote's Journal" (Feb. 13, 1854). For an earlier parallel with regard to general ideas in America and France see *Oeuvres* (M): *Démocratie,* II, 25–26. Here again, in the *Ancien Régime,* England was assimilated with America.

inseparably linked as the causes of all the diseases of which the old regime had died and of the vicious cycle into which France had been thrown. In tracing the impoverishment of the French nobility, Tocqueville could not refrain from pointing with satisfaction to the one aristocracy which retained its wealth because it retained its political instincts. This seemed clear when he considered the distribution of landed estates and the allotment of the burden of taxes in England as compared with France. Status in England went with the land, not the person. Thus the sale of fiefs to commoners in England aided the confusion of rank through wealth, while in France the distinction between noble and *roturier* was retained. In addition, "political liberty, the custom of assemblies, rendered this transformation easier [in England] than in France, common concerns naturally drawing interested parties together and tending to mingle those who had a common interest." It allowed "the political power and social influence (in short, the privileges) of wealth and particularly of landed wealth to continue." [45]

Similarly, the evil of the French tax system lay not only in the inequality of distribution but in the fact that the nobility had traded its contact with the lower classes in return for exemptions. The British upper class had, on the contrary, assumed the largest portion of responsibility for taxes and the support of the poor—not out of generosity, but because of a strong instinct for retaining control of political life: "It was willing to sacrifice anything for power. For centuries the only alterations in the taxes were made in favor of the poorer classes . . . In the eighteenth century, in England, the only exemptions from taxes were enjoyed by the poor, in France by the rich." [46] He also implicitly admitted the deficiency of his own earlier perception. The poor law now seemed a pillar of the constitution instead of the breeding place of social instability.

Tocqueville saw an identical lack of political common sense and political virtue in every class under the old regime. His theme of the political atrophy of the nobility was to have culminated in a comparison of the ideological defense of the English constitution

[45] *Ancien Régime*, II, 360.
[46] *Ancien Régime*, I, 160.

after 1789 with the theoretical vacuum in France. He contended that even during the "aristocratic revolution" of 1787–88 the rights of man and citizen terminology permeated the arguments of king and nobility alike. Both were psychologically helpless when the third estate took up the identical slogans.[47] He could detect in the *cahiers* of the nobility in 1789 no intelligent argument for the defense of the very class that jealously clung to the honorary distinctions that had aroused the most intense resentment while consenting to political and social reform. Even the reflex of self-defense had failed.[48]

The same explanation was given to the role of the Enlightenment in its attack both on institutions and religious dogma in the old regime. Tocqueville considered political inexperience to be the prime cause for the success of that utopian thought which had pushed the Revolution beyond the limits of the political liberty achieved in 1789. Since Frenchmen of letters before the Revolution took no part in public affairs, had no public functions to discharge, and were without any sense of responsibility for the direction of the nation, the political world remained divided into two separate provinces: administration without discussion and theory without application. Tocqueville was much more incensed by the authoritarian outlook of many eighteenth-century writers than by their confidence in human reason. He compared their contempt for the ignorant herd with the respect for the "sentiments of the majority" among the English and Americans—even at the cost of sheer historical anachronism.[49] This was incidentally his final reference to that "majority" which the *Démocratie* had so prominently linked with tyranny.

His basic argument was not that the same ideas might not have come from individual Englishmen as well as Frenchmen, but that French political conditions afforded no measuring rod to determine what political theories might reasonably be put into practice. Tocqueville reiterated his doctrine that it was unsafe to disconnect either the individual or society from political activity; once one ceased to act in affairs, the gauge of political reason was lost. English writers and

[47] *Ancien Régime,* II, 59–60.
[48] *Ancien Régime,* I, 196–197, and II, 84–85, 108–109.
[49] *Ancien Régime,* I, 306.

statesmen, on the other hand, enjoyed the power to apply their minds to actual circumstances and could appeal to public opinion through the free press. In the 1836 *Westminster Review* article he had attributed the difference in the degree of power wielded by writers in England and France to that overwhelming passion for wealth which had absorbed the English public mind. Now the free play of political life was given full credit for the difference; the effect of the acquisitive instinct on political philosophy was not even mentioned.

England played an identical role in the discussion of the growth of irreligion in the *Ancien Régime*. In his rough drafts for the *Démocratie* of 1840, Tocqueville had observed that the English middle classes were remarkably persistent in their traditional religious beliefs and practices. Despite their intense concern with material gain, they were equally impervious to the iconoclasm of their neighbors and to the skepticism of some of their own literary and philosophical geniuses.[50] When this observation was finally published, in the *Ancien Régime,* Tocqueville applied it to the eighteenth century, eliminated its class connotation, and dropped all reference to English materialism. He added a clearly defined political explanation of the contrast between England and France: "Throughout the eighteenth century unbelief had champions in England. Able writers, profound thinkers embraced its cause. But they could never make it triumph as in France, because all who had anything to lose by revolutions hastened to the support of the established beliefs." [51]

In the *Westminster Review* article Tocqueville had drawn an analogy between the Anglican Church in 1836 and the Gallican in 1789. Both were hated and vulnerable because of their institutional links with constitutions full of abuses. In 1856 Tocqueville turned from the decrepitude of the Anglican Church to the resilience of the Anglicans:

Great political parties, such as exist in every free country, found it to be in their interest to espouse the cause of the Church; Bolingbroke himself was seen to become the ally of the bishops. Animated by this example,

[50] Yale Mss(T) C.V.g: copy of rough drafts for the *Démocratie* of 1840, paq. 9, cahier 1, pp. 171–173.
[51] *Ancien Régime,* I, 206.

and encouraged by a consciousness of support, the clergy fought with energy in its own defense. The Church of England, in spite of the vice of its constitution and the various abuses which abounded within it, victoriously sustained the blow. Hostile theories after having been discussed and refuted were finally rejected by the exertions of society itself, without the intervention of the government.[52]

Tocqueville's blanket characterization of eighteenth-century men of letters as speculative utopians is no longer viable.[53] But historians in attacking his position have frequently ignored the *Ancien Régime*'s emphasis on the social conditions which fostered iconoclasm in France. He differs at this point from his apparent forebear Edmund Burke, for whom the men of abstractions had destroyed a basically sound social order.

On the Continent, despotism not democracy, in England liberty not aristocracy, were the points of departure in the *Ancien Régime*. Where the essay of 1836 concluded with the thought that "the French had conceived earlier and more clearly than any the democratic idea of liberty," the *Ancien Régime*'s summation identified France as a country of Europe "where all political life was extinguished most completely and for the longest time." [54] The *Ancien Régime* marked a complete break with Tocqueville's original identification of the old regime as described in the introduction to the *Démocratie*. Fusing the English and American images, Tocqueville muted his initial dichotomy between "aristocracy" and "democracy" as the key terms of analysis. In the *Démocratie* these deliberately ambiguous concepts had divided the multitude of social phenomena between them. The use of "democracy" was particularly inexact and confusing.[55] Sometimes it referred to a political structure, but more often simply evoked

---

[52] *Ancien Régime*, I, 206.
[53] See Herr, *Tocqueville and the Old Regime*, 121–122.
[54] *Ancien Régime*, I, 65, 245.
[55] Arne Naess and others, in *Democracy, Ideology and Objectivity: Studies in the Semantics and Cognitive Analysis of Ideological Controversy* (Oslo, 1956), 53–54, were unable to locate in the *Démocratie* "a concept [of democracy] that could justifiably be called Tocqueville's concept."

the picture of a vast leveling movement, a providential fact engulfing the entire range of thought and action. In the notes for the *Démo-cratie* of 1840 Tocqueville had considered drawing a distinction between *démocratie* and *égalité:* "When I understand [the new society] in the political sense, I say *Démocratie.* When I want to speak of the effects of equality, I say *égalité.*" [56] This clarification, whether because it would have aesthetically weakened the impact of the term, or for some other reason, remained buried in his papers and his book went to press with "equality" and "democracy" used interchangeably. When he wrote the *Ancien Régime* Tocqueville seemed to be trying to banish by omission the ambiguity, which had begun to haunt his political conscience. The terms "democracy" and "democratic" were used scarcely more than a dozen times in the entire work. Discussing the same topic, the *Westminster Review* article had employed them twice as many times in one tenth the space. In one of the last dated chapter plans of his unfinished sequel to the *Ancien Régime* he finally enclosed democracy, in the political sense, within the bounds of liberty alone: "The words 'democracy,' 'monarchy,' 'democratic government' can mean only one thing, according to the true sense of these words: a government where the people participate to a greater or to a lesser extent. Its sense is intimately tied to the idea of political liberty. To characterize as democratic a government where political liberty is absent is a palpable absurdity according to the natural sense of these words." [57]

Whatever the merits of the *Ancien Régime* in its treatment of France Tocqueville never claimed to have investigated the English sources in depth as he did in the case of his own country. If the study ignored the intricacies of the structure of politics and administration

[56] Yale Mss C.V.k, paq. 7, cahier 1, pp. 50–51. But see Tocqueville to J. S. Mill, Nov. 14, 1839, *Oeuvres* (M): *Corr angl.,* I, where he referred to the work as the influence of equality on men's ideas and feelings.

[57] *Ancien Régime,* II, 199, dated December 1857. Tocqueville, in the Preface to the *Ancien Régime,* referred once to "democratic societies which are not free," but in the text, "despotism" and "equality" were usually used where *démocratie* or *démocratique* would have appeared twenty years before.

in Georgian England and coated it with a broad Victorian brush, one must recognize that French society was its primary subject. In addition, the author's vantage point and polemic intent meant that where Tocqueville's fundamental loyalties were at stake, as when he dealt with the administrative and political mentalities, the juxtaposition of England and France came disturbingly close to an unreal Manichaean dualism that was unjust to both societies. England and a France merged with Germany on certain fundamental points, were demonstrations of political alternatives as well as the subjects of comparative history.

Tocqueville referred to a feeling of terror twice in his works. The first described his reaction to the enormity of the egalitarian onslaught in the introduction to the *Démocratie;* the second, his realization while reading the *cahiers* of 1789 for his *Ancien Régime,* that the sum of their individual demands amounted to the doom of every existing institution even before the Revolution began. No Frenchman could put down the *Ancien Régime* without noticing with equal terror that its author had assailed almost every class, every institution, and every event in recent French history. There was one exception. France, by a conscious and deliberate act in 1789, had chosen to defy her past and proclaim her capacity for political liberty. It was a moment his nation could reject but never forget. The chain of history had been broken once. It could be broken again.

This note of hope in the last completed chapter of his unfinished work pierced through the dreary implications of the *Ancien Régime.* It was closer to faith than to reason, a secular faith in the art of the possible. As Max Weber said, "Only he has the calling for politics who is sure that he shall not crumble when the world from his point of view is too base or stupid for what he wants to offer. Only he who in the face of all this can say 'In spite of all!' has the calling for politics." [58] Tocqueville remained true to his calling.

---

[58] "Politics as a Vocation," in *From Max Weber: Essays in Sociology,* ed. and transl. H. H. Gerth and C. Wright Mills (London, 1947), 128.

XI ❖ *Tocqueville and England*

THE DECADE following the publication of the *Ancien Régime* and the last visit to England marked the height of Tocqueville's influence in England. The *Ancien Régime* arrived at the moment in English historiography when "the eighteenth century was so remote that the structural differences between the world of 1760 and 1860 could be entirely overlooked."[1] Tocqueville's description of the English aristocracy blended perfectly with the first chapter of Macaulay's *History of England*. The combination of a new synthesis of French history, of a focus on England's splendid isolation from the revolutionary virus, and a vibrant style proved to be irresistible. Not one of the major English reviews took issue with his interpretation of developments on either side of the Channel. The *Ancien Régime* at once became for both university professors and their students the standard interpretation of the epoch.[2]

Tocqueville's second great work reinforced and revived the influence of the first. A generation which had been raised on the *Démocratie* was coming to the fore. Sir Charles Dilke and Leslie Stephen dreamt of writing masterpieces which would be sequels to Tocqueville's analysis of the egalitarian era. Lord Acton visited Tocqueville in Paris as part of his special education under the German historian Ignaz von Döllinger. Henry Sidgwick, Sir Thomas Erskine May, William Lecky, and James Bryce incorporated Tocque-

---

[1] Herbert Butterfield, *George III and the Historians,* rev. ed. (New York, 1959), 151.

[2] See Charles Kingsley, *Three Lectures Delivered at the Royal Institution on the* Ancien Régime (London, 1867), and Marcel, *Essai politique,* 118.

ville's thought into their own historical and political works. Sir
Henry Sumner Maine, Frederick Denison Maurice, and Frederick
William Maitland came under his influence.

It was above all in the political world that Tocqueville's influence
swelled in the years following his death. He affected Gladstone's
views on colonial government and through Richard Cobden, Sir
William Molesworth, and Dilke left a mark on imperial policy.
The *Démocratie* played an important part in the bitter controversy
over the British government's attitude toward the Civil War in
America. It furnished material for those who viewed the breakdown
of the Union as inevitable and for those who had faith in a northern
victory.[3] It was at the center of British political controversy that
Tocqueville's impact was greatest. Domestic conditions conspired to
bring about his posthumous return to Parliament. In 1859 Sir James
Graham quoted him in a speech on franchise reform. In 1860, on
the same subject, W. H. Gregory read whole pages of the *Démocratie*
to the House of Commons, and three other members followed his
choice of authority. By the time the Reform Bill debates reached
their climax in 1866–67, Tocqueville was probably the most frequently invoked foreigner in both houses, with Robert Lowe, C. P.
Villiers, John Stuart Mill, Gathorne Hardy, Lords Elcho, Grey,
Houghton, and Gregory again drawing on his name or his ideas to
plead their cause. He supplied equal ammunition for and against

---

[3] See J. L. Hammond and M. R. D. Foot, *Gladstone and Liberalism* (London,
1952), 56–57; Richard Cobden, *Speeches on Questions of Public Policy, by Richard
Cobden, M.P.*, ed. John Bright and J. E. T. Rogers (London, 1870), II, 113; Sir
William Molesworth, *Selected Speeches of Sir William Molesworth* (London, 1903),
380–390; Pope-Hennessy, *Monckton Milnes: The Flight of Youth, 1851–1885*, 165–
166; [George Cornewall Lewis], "The Election of President Lincoln and Its Consequences," *Edinburgh Review*, CXIII (April 1861), 574; "The American Revolution,"
ibid., CXVI (October 1862), 563, 584, 590; "Democracy on Its Trial," *Quarterly
Review*, CX (July 1861), 254, 281; [J. S. Mill], "The Slave Power," *Westminster
Review*, LXXVIII (October 1862), 491; "The American Constitution at the Present
Crisis," *National Review*, XIII (October 1861), 465, 475–476; "The American War,"
ibid., XIV (April 1862), 502; "The Slave Power and the Secession War," *ibid.*, XV
(July 1862), 175; "The Close of the American War," *Quarterly Review*, CXVIII
(July 1865), 128; "The Value of India to England," *ibid.*, CXX (July 1866), 198–
201, 214, 220.

both the Liberal bill of 1866 and the Conservative one the following year. At one point, on two successive nights, four Tocqueville-based speeches divided equally, for and against.[4]

A nation teetering on the edge of democracy felt itself instinctively in need of a temperate apostle. In the flurry of comparative analyses and polemic literature provoked by a decade of controversy, few authors felt their works to be complete without at least a passing reference to the *Démocratie* or the *Ancien Régime*.[5] An acute awareness of certain tendencies on the Continent had enabled Tocqueville to demonstrate that the spirit of liberty did not flow automatically or even naturally from the principles of equality and popular sovereignty, but from values and institutions which might be compatible but were not identical with them. England had first to be convinced that it could have both liberty and equality before it was ready for

[4] See *Hansard's Parliamentary Debates,* 3rd ser. Vol. 146: June 30, 1857, p. 657; Vol. 153: March 28, 1859, pp. 973–974, 979–980. Vol. 157: March 22, 1860, pp. 1038–39; April 23, 1860, pp. 2218–19. Vol. 158: May 3, 1860, pp. 577–592; May 3, 1860, pp. 600–601. Vol. 178: May 3, 1865, p. 1427. Vol. 182: March 13, 1866, pp. 164–178; April 13, 1866, pp. 1261–62; April 19, 1866, pp. 1679–80, 1745–46; April 20, 1866, p. 1792; April 26, 1866, pp. 2104–07. Vol. 188: July 22, 1867, p. 1817; July 23, 1867, pp. 1917–33, 1978. See also Henry Fawcett's speech on the same subject in vol. 202, June 15, 1870, p. 172. Tocqueville's name was still invoked as late as 1888 and 1893 in the debates on local government reform.

[5] See, for example, Hugh Seymour Tremenheere, *The Constitution of The United States Compared with Our Own* (London, 1854), xiii, xvi, 167; J. S. Mill, *Considerations on Representative Government* (London, 1861), 15; Henry George (Earl) Grey, *Parliamentary Government Considered with Reference to Reform* (London, 1864), 84, 162, 173–174; Robert Lowe, *Speeches and Letters on Reform, with a Preface* (London, 1867), Preface; the essays by G. C. Brodrick, Leslie Stephen, Bernard Cracroft, Goldwin Smith, and James Bryce in *Essays on Reform* (London, 1867); "The Political Tendencies of America," *National Review,* II (April 1856), 462–463; "Earl Grey on Reform," *ibid.,* VI (April 1858), 442–443; "The State of Parties," *ibid.,* VII (July 1858), 229–230; "The Reform Bill: Its Real Bearing and Ultimate Results," *ibid.,* X (April 1860), 439; Sheldon Amos, "Democracy in England," *Fortnightly Review,* I (June 1, 1865), 236–237; "Representative Reform," *Edinburgh Review,* CVI (July 1857), 280–281; "Earl Grey on Parliamentary Government," *ibid.,* CVIII (July 1858), 283; "Democracy," *Westminster Review,* LXXXVIII (October 1867), 480–481, 488, 500; "Democratic Government in Victoria," *ibid.,* LXXXIX (April 1868), 502, 505; "Reform," *Quarterly Review,* CV (January 1859), 259, 261–262; "The Four Reform Orators," *ibid.,* CXXII (April 1867), 557; "Reform Essays," *ibid.,* CXXIII (July 1867), 264.

its "leap in the dark." It is no wonder that Matthew Arnold, ten years after Tocqueville's death, viewed him as probably the most typically English French liberal.[6]

In the peaceful aftermath of the stormy debates of 1866–67, the prospect of triumphant democracy ceased to arouse either fervor or terror. Franchise and ballot reforms and the mass-party caucus were instituted without disaster to the constitution or society. The Frenchman who had amazed his English contemporaries by the lofty seriousness with which he analyzed the turbulent American democracy seemed almost too solemn to an audience which forgot or smiled at the fears of their fathers. Democracy did not seem as potent a moral and political force as Tocqueville had made it out to be. In many ways the masses seemed less massive, and social and economic equality less imminent in the 1880's than they had appeared in the 1830's. James Bryce typified the mood of English liberalism toward the end of the century when he wrote in his *American Commonwealth,* that Tocqueville, so long singled out for his calm appraisal of the merits and deficiencies of the democratic age, had in fact been too emotional about its potentialities. His works had come to be regarded largely as two extremely quotable but outdated analyses of America and France.[7] Tocqueville's influence also seemed to wane in proportion to the adjustment made by liberalism to the idea of the welfare state and the necessity of centralization to implement it. The Webbs were impressed by his vision of the inevitability of equality, but they had no qualms about inferring their own collectivist economic and social consequences from it. A revival of interest in Tocqueville's political philosophy came only with the crisis of parliamentary democracy following World War I, and by Harold Laski and J.-P. Mayer his name was coupled with Marx as one of

[6] "Sainte-Beuve," in *Essays, Letters, and Reviews by Matthew Arnold,* ed. Fraser Neiman (Cambridge, Mass., 1960), 166–167.

[7] See Bryce, *The American Commonwealth* (London, 1888), I, 5, and compare Basil Hall, "Tocqueville on the State of America," *Quarterly Review,* LVII (September 1836), 132–162, with "Characteristics of Democracy," *ibid.,* CLXII (April 1886), 518–543, or with the explicit juxtaposition of Bryce and Tocqueville in *Macmillan's Magazine,* February 1889, or the *Edinburgh Review,* April 1889.

the profoundest social thinkers of the nineteenth century. Many of the assumptions inherited from the nineteenth century concerning European social evolution once more became problematical and divergent definitions of democracy and liberty acquired intense political significance. With the reinvestigation of the liberal point of departure Tocqueville's writings increased steadily in stature and popularity.

Tocqueville's conclusions were readily incorporated into the political and intellectual life of nineteenth century England because he had assimilated many of its values into his own outlook. The British Isles were the source of some of his greatest insights, especially into the historical connection between the rise of democracy and the extension of bureaucratic centralization. They furnished him with two examples from which he eventually drew a theory of the evolution of aristocracies. They gave him a comparative basis for a theory of the relation of ideas to social change, of the causes of and antidotes for revolutions. His ideas on institutional and economic reform, on colonization, and on the ingredients of a great foreign policy bore the English trademark. If at times he inveighed against a lifeless imitation of an insolent rival, more often than not what the rival was doing became the basis for his own solutions to French problems.

England, because of the peculiar nature of her constitutional development, could not provide Tocqueville with a clear and logical framework on which to model political institutions in a democratic age. But there were facets of the English political situation which were vital to his arguments and which America could not duplicate. England clearly presented a case in which the disintegration of medieval society had not led to the permanent alienation of its constituent classes, and it still afforded viable political machinery for the transfer of political power by peaceful means. England, more than America, proved that a nation could successfully combine national cohesion with a maximum of local self-government and could remain free while sustaining the tremendous economic transformation that placed her at the forefront of the industrial revolution. England enabled Tocqueville to turn with relief from the incipient class conflicts that smoldered on the Continent, but its prosperous and proprietary society probably kept him from grappling more profoundly with the affront to human liberty known as the "social problem," and from seriously inquiring into the real political and libertarian potentialities of increasingly collectivist societies.

As long as he thought that its principles could affect the development of the Continent, Tocqueville was not politically divorced from his own age. He found there the opportunity to continue to influence the course of events, however diminished his range. It is not unlikely that in a nation which was still congenial to aristocratic leadership, and where almost every political figure was still a gentleman, Tocqueville would have fulfilled the ambitions which turned to ashes for him in France. To the end, he maintained that political action carried with it a sense of freedom and power in choosing one's future which could never be forgotten once it was experienced. Although its intrinsic worth was ultimately a matter of experience, uncommunicable by description alone, Tocqueville insisted on directing attention to societies where it existed, and to the conditions in which it would flourish or perish.

Finally, England provided Tocqueville with a refuge from the intellectual and moral isolation of his last years. To fully comprehend what England meant to him in this respect, one must recall how deeply and completely an *homme politique* he was, how he reacted to political developments as another might only to the most personal situations. One must recognize how profoundly, in the last years of his life, Tocqueville felt himself a foreigner, or rather a shadow from the past among his own countrymen. He clung to that remnant of interaction which had always been his link with reality. "I imagine," he confided to a friend,

that the spiritual predicament in which men like us find ourselves must be rather like that of the Jews in the Middle Ages, when they felt themselves strangers everywhere, no matter where they went, obstinate sectarians of a religion which was no longer believed in, and still hoping for a Messiah whom no one around them expected. If we resemble them in this way we must resemble them in another; their isolation on the earth rendered them dearer to each other; they sought one another out from one end of the world to the other, and made for themselves a kind of *patrie mobile,* which they brought with them to any place at which they met.[8]

If the consensus of his friends assured him that his words and thoughts were responded to, England assured him that they were significant. For one so careful to avoid the charge of utopianism and so convinced of the necessity of connecting thought and action, it was manifest proof that his liberalism was not everywhere the creed of an embattled remnant. He was grateful for "the impulse given to the human spirit in England by political life," and as grateful for the impulse which it gave to his own. The man, as he wrote in another context, was as involved as the writer. At the end of his life England was morally and politically, as well as intellectually, his second homeland.

[8] Fragment of an unpublished letter quoted by Albert Gigot, "M. de Tocqueville," *Le Correspondant,* LI (December 1860), 715–716.

Appendix
Abbreviations
Bibliography
Index

Appendix

PARALLELS IN THE WRITINGS AND CAREERS OF
TOCQUEVILLE AND BEAUMONT

Alexis Charles Henri Clerel de
Tocqueville
(1805–1859)

Gustave Auguste de la Bonninière
de Beaumont
(1802–1865)

Magistrates under Charles X.

Joint studies of English history,
economics (1828–1830).

Journey to America (May 1831–
February 1832).

Joint authorship, *Du système pénitentiaire aux Etats-Unis* (1833).

Plans for a joint work on *Institutions
et moeurs américains*. Abandoned for
individual works:

De la démocratie en Amérique
(1835, 1840) (Prix Montyon).

Marie, ou l'esclavage aux Etats-Unis
(1835).

Journey to England and Ireland (1835)

"Mémoire sur l'influence du point
de départ sur l'avenir de la société
des Etats-Unis" (1837).

"Mémoire sur la condition sociale
et politique des nègres esclaves et des
gens de couleur aux Etats-Unis"
(1837).

"Political and Social Condition of
France" (1836).

*L'Irlande sociale, politique et reli-
gieuse* (1839) (Prix Montyon).

Members of the Académie des sciences morales et politiques.

Elected to Chamber of Deputies: Tocqueville for Valognes (1839); Beaumont for Mamers (1840).

Journey to Algeria as members of a special parliamentary subcommittee (1841).
Parallel speeches on foreign and domestic policy (1840–1848).

Members of the National Assembly: Tocqueville for la Manche; Beaumont for Sarthe (1848–1851).

Members of the Constitutional Commission (1848).

Tocqueville	Beaumont
Chosen representative to the projected conference at Brussels for Austro-Italian affairs (never held) (1848).	Special ambassador to London (1848).
	Simultaneous resignation of diplomatic appointments on the election of Louis Napoleon as president (December 1848).
Foreign minister (June–October 1849).	Ambassador to Vienna (September–November 1849).
Both arrested in the *coup d'état* of December 2, 1851, and retirement from politics.	
L'Ancien Régime et la Révolution (1856).	"La Russie et les Etats-Unis" (1854). "Notice sur l'état présent de l'Irlande" (1863).
	Oeuvres Complètes d'Alexis de Tocqueville, ed. Gustave de Beaumont (1861–1866).

Abbreviations

The following Tocqueville and Beaumont papers are cited in abbreviated form:

Yale Mss — The Tocqueville and Beaumont Collection, at Yale University Library. The abbreviation Yale Mss is followed by (T) for Tocqueville's papers or (B) for Beaumont's, plus the catalogue number.

Oeuvres (B) — *Oeuvres complètes d'Alexis de Tocqueville,* ed. Gustave de Beaumont, 9 vols. (Paris: Michel Lévy, 1860–1866). The following volumes are cited in the notes. In each case the abbreviation *Oeuvres* (B) is followed by the volume number only.

     V. *Correspondance et oeuvres posthumes de* [sic] *Alexis de Tocqueville,* 2nd ed. (1866).

    VI. *Correspondance d'Alexis de Tocqueville,* 2nd ed. (1867).

   VII. *Nouvelle correspondance entièrement inédite d'Alexis de Tocqueville* (1866).

  VIII. *Mélanges, fragments historiques et notes sur l'Ancien Régime, la Révolution et l'Empire, voyages, pensées entièrement inédits* (1865).

    IX. *Etudes économiques politiques et littéraires* (1866).

Oeuvres (M) — *Alexis de Tocqueville: Oeuvres complètes.* Edition définitive publiée sous la direction de J.-P. Mayer, sous le patronage de la Commission Nationale pour l'édition des ouevres de Tocqueville (Paris: Gallimard, 1951—). This definitive edition, now in process of publication, has been published so far in the following tomes and volumes, which are cited in the notes as *Oeuvres* (M) followed by a distinguishing part of the title.

Tome   I. *De la démocratie en Amérique,* 2 vols. (1951). Introduction par Harold J. Laski.

Tome II. *L'Ancien Régime et la Révolution,* 2 vols. (1953). Introduction par Georges Lefebvre. Volume II is subtitled *Fragments et notes inédites sur la Révolution.* Texte établi et annoté par André Jardin.

Tome III. Vol. I. *Ecrits et discours politiques* (1962). Texte établi et annoté par André Jardin. In troduction par J.-J. Chevallier et André Jardin.

Tome V. Vol. I. *Voyages en Sicile et aux Etats-Unis* (1957). Texte établi, annoté et préfacé par J.-P. Mayer.

Vol. II. *Voyages en Angleterre, Irlande, Suisse et Algérie* (1958). Texte établi et annoté par J.-P. Mayer et André Jardin.

Tome VI. Vol. I. *Correspondance anglaise: Correspondance d'Alexis de Tocqueville avec Henry Reeve et John Stuart Mill* (1954). Texte établi et annoté par. J.-P. Mayer et Gustave Rudler. Introduction par J.-P. Mayer.

Tome IX. *Correspondance d'Alexis de Tocqueville et d'Arthur de Gobineau* (1959). Texte établi et annoté par M. Degros. Introduction par J.-J. Chevallier.

Translations from the French are the author's unless otherwise indicated.

Bibliography

A WORD must be said about the two editions of Tocqueville's works used in this study. Gustave de Beaumont edited the Tocqueville papers after his death, and nine volumes were published between 1861 and 1866 as a final tribute by Beaumont to his lifelong friend. Unfortunately he saw fit to delete whatever might not enhance Tocqueville's reputation as a stylist or might too closely touch living contemporaries. He went so far as to efface or change phrases and made numerous errors of dating. Beaumont's edition has, therefore, been employed only where the new edition has not yet superseded it.

A new and extended edition of Tocqueville's work is now in progress under the direction of J.-P. Mayer. With the exception of a few errors and omissions it may be considered to be definitive. For a description of the volumes of the *Oeuvres* yet to be published, consult Charles Pouthas, "Plan et programme des *Oeuvres, papiers et correspondances d'Alexis de Tocqueville*," in *Alexis de Tocqueville: Livre du centenaire, 1859–1959*, 35–43.

At present the main body of Tocqueville's manuscripts is in the control of the Tocqueville Commission and is ordinarily unavailable for purposes of research. By far the most important group of manuscripts outside those of the Tocqueville Commission's collection is the Tocqueville and Beaumont Collection in the Yale University Library. This collection is primarily due to the efforts of G. W. Pierson. It includes copies and originals of Tocqueville's correspondence, along with diaries, essays, and notes. It also contains the notes and drafts related to the composition of Beaumont's *L'Irlande,* together with a substantial portion of the Tocqueville–Beaumont correspondence. The catalogue of the collection at Yale, recently revised and extended by Pierson, contains a detailed inventory of the manuscripts.

Apart from the works of Tocqueville and Beaumont, which are listed separately, all entries in the bibliography follow in alphabetical sequence.

I. Manuscripts

Archives nationales, C 918. Procès-verbaux du Comité de Constitution de 1848, registres I, II: "Délibérations du Comité de Constitution à l'Assemblée nationale, 19 mai–17 juin 1848."

Yale University Library. Tocqueville and Beaumont Collection.

Harvard University, Houghton Library. Charles Sumner and Jared Sparks collections.

II. The Works of Alexis de Tocqueville

"A MM. les électeurs de l'arrondissement de Valognes," 24 juin 1842, in *Chambre des députés. Elections 1840–1842,* I. Bibliothèque nationale, cat. no. Le^{54} 1527.

"Adresse aux citoyens de Valognes," March 19, 1848, in *Assemblée constituante, élections, la Manche,* 1848.

Correspondence and Conversations of Alexis de Tocqueville with Nassau William Senior from 1834 to 1859, ed. M. C. M. Simpson, 2nd ed., 2 vols. London: Henry S. King, 1872.

De la démocratie en Amérique, 4 vols. Paris: Charles Gosselin, 1835–1840.

"De l'influence des chemins de fer sur l'agriculture," *Journal d'agriculture pratique,* VIII (February 1845), 378–382.

Democracy in America, ed. Phillips Bradley, transl. Henry Reeve, 2 vols. New York: Alfred A. Knopf, 1945.

"Des révolutions dans les sociétés nouvelles," *Revue des deux mondes,* ser. 4, vol. XXII (April 1840), 322–334.

Journey to America, ed. J.-P. Mayer, transl. George Lawrence. New Haven: Yale University Press, 1960.

Journeys to England and Ireland, ed. J.-P. Mayer, transl. George Lawrence and K. P. Mayer. London: Faber and Faber, 1958; New Haven: Yale University Press, 1958.

Lanzac de Laborie, Léon d'Estresse de, "L'Amitié de Tocqueville et de Royer-Collard," *Revue des deux mondes,* 7th per., vol. LVIII (1930), 876–911.

Mayer, Jacob-Peter, ed., "Alexis de Tocqueville: Sur la démocratie en

Amérique. Fragments inédites," *Nouvelle Revue française,* no. 76 (April 1959), 761–768.

―――― "De Tocqueville: Unpublished Fragments," *Encounter,* XII (April 1959), 17–22.

―――― "Sur la démocratie en Amérique," *Revue internationale de philosophie,* XIII (1959), 300–312.

Memoir, Letters, and Remains of Alexis de Tocqueville, 2 vols. Boston: Ticknor and Fields, 1862.

"Mémoire sur l'influence du point de départ sur l'avenir de la société des Etats-Unis," *Mémoires de l'Académie royale des sciences morales et politiques de l'Institut de France,* ser. 2, vol. I. Paris: Firmin Didot, 1837.

"Mémoire sur le paupérisme," *Mémoires de la Société académique de Cherbourg,* 293–344. Cherbourg: Boulanger, Beaufort, 1835.

Oeuvres complètes, ed. Gustave de Beaumont, 9 vols. Paris: Michel Lévy, 1861–1866. Individual volumes are listed in the Abbreviations.

Oeuvres complètes, ed. J.-P. Mayer. Paris: Gallimard, 1951―. Individual tomes and volumes are listed in the Abbreviations.

"Political and Social Condition of France, First Article," *London and Westminster Review,* III and XXV (April 1836), 137–169.

The Recollections of Alexis de Tocqueville, ed. J.-P. Mayer, transl. Alexander Teixeira de Mattos. London: Harvill Press, 1948.

Souvenirs d'Alexis de Tocqueville, ed. Luc Monnier. Paris: Gallimard, 1942.

The State of Society in France before the Revolution of 1789, and the Causes Which Led to That Event, transl. Henry Reeve, 3rd ed. London: John Murray, 1888.

III. The Works of Gustave de Beaumont

Commission de colonisation de l'Algérie, *Rapport fait au nom de la seconde sous-commission . . . le 20 juin 1842. Organisation civile, administrative, municipale, et judiciaire.* Paris: Imprimerie royale, 1843.

De l'intervention du pouvoir dans les élections. Paris: Paulin, 1843.

De la politique extérieure de la France au 29 octobre 1840. Paris: Charles Gosselin, 1840.

"Discussion . . . sur l'organisation du travail," *Séances et travaux de l'Académie des sciences morales et politiques: Compte rendu,* VIII (1845), 189–202.

Du système pénitentiaire aux Etats-Unis et de son application en France, suivi d'un appendice sur les colonies pénales et notes statistiques par MM. Gustave de Beaumont et Alexis de Tocqueville, avocats à la cour royale de Paris, membres de la société historique de Pennsylvanie. Paris: H. Fournier Jeune, 1833.

Du système pénitentiaire aux Etats-Unis et de son application en France suivi d'un appendice sur les colonies pénales et de notes statistiques, 3rd ed. Augmentée du rapport de M. de Tocqueville sur le projet de réforme des prisons et du texte adoptée par la Chambre des députés. Paris: Charles Gosselin, 1845.

L'Irlande sociale, politique et religieuse. 3rd ed., 2 vols. Paris: Charles Gosselin, 1839.

Ireland: Social, Political, and Religious, ed. W. C. Taylor, 2 vols. London: Richard Bentley, 1839.

Marie, ou l'esclavage aux Etats-Unis: Tableau des moeurs américaines, 2 vols. in one. Paris: Charles Gosselin, 1835; 3rd ed., 1839; 4th ed., 1840.

Marie, or Slavery in the United States, transl. Barbara Chapman. Stanford: Stanford University Press, 1958.

"Mémoire sur la condition sociale et politique des nègres esclaves et des gens de couleur aux Etats-Unis," *Mémoires de l'Académie royale des sciences morales et politiques de l'Institut de France,* ser. 2, vol. I. Paris: Firmin Didot, 1837.

"Notice sur l'état présent de l'Irlande, 1862–1863," *Séances et travaux de l'Académie des sciences morales et politiques: Compte rendu,* LXIV (1863), 237–280; LXV (1863), 377–392.

"Rapport sur l'ouvrage de M. G. Cornewall Lewis . . . *Essays on the Influence of Authority in Matters of Opinion,*" *Séances et travaux de l'Académie des sciences morales et politiques: Compte rendu,* XXIII (1853), 201–220.

"La Russie et les Etats-Unis sous le rapport économique," *Revue des deux mondes,* ser. 2, vol. V (1854), 1163–83.

IV. OTHER WORKS

Adams, Herbert B., *Jared Sparks and Alexis de Tocqueville,* Johns

Hopkins University Studies in Historical and Political Science, ser. 16, no. 12, Baltimore: The Johns Hopkins Press, 1898.

Aiken, P. F., *A Comparative View of the Constitutions of Great Britain and the United States of America in Six Lectures.* London: Longman, 1842.

Alexis de Tocqueville: Livre du centenaire, 1859–1959. Paris: Editions du Centre national de la recherche scientifique, 1960.

Alhoy, M., and others, *Biographie parlementaire des représentants du peuple à l'Assemblée nationale constituante.* Paris: Mme. Vᵉ Louis Janet, n.d.

Amann, Peter, "Taine, Tocqueville, and the Paradox of the Ancien Régime," *Romanic Review,* LII (October 1961), 183–195.

"The American Constitution at the Present Crisis," *National Review,* XIII (October 1861), 465–493.

"American Orators and Statesmen," *Quarterly Review,* LXVII (December 1840), 1–53.

"The American Revolution," *Edinburgh Review,* CXVI (October 1862), 549–594.

"The American War," *National Review,* XIV (April 1862), 492–507.

Amos, Sheldon, "Democracy in England," *Fortnightly Review,* I (June 1, 1865), 228–238.

Ampère, J. J., "Alexis de Tocqueville," in *Mélanges d'histoire littéraire,* 2 vols. Paris: Michel Lévy, 1867.

—— and A. M. Ampère, *Correspondance et souvenirs,* 5 vols. Paris: J. Hetzel, 1875.

Annales de la charité, 1845–1855.

Annuaire des cinq départements de la Normandie, 1835–1860.

Annuaire du département de la Manche, 1842–1852. St. Lô: Elie.

The Aristocracy of Britain and the Laws of Entail and Primogeniture Judged by Recent French Writers. London: Dyer, 1844.

Arnold, Matthew, *Mixed Essays, Irish Essays and Others.* New York: Macmillan, 1883.

Aron, Raymond, "Idées politiques et vision historique de Tocqueville," *Revue française de science politique,* X (September 1960), 509–526.

Bagehot, Walter, *The English Constitution.* London: Chapman and Hall, 1867.

Bain, Alexander, *An Autobiography.* London: Longmans, Green, 1904.

Barrington, Russell (Mrs.), *The Works and Life of Walter Bagehot*, 10 vols. London: Longmans, Green, 1915.

Barrot, Odilon, *Mémoires posthumes*, 4 vols. Paris: Charpentier, 1874–1876.   ,

Barth, Niklas Peter, *Die Idee der Freiheit und der Demokratie bei Alexis de Tocqueville*. Arau: Eugen Keller, 1954.

Bastid, Paul, *Doctrines et institutions politiques de la Seconde République*, 2 vols. Paris: Hachette, 1945.

—— *Les Institutions politiques de la monarchie parlementaire française, 1814–1848*. Paris: Sirey, 1954.

Beloff, Max, "Can England Avoid Revolution?" *The Listener*, LIX (May 29, 1958), 891–892.

Biographie des deputés précédée d'une histoire de la législature de 1842 à 1846 par deux journalistes. Paris: Pagnerre, 1846.

Biographie des 900 représentants à la constituante et des 750 représentants à la législative: session de 1849. Paris: Victor Lecou, n.d.

Blackie, J. S., *On Democracy*. Edinburgh: Edmonston and Douglas, 1867.

Bloch, Marc, *La Société féodale: Les Classes et le gouvernement des hommes*. L'Evolution de l'humanité: Synthèse collective, 34 *bis*. Paris: Albin Michel, 1940.

Bourgeois, Emile, *History of Modern France, 1815–1913*, 2 vols. Cambridge, Eng.: Cambridge University Press, 1919.

Bowle, John, *Politics and Opinion in the Nineteenth Century*. London: Jonathan Cape, 1954.

Bowley, Marian, *Nassau Senior and Classical Economics*. London: Allen and Unwin, 1937.

Briggs, Asa, *The Age of Improvement*. London: Longmans, Green, 1959.

—— *Victorian People: A Reassessment of Persons and Themes, 1851–67*. Chicago: University of Chicago Press, 1954.

British Museum Catalogue of Additions to the Manuscripts. The Gladstone Papers. London: Trustees of the British Museum, 1953.

Brose, Olive J., *Church and Parliament: The Reshaping of the Church of England, 1828–1860*. Stanford: Stanford University Press, 1959.

Brougham, (Lord) Henry, *Discours sur le droit de visite*, transl. A. Claudet. Paris, 1843.

—— (Isaac Tomkins, pseud.) *Thoughts upon the Aristocracy of England*. London, 1835.

Brunius, Teddy, *Alexis de Tocqueville, the Sociological Aesthetician*, Swedish Studies in Aesthetics, 1. Uppsala: Almqvist and Wicksell, 1960.

Bryce, James, *The American Commonwealth*, 3 vols. London: Macmillan, 1888.

—— *Modern Democracies*, 2 vols. New York: Macmillan, 1921.

—— *The Predictions of Hamilton and de Tocqueville*, Johns Hopkins University Studies in Historical and Political Science, ser. 5, no. 9. Baltimore: Johns Hopkins University, 1887.

"Bryce's American Commonwealth," *Edinburgh Review*, CLXIX (April 1889), 481–518.

Bulwer-Lytton, Edward, *England and the English*, 2 vols. New York: J. and J. Harper, 1833.

Butterfield, Herbert, *George III and the Historians*, rev. ed. New York: Macmillan, 1959.

Cavour, Camillo Benso, *Dario inedito con note autobiografiche del conte di Cavour*. Rome: Voghere Carlo, 1888.

—— *Scritti di economia*. Milan: Feltrinelli, 1962.

"Characteristics of Democracy," *Quarterly Review*, CLXII (April 1886), 518–543.

Charléty, S. C. G., *La Monarchie de juillet, 1830–1848*, Histoire de France contemporaine. Paris: Hachette, 1921.

Chevallier, Jean-Jacques, *Les grandes oeuvres politiques de Machiavel à nos jours*. Paris: Armand Colin, 1949.

Chinard, Gilbert, *Alexis de Tocqueville et le Capitaine Basil Hall*, Bulletin de l'institut français de Washington, 15 (December 1942).

"The Close of the American War," *Quarterly Review*, CXVIII (July 1865), 106–136.

Cobden, Richard, *Speeches on Questions of Public Policy, by Richard Cobden, M.P.*, ed. John Bright and J. E. T. Rogers, 2 vols. London: Macmillan, 1870.

Codman, John, *A Narrative of a Visit to England*. Boston: Perkins and Marvin, 1836.

Cole, Margaret, *The Story of Fabian Socialism*. Stanford: Stanford University Press, 1961.

"Contemporary Literature," *Westminster Review*, CXXVIII (November 1887), 1040–41.

Copans, S. J., "Tocqueville's Later Years," *Romanic Review*, XXXVI (April 1945), 113–121.

Cottu, Charles, *De l'administration de la justice criminelle en Angleterre et de l'esprit du gouvernement anglais*. Paris: H. Nicolle, 1820.

Cuvillier, Armand, *Hommes et idéologies de 1840*. Paris: Marcel Rivière, 1956.

Dawson, William Harbutt, *Richard Cobden and Foreign Policy*. London: George Allen and Unwin, 1926.

"Democracy," *Westminster Review*, LXXXVIII (October 1867), 479–505.

"Democracy on Its Trial," *The Quarterly Review*, CX (July 1861), 247–288.

"Democratic Government in Victoria," *Westminster Review*, LXXXIX (April 1868), 480–523.

Deries, Madeleine, "Un Toast de Tocqueville," *La Révolution de 1848*, XVI (1920), 52–53.

"De Tocqueville's Society in France before the Revolution." *Spectator Supplement*, August 2, 1856, 829–831.

Dicey, A. V., "Alexis de Tocqueville," *National Review*, XXI (August 1893), 771–784.

———— *Introduction to the Study of the Law of the Constitution*, 5th ed. London: Macmillan, 1897; 6th ed., 1902; 10th ed., 1959.

———— *Lectures on the Relation between Law and Public Opinion in England during the Nineteenth Century*. London: Macmillan, 1914.

Dictionnaire de parlementaires français, 5 vols. Paris: Bourloton, 1891.

Dilke, Sir Charles Wentworth, *Problems of Greater Britain*. London: Macmillan, 1890.

Dollot, René, "Gobineau, Tocqueville et la rivalité anglo-russe en Asie centrale," *Revue d'histoire diplomatique*, LXXV (January–March 1961), 73–79.

Duff, Sir M. E. G., *Sir Henry Maine: A Brief Memoir of His Life*. London: John Murray, 1892.

Dunoyer, Charles, "Du système de la centralisation, de sa nature, de son influence, de ses limites et des réductions utiles qu'il est destiné à subir," *Journal des économistes*, I (1842), 353–389.

Dupuynode, Gustave, "De la centralisation," *Journal des économistes,* XX (April–July 1848), 409–418; XXI (August–November 1848), 16–24.

Duroselle, J.-B., *Les Débuts du catholicisme sociale en France (1822–1870).* Paris: Presses universitaires de France, 1951.

Duvergier de Hauranne, P., "L'Irlande sociale, politique et religieuse, par M. Gustave de Beaumont," *Revue des deux mondes,* ser. 4, vol. XXII (April 1840), 5–38.

"Earl Grey on Reform," *National Review,* VI (April 1858), 424–443.

Eastlake, Lady Elizabeth, *Mrs. Grote: A Sketch,* 2nd ed. London: John Murray, 1880.

The Economist: Or the Political, Commercial, Agricultural, and Free-Trade Journal, 1843–44, 1856. London.

Elkington, Margery E., *Les Relations de société entre l'Angleterre et la France sous la Restauration (1814–1830),* Bibliothèque de la Revue de littérature comparée, 56. Paris: Champion, 1929.

Engel-Jánosi, Friedrich, *Four Studies in French Romantic Historical Writings,* The Johns Hopkins University Studies in Historical and Political Science, ser. 71, no. 2. Baltimore: The Johns Hopkins Press, 1955.

Engels, Friedrich, "The Condition of the Working Class in England in 1844," in *Karl Marx and Friedrich Engels on Britain,* 1–336. Moscow: Foreign Languages Publishing House, 1953.

"English Charity," *Quarterly Review,* CVI (April 1835), 473–539.

Essays on Reform. London: Macmillan, 1867.

Extracts from the Information Received by His Majesty's Commissioners as to the Administration and Operation of the Poor Laws. London: B. Fellowes, 1833.

Fabian, Bernhard, *Alexis de Tocquevilles Amerikabild: Genetische Untersuchungen über Zusammenhange mit der zeitgenossischen insbesondere der englischen Amerika-Interpretation.* Heidelberg: Carl Winter, 1957.

Faguet, Emile, *Politiques et moralistes du XIX siècle,* 3 vols. Paris: Lecene et Oudin, 1900.

Finer, S. E., *The Life and Times of Sir Edwin Chadwick.* London: Methuen, 1952.

Fisher, H. A. L., ed., *The Collected Papers of Frederic William Maitland,* 3 vols. Cambridge, Eng.: Cambridge University Press, 1911.

"The Four Reform Orators," *Quarterly Review*, CXXII (April 1867), 541–573.

"France before and since the Revolution of 1789," *Fraser's Magazine for Town and Country*, LIV (September 1856), 363–374.

"France before the Revolution of '89," *Westminster Review*, LXVI (October 1856), 462–494.

"The French Constitutionalists," *Quarterly Review*, CII (July 1857), 6–31.

Galbraith, John S., "Myths of the 'Little England' Era," *American Historical Review*, LXVII (October 1961), 34–48.

Gargan, Edward T., *Alexis de Tocqueville: The Critical Years, 1848–1851*. Washington, D.C.: Catholic University of America Press, 1955.

―――― "The Formation of Tocqueville's Historical Thought," *Review of Politics*, XXIV (January 1962), 48–61.

―――― "Some Problems in Tocqueville Scholarship," *Mid-America*, XLI (January 1959), 3–26.

―――― "Tocqueville and the Problem of Historical Prognosis," *The American Historical Review*, LXVIII (January 1963), 332–345.

Garnier-Pagès, L. A., *Histoire de la Révolution de 1848*, 8 vols. Paris: Pagnerre, 1861.

Gash, Norman, "English Reform and French Revolution in the Election of 1830," in *Essays Presented to Sir Lewis Namier*, ed. Richard Pares and A. J. P. Taylor. London: Macmillan, 1956.

―――― *Politics in the Age of Peel: A Study in the New Technique of Parliamentary Representation, 1830–1850*. London: Longmans, Green, 1953.

Gigot, Albert, "M. de Tocqueville," *Le Correspondant*, LI (December 1860), 690–726.

Giraudeau, Louis, and others, *Biographie des représentants du peuple à l'assemblée nationale constituante*. Paris: Au Bureau de notre histoire, 1848.

Gojat, Georges, "Les Corps intermédiaires et la décentralisation dans l'oeuvre de Tocqueville," in *Libéralisme, traditionalisme, décentralisation*, ed. R. Pelloux, Cahiers de la Fondation nationale des sciences politiques, 31. Paris: Armand Colin, 1952.

Goldstein, Doris S., "Church and Society: A Study of the Religious Outlook of Alexis de Tocqueville." Unpub. diss., Bryn Mawr College, 1955.

——— "The Religious Beliefs of Alexis de Tocqueville," *French Historical Studies*, I (December 1960), 379–393.

Gorla, Gino, *Commento a Tocqueville. L'idèa dei diritti.* Milan: A. Guiffre, 1948.

Greg, W. R., "De Tocqueville's France before the Revolution of 1789," *The Times* (London), September 3 and 10, 1856.

——— "M. de Tocqueville," in *Literary and Social Judgments*, 4th ed., 2 vols. London: Trubner, 1877.

Greville, Charles C. F., *The Greville Memoirs, 1814–1860*, Strachey and Fulford edition, 8 vols. London: Macmillan, 1938.

——— and Henry Reeve, *The Letters of Charles Greville and Henry Reeve, 1836–1865*, ed. Rev. A. H. Johnson. London: T. F. Unwin, 1924.

Grey, Henry George (Earl), *Parliamentary Government Considered with Reference to Reform.* London: John Murray, 1864.

Grote, George, *Seven Letters concerning the Politics of Switzerland pending the Outbreak of the Civil War in 1847*, ed. H. G. [Harriet Grote]. London: John Murray, 1876.

Grote, Harriet, *The Case of the Poor against the Rich, Fairly Considered by a Mutual Friend.* London: 1850.

——— *The Personal Life of George Grote*, 2nd ed. London: John Murray, 1873.

Guizot, François P. G., *Cours d'histoire moderne: Histoire de la civilisation en France depuis la chute de l'empire romain jusqu'en 1789.* 5 vols. Paris: Pichon et Didier, 1829–1832.

——— *Mémoires pour servir à l'histoire de mon temps*, 8 vols. Paris: Michel Lévy, 1867.

Gunnell, Doris, *Sutton Sharpe et ses amis français, avec des lettres inédites*, Bibliothèque de la Revue de littérature comparée, 26. Paris: Honoré Champion, 1925.

Hainds, J. R., "John Stuart Mill and the Saint Simonians," *Journal of the History of Ideas*, VII (January–October 1946), 103–112.

Halévy, Elie, *A History of the English People in the Nineteenth Century*, 6 vols. London: E. Benn, 1950. See especially vol. III, *The Triumph of Reform, 1830–1841*, and vol. IV, *The Victorian Years, 1841–1895*.

———— "Before 1835," in *A Century of Municipal Progress,* ed. Harold J. Laski, Ivor Jennings, and W. A. Robson. London: Allen and Unwin, 1935.

———— *The Growth of Philosophic Radicalism,* transl. Mary Morris. New York: Macmillan, 1928.

[Hall, Basil], "Tocqueville on the State of America," *Quarterly Review,* LVII (September 1836), 132–162.

Hammond, John L., *Gladstone and the Irish Nation.* London: Longmans, Green, 1938.

———— "The Social Background: 1835–1935," in *A Century of Municipal Progress,* ed. Harold J. Laski, Ivor Jennings, and W. A. Robson. London: Allen and Unwin, 1935.

———— and M. R. D. Foot, *Gladstone and Liberalism.* London: English University Press, 1952.

———— and Barbara Hammond, *The Age of the Chartists, 1832–1854: A Study of Discontent.* London: Longmans, Green, 1930.

Hansard's Parliamentary Debates. Third series, volumes for 1841–1893.

Hauser, Henri, and others, *Du libéralisme à l'impérialisme (1860–1878),* Peuples et civilisations, 17. Paris: Félix Alcan, 1939.

Hawkins, R. L., "Unpublished Letters of Alexis de Tocqueville," *Romanic Review,* XIX (July–September 1928), 195–217; XX (October–December 1929), 351–356.

Herr, Richard, *Tocqueville and the Old Regime.* Princeton: Princeton University Press, 1962.

Holdsworth, W. S., *A History of English Law,* ed. A. L. Goodheart and H. G. Hanbury, vol. XIII. London: Methuen, 1932.

———— *Some Makers of English Law.* Cambridge, Eng.: Cambridge University Press, 1938.

Holland, Frederic May, *Liberty in the Nineteenth Century.* New York and London: G. P. Putnam, 1899.

Hughes, H. Stuart, *Consciousness and Society: The Reorientation of European Social Thought, 1890–1930.* New York: Alfred A. Knopf, 1958.

Ideas and Beliefs of the Victorians: An Historic Revaluation of the Victorian Age. [London]: Sylvan Press [1949].

"Ireland," *Edinburgh Review,* CXIX (January 1864), 279–304.

"Ireland, social, political and religious," *Dublin University Magazine* LXXIX (July 1839), 107–120; LXXX (August 1839), 210–227.

Jenks, Edward, *A Short History of Common Law*. Boston: Little, Brown, 1913.

Jennings, Sir W. Ivor, *The Law and the Constitution*. London: University of London Press, 1943.

——— *Principles of Local Government Law*, 4th ed. London: University of London Press, 1960.

Jones, Ernest, *Democracy Vindicated*. Manchester, Eng.: John Heywood, 1867.

Jones, Ethel, *Les Voyageurs français en Angleterre de 1815 à 1830*. Paris: E. de Boccard, 1930.

Journal de Cherbourg: Organe des veux et des intérêts du peuple. Cherbourg, 1848.

Journal des débats politiques et littéraires. Paris, 1849.

Kay-Shuttleworth, James, *Thoughts and Suggestions on Certain Social Problems*. London: Longmans, Green, 1873.

Kent, Sherman, *Electoral Procedure under Louis Philippe*. Yale Historical Studies, 10. New Haven: Yale University Press, 1937.

Kingsley, Charles, *Three Lectures Delivered at the Royal Institution on the Ancien Régime as It Existed on the Continent before the French Revolution*. London: Macmillan, 1867.

Laski, Harold J., "Alexis de Tocqueville and Democracy," in *The Social and Political Ideas of Some Representative Thinkers of the Victorian Age,* ed. F. J. C. Hearnshaw. London: George C. Harrap, 1933.

——— *The Rise of European Liberalism: An Essay in Interpretation*. London: Allen and Unwin, 1936.

Lavergne, Léonce de, *Essai sur l'économie rurale de l'Angleterre, de l'Ecosse et de l'Irlande*. Paris: Guillaumin, 1854.

Lawlor, Sister Mary, "Alexis de Tocqueville's 'Etat social et politique de la France.'" Unpub. diss., Catholic University of America, 1953.

——— *Alexis de Tocqueville in the Chamber of Deputies: His Views on Foreign and Colonial Policy*. Washington, D.C.: Catholic University of America Press, 1959.

Lawson, F. H., "Dicey Revisited," *Political Studies,* VII (1959), 109–126, 207–221.

Lecky, William E. H., *Democracy and Liberty,* 2 vols. New York: Longmans, Green, 1899.

———— *A History of England in the Eighteenth Century,* 8 vols. New York: Appleton, 1890.

Leroy, Maxime, "Alexis de Tocqueville," *Politica,* I (August 1935), 393–424.

Levy, S. Leon, *Nassau Senior, the Prophet of Modern Capitalism.* Boston: Bruce Humphries, 1943.

Lewis, Sir George Cornewall, "Earl Gray on Parliamentary Government," *Edinburgh Review,* CVIII (July 1858), 271–297.

———— "The Election of President Lincoln and Its Consequences," *Edinburgh Review,* CXIII (April 1861), 555–587.

———— *An Essay on the Influence of Authority in Matters of Opinion.* London: J. W. Parker, 1849.

———— *Letters of the Right Honorable Sir George Cornewall Lewis, Bart., to Various Friends,* ed. Sir George F. Lewis. London: Longmans, Green, 1870.

———— *On Local Disturbances in Ireland and on the Irish Church Question.* London: B. Fellowes, 1836.

L'Hommedé, Edmond, *Un Département français sous la monarchie de juillet: le conseil général de la Manche et Alexis de Tocqueville.* Paris: Bovin, 1933.

Lingard, John, *Abrégé de l'histoire d'Angleterre de John Lingard.* Paris: 1827.

———— *The History of England from the First Invasion by the Romans to the Accession of William and Mary,* 6th ed., 10 vols. London: Charles Dolman, 1855.

Lipman, V. D., *Local Government Areas, 1834–1945.* Oxford: Blackwell, 1949.

Lipset, Seymour Martin, *Political Man: The Social Basis of Politics.* Garden City, N.Y.: Doubleday, 1960.

———— Martin A. Trow, and James S. Coleman, *Union Democracy: The Internal Politics of the International Typographical Union.* Glencoe, Ill.: Free Press, 1956.

Lively, Jack, *The Social and Political Thought of Alexis de Tocqueville.* Oxford: Clarendon Press, 1962.

Loménie, Louis de, "Alexis de Tocqueville," in *Esquisses historiques et littéraires*. Paris: C. Lévy, 1879.

Lowe, Robert, *Speeches and Letters on Reform, with a Preface*. London: Bush, 1867.

Lowry, Howard Foster, and others, eds., *The Note Books of Matthew Arnold*. London and New York: Oxford University Press, 1952.

"M. Beaumont on the Americans," *Quarterly Review*, LIII (April 1835), 289–312.

"M. de Tocqueville's France before the Revolution," *Edinburgh Review*, CIV (October 1856), 531–561.

McDowell, Robert B., *Public Opinion and Government Policy in Ireland, 1801–1846*. London: Faber and Faber, 1952.

McInnis, Edgar, "A Letter from Alexis de Tocqueville on the Canadian Rebellion of 1837," *Canadian Historical Review*, XIX (1938), 394–397.

MacKay, Thomas, *A History of the English Poor Law, Volume III, from 1834 to the Present Time*. London: P. S. King, 1899.

—— *The Reminiscences of Albert Peel*. London: John Murray, 1908.

Maine, Sir Henry Sumner, "Nature of Democracy," in *Popular Government*. London: John Murray, 1918.

Maitland, Frederic William, *The Life and Letters of Leslie Stephen*. New York: G. P. Putnam, 1906.

Mansergh, Nicholas, *Ireland in the Age of Reform and Revolution: A Commentary on Anglo-Irish Relations and on Political Forces in Ireland, 1840–1921*. London: Allen and Unwin, 1940.

Manuel, Frank E., *The New World of Henri Saint-Simon*. Cambridge, Mass.: Harvard University Press, 1956.

Marcel, R. Pierre, *Essai politique sur Alexis de Tocqueville avec un grand nombre de documents inédits*. Paris: Félix Alcan, 1910.

Marchand, Leslie A., *The Athenaeum: A Mirror of Victorian Culture*. Chapel Hill, N.C.: University of North Carolina Press, 1941.

Martel, André, "Tocqueville et les problèmes coloniaux de la monarchie de juillet," *Revue d'histoire économique et sociale*, XXXII (April 1954), 367–388.

Martin, Sir Theodore, *The Life of His Royal Highness, the Prince Consort*, 5 vols. London: Smith, Elder, 1880.

Marx, Karl, and Friedrich Engels, *Historisch-Kritische Gesamtausgabe:*

Werke/Schriften/Briefe, Band I, Vol. I: *Karl Marx, Werke und Schriften bis Anfang 1844, Nebst Briefen und Documenten.* Frankfurt am Main: Marx-Engels-Archiv-Verlagsgesellschaft, 1927.

Mathew, David, *Acton: The Formative Years.* London: Eyre and Spottiswoode, 1946.

Maurice, Frederick, *The Life of Frederick Denison Maurice Chiefly Told in His Own Letters,* 2 vols. New York: Charles Scribner, 1884.

Maxwell, Sir Herbert, *The Life and Letters of George William Frederick, Fourth Earl of Clarendon,* 2 vols. London: E. Arnold, 1913.

May, Sir Thomas Erskine, *Democracy in Europe,* 2 vols. London: Longmans, Green, 1877.

Mayer, Jacob-Peter. *Alexis de Tocqueville: A Biographical Essay in Political Science,* transl. M. Bozman and C. Hahn. New York: Viking, 1940.

—— *Alexis de Tocqueville: A Biographical Study in Political Science, with a New Essay,* "Tocqueville after a Century." New York: Harper Torchbooks, 1960.

—— "Alexis de Tocqueville and His British Friends," *The Times* (London), July 29, 1955.

—— "Alexis de Tocqueville: A Commentated Bibliography," and "Tocqueville Today," *Revue internationale de philosophie,* XIII (1959), 313–319, 350–353.

—— "Alexis de Tocqueville and John Stuart Mill," *The Listener,* XLIII (March 16, 1950), 471–472.

—— "Tocqueville as a Political Sociologist," *Political Studies,* I (1953), 132–142.

Michel, Henri, *L'Idée de l'Etat: Essai critique sur l'histoire des théories sociales et politiques en France depuis la Révolution,* 3rd ed. Paris: Hachette, 1898.

Mill, John Stuart, *An Autobiography of John Stuart Mill.* New York: Columbia University Press, 1924.

[——] "Centralisation," *Edinburgh Review,* CXV (April 1862), 323–358.

—— *Considerations on Representative Government.* London: Parker, Son, and Bourn, 1861.

[——] "Democracy in America," *Edinburgh Review,* LXXII (October 1840), 1–48.

—— *Dissertations and Discussions: Political, Philosophical, and Historical,* 4 vols. Boston: William V. Spencer, 1868.

—— *The Letters of John Stuart Mill,* ed. Hugh S. R. Elliot, 2 vols. London: Longmans, Green, 1910.

—— *Principles of Political Economy with Some of Their Applications to Social Philosophy,* 2 vols. London: John W. Parker, 1848.

[——] "The Slave Power," *Westminster Review,* LXXVIII (October 1862), 489–510.

[——] "State of Society in America," *London Review,* II (January 1836), 365–389.

—— "De Tocqueville on Democracy in America," *London Review,* II (October 1835), 85–129.

[Milnes, R. Monckton, Lord Houghton], "Alexis de Tocqueville," *Quarterly Review,* CX (October 1861), 517–544.

Molesworth, Sir William, *Selected Speeches of Sir William Molesworth.* London: John Murray, 1903.

"Monarchy and Democracy," *Quarterly Review,* CXLIX (January 1880), 230–251.

Moneypenny, F. W., and G. E. Buckle, *The Life of Benjamin Disraeli, Earl of Beaconsfield,* 2 vols. New York: Macmillan, 1917.

Le Moniteur universel (Paris), 1839–1852.

Montalembert, C. F. R., comte de, *De l'avenir politique de l'Angleterre,* 2nd ed. Paris: Didier, 1856.

—— *Un Débat sur l'Inde au parlement anglais.* London: W. Jeffs, 1858.

Morley, John, *The Life of Richard Cobden.* London: Chapman and Hall, 1881.

—— *The Life of William Ewart Gladstone,* 3 vols. London: Macmillan, 1903.

Mornet, Daniel, *Les Origines intellectuelles de la Révolution française, 1715–1787.* Paris: Armand Colin, 1933.

"Mrs. Butler's American Journal," *Edinburgh Review,* LXI (July 1835), 379–406.

Mueller, Iris Wessel, *John Stuart Mill and French Thought.* Urbana: University of Illinois Press, 1956.

Naess, A., J. Christophersen, and K. Kval, *Democracy, Ideology and Objectivity: Studies in the Semantics and Cognitive Analysis of*

Ideological Controversy. Oslo: Oslo University Press, 1956; Oxford: Basil Blackwell, 1956.

Namier, Sir Lewis B., *England in the Age of the American Revolution*. London: Macmillan, 1930.

"The Nature of Democracy," *Quarterly Review*, CLVIII (October 1884), 297–333.

Ohaus, Werner, *Volk und Völker im Urteil von Alexis de Tocqueville*. Berlin: E. Ebering, 1938.

Packe, Michael St. John, *The Life of John Stuart Mill*. New York: Macmillan, 1954.

Palm, Franklin Charles, *England and Napoleon III: A Study of the Rise of a Utopian Dictator*. Durham, N.C.: Duke University Press, 1948.

Palmer, R. R., *The Age of the Democratic Revolution: A Political History of Europe and America, 1760–1800.* Princeton: Princeton University Press, 1959.

Pares, Richard, *King George III and the Politicians*. Oxford: Clarendon Press, 1953.

"Parliamentary Reform and the Government," *Fraser's Magazine for Town and Country*, LXXIII (June 1866), 683–704.

Paul, Herbert, ed., *Letters of Lord Acton to Mary Gladstone*. New York: Macmillan, 1904.

[Peel, Sir Robert], *A Correct Report of Sir Robert Peel's Speeches at Glasgow, January 1837*. London: 1837.

"Penitentiary System in America and France," *Monthly Review*, CXXX (April 1833), 504–525.

Pierce, Edward L., *Memoir and Letters of Charles Sumner*, 4 vols. Boston: Roberts Brothers, 1893.

Pierson, George Wilson, "Gustave de Beaumont: Liberal," *Franco-American Review*, I (1936–37), 307–316.

———— *Tocqueville and Beaumont in America*. New York: Oxford University Press, 1938. Abridged by Dudley C. Lunt as *Tocqueville in America*, with a new Bibliographical Note. Garden City: Doubleday Anchor Books, 1959.

"The Political Tendencies of America," *National Review*, II (April 1856), 433–468.

Pope-Hennessy, James, *Monckton Milnes: The Years of Promise, 1809–1851*. London: Constable, 1949.

———— *Monckton Milnes: The Flight of Youth, 1851–1885*. London: Constable, 1951.

"Popular Government," *Edinburgh Review*, CLXIII (January 1886), 266–291.

Prévost-Paradol, Lucien Anatole, *Essais de politique et de littérature*. Paris: Hachette, 1865.

"Privileges of Parliament—Publication of Printed Papers," *Quarterly Review*, LXI (January 1838), 122–149.

"The Prospects of the Confederates," *Quarterly Review*, CXV (April 1864), 289–311.

Quentin-Bauchart, Pierre, *La Crise sociale de 1848: Les Origines de la Révolution*. Paris: Hachette, 1920.

Raudot, Claude Marie, "L'Administration locale en France et en Angleterre," *Le Correspondant*, LVIII (February 1863), 300–320.

Raumer, Friedrich von, *England in 1835*, transl. S. Austin and H. E. Lloyd. Philadelphia: Carey, Lea, and Blanchard, 1836.

Redier, Antoine, *Comme disait M. de Tocqueville . . .* 3rd ed. Paris: Perrin, 1925.

Reeve, Henry, *Memoirs of the Life and Correspondence of Henry Reeve*, ed. John Knox Laughton, 2 vols. London: Longmans, Green, 1898.

———— "Alexis de Tocqueville," in *Royal and Republican France*, 2 vols. London: Longmans, Green, 1872.

"Reform," *Quarterly Review*, CV (January 1859), 255–274.

"The Reform Bill: Its Real Bearing and Ultimate Results," *National Review*, X (April 1860), 421–446.

"Reform Essays," *Quarterly Review*, CXXIII (July 1867), 244–277.

Reid, T. Wemyss, *The Life, Letters, and Friendships of Richard Monckton Milnes, First Lord Houghton*, 2 vols. New York: Cassell, 1891.

Rémusat, Charles de, "De la centralisation en France," *Revue des deux mondes*, 2nd per., vol. XXIX (October 1860), 798–837.

———— "De l'esprit de réaction: Royer-Collard et Tocqueville," *Revue des deux mondes*, 2nd per., vol. XXXV (1861), 777–813.

———— *Mémoires de ma vie*, 3 vols. to date. Paris: Plon, 1958—.

———— *Politique libérale ou Fragments pour servir à la défense de la révolution française*. Paris: Michel Lévy, 1875.

Renan, Ernest, *Correspondance, 1846–1871*. Paris: Calmann-Lévy, 1926.

Report from His Majesty's Commissioners for Inquiring into the Ad-

ministration and Practical Operation of the Poor Laws. London: B. Fellowes, 1834.

"Representative Reform," *Edinburgh Review,* CVI (July 1857), 254–286.

Revans, John, *Evils of the State of Ireland: Their Causes and Their Remedy—A Poor Law.* London: Hatchard, n.d.

Riesman, David, "Tocqueville as Ethnographer," *The American Scholar,* XXX (Spring 1961), 174–184.

Roberts, David, *Victorian Origins of the British Welfare State.* New Haven: Yale University Press, 1960.

Robson, William A., *Justice and Administrative Law: A Study of the British Constitution.* London: Stevens, 1947.

Ruggiero, Guido de, *The History of European Liberalism,* transl. R. G. Collingwood. London: Oxford University Press, 1927.

Salomon, Albert, "Alexis de Tocqueville: Moralist and Sociologist," *Social Research,* II (1935), 405–438.

———— "Tocqueville 1959," *Social Research,* XXVI (Winter 1959), 449–470.

———— "Tocqueville's Philosophy of Freedom: A Trend towards Concrete Sociology," *Review of Politics,* I (1939), 400–431.

Savary, Charles, *Alexis de Tocqueville: sa vie et ses ouvrages.* Paris: Gustave Retaux, 1868.

Say, Jean Baptiste, *Cours complet d'économie politique pratique,* 6 vols. Paris: Rapilly, 1828–29.

Schapiro, J. Salwyn, *Liberalism and the Challenge of Fascism: Social Forces in England and France (1815–1870).* New York: McGraw-Hill, 1949.

Schlatter, Richard, *Private Property: The History of an Idea.* New Brunswick, N.J.: Rutgers University Press, 1951.

"Secondary Punishments—Transportation," *Edinburgh Review,* LVIII (April 1834), 336–362.

Senior, Nassau William, "The Continent in 1854," *North British Review,* XLIV (February 1855), 289–342.

———— *An Outline of the Science of Political Economy.* London: W. Clowes, 1836.

———— *Conversations with Distinguished Persons during the Second Empire, from 1860 to 1863,* 2 vols. London: Hurst and Blackett, 1880.

—— *Conversations with M. Thiers, M. Guizot, and Other Distinguished Persons during the Second Empire by the late Nassau William Senior,* ed. M. C. M. Simpson, 4 vols. London: Hurst and Blackett, 1880.

—— *Historical and Philosophical Essays,* 2 vols. London: Longman, Green, Longman, Roberts, and Green, 1865.

—— *Industrial Efficiency and Social Economy,* ed. S. Leon Levy, 2 vols. New York: Henry Holt, 1928.

—— *Journals, Conversations, and Essays relating to Ireland,* 2 vols. London: Longmans, Green, 1868.

—— *Journals Kept in France and Italy from 1848 to 1852,* ed. M. C. M. Simpson, 2nd ed., 2 vols. London: Henry S. King, 1871.

—— "Lamartine's *Histoire de la Révolution de 1848,*" *Edinburgh Review,* XCI (January 1850), 228–297.

—— *Letters on the Factory Act.* London: B. Fellowes, 1837.

—— *Statement of the Provision for the Poor and of the Condition of the Laboring Classes in a Considerable Portion of America and Europe.* London: B. Fellowes, 1835.

Seymour, Charles, *Electoral Reform in England and Wales. The Development and Operation of the Parliamentary Franchise, 1832–1885.* New Haven: Yale University Press, 1915.

Shaw, Bernard, and others, *Fabian Essays in Socialism.* London: Fabian Society, 1889.

Sheppard, F. H. W., *Local Government in St. Marylebone, 1688–1835.* London: University of London, Athlone Press, 1958.

Sidgwick, Henry, *The Development of European Polity.* London: Macmillan, 1920.

—— *Miscellaneous Essays and Addresses.* London: Macmillan, 1904.

Simon, C.-G., *Observations recueillées en Angleterre en 1835.* Paris: I. Pesron, n.d.

Simpson, F. A., *Louis Napoleon and the Recovery of France.* London: Longmans, Green, 1923.

Simpson, Mary Charlotte Mair, *Many Memories of Many People,* 4th ed. London: Edward Arnold, 1898.

"The Slave Power and the Secession War," *National Review,* XV (July 1862), 167–198.

Smith, Charles E., ed., *Journals and Correspondence of Lady Eastlake,* 2 vols. London: John Murray, 1895.

Smith, Frank, *The Life and Work of Sir James Kay-Shuttleworth.* London: John Murray, 1923.

Smith, Goldwin, "The American Commonwealth," *Macmillan's Magazine,* LIX (February 1889), 241–253.

Smith, J. Toulmin, *The Parish: Its Obligations and Powers, Its Officers and Duties,* 2nd ed. London: H. Sweet, 1857.

Soltau, Roger, *French Political Thought in the Nineteenth Century.* New Haven: Yale University Press, 1931.

Somerset, Duke of, *Monarchy and Democracy: Phases of Modern Politics.* London: James Bain, 1880.

Staël-Holstein, A. de, *Letters on England,* 2nd ed. London: Treuttel et Würtz, 1830.

———— *Lettres sur l'Angleterre.* Paris: Treuttel et Würtz, 1825.

"The State of Parties," *National Review,* VII (July 1858), 220–243.

"The State of Society in France before the Revolution of 1789," *Athenaeum,* no. 1502 (August 9, 1856), 988–990.

"The State of Society in France before the Revolution of 1789," *Economist,* XIV (August 9, 1856), 872–873.

Stephen, James, *Lectures on the History of France,* 3rd ed., 2 vols. London: Longmans, Green, 1857.

Strauss, E., *Irish Nationalism and British Democracy.* London: Methuen, 1951.

Stubbs, William, *The Constitutional History of England,* 4th ed., 3 vols. Oxford: Clarendon Press, 1896.

Sumner, Charles, *The Works of Charles Sumner,* 15 vols. Boston: Lee and Shepard, 1875.

Suter, Jean François, "Tocqueville et le problème de démocratie," *Revue internationale de philosophie,* XIII (1959), 330–340.

Swart, Koenraad A., " 'Individualism' in the Mid-Nineteenth Century (1826–1860)," *Journal of the History of Ideas,* XXIII (January–March 1962), 77–86.

Swetchine, Sophie, *Lettres inédites.* Paris: Auguste Vaton, 1866.

Tawney, R. H., *Equality.* London: Allen and Unwin, 1952.

Thierry, Augustin A., *Augustin Thierry (1795–1856) d'après sa correspondance et ses papiers de famille.* Paris: Plon-Nourrit, 1922.

Thureau-Dangin, Paul, *Histoire de la monarchie de juillet,* 7 vols. Paris: Plon, 1904.

Ticknor, George, *Life, Letters and Journals of George Ticknor,* 10th ed., 2 vols. Boston: Houghton, Osgood, 1880.

The Times (London), 1833–1857.

"Tocqueville on Democracy," *British and Foreign Review,* X (April 1840), 541–575.

"Tocqueville's *Democracy in America,*" British and Foreign Review, II (January 1836),304–327.

Touchard, Jean, *Histoire des idées politiques.* Paris: Presses Universitaires de France, 1959.

Tremenheere, Hugh Seymour, *The Constitution of the United States Compared with Our Own.* London: John Murray, 1854.

Trilling, Lionel, *Matthew Arnold.* New York: Columbia University Press, 1949.

Turberville, A. S., "Aristocracy and Revolution: The British Peerage, 1789–1832," *History,* XXVI (March 1942), 240–263.

"The Value of India to England," *Quarterly Review,* CXX (July 1866), 198–220.

Villeneuve-Bargemont, Vicomte Alban de, *Economie politique chrétienne, ou recherches sur la nature et les causes du paupérisme en France et en Europe,* 3 vols. Paris: Paulin, 1834.

Vivien, Alexandre F. A., "Mémoire sur la défense des indigents dans les procès civils et criminels . . . suivie d'observations presentées par MM. Cousin, Dupin, de Beaumont et Giraud," *Séances et travaux de l'Académie des sciences morales et politiques: Compte rendu,* XII (1847), 446–469.

Wach, Joachim, "The Role of Religion in the Social Philosophy of Alexis de Tocqueville," *Journal of the History of Ideas,* VII (January–October 1946), 74–90.

Webb, R. K., *Harriet Martineau: A Radical Victorian.* New York: Columbia University Press, 1960.

Webb, Sidney and Beatrice, *English Local Government from the Revolution to the Municipal Corporations Act,* 9 vols. London: Longmans, Green, 1906–1929.

Vol. I. *The Parish and the Country,* 1906.

Vols. II, III. *The Manor and the Borough,* 1908.

Vol. IV. *Statutory Authorities for Special Purposes,* 1922.

Vol. V. *The Story of the King's Highway,* 1913.

Vol. VI. *English Prisons,* 1922.

Vol. VII. *English Poor Law History, Part I: The Old Poor Law,* 1927.

Vols. VIII–IX. *English Poor Law History, Part II: The Last Hundred Years.* 1929.

Weber, Anatole, *Essai sur le problème de la misère.* Paris: Marcel Rivière, 1913.

Weber, Max, *From Max Weber: Essays in Sociology,* ed. and transl. H. H. Gerth and C. Wright Mills. London: Kegan Paul, Trench, Trubner, 1947.

Webster, Charles Kingsley, *The Foreign Policy of Lord Palmerston.* London: G. Bell, 1951.

Wilson, Francis G., "Tocqueville's Conception of the Elite," *Review of Politics,* IV (July 1942), 271–286.

Whyte, A. J., *The Early Life and Letters of Cavour, 1810–1848.* London: Oxford University Press, 1925.

Wrong, E. M., *Charles Buller and Responsible Government.* Oxford: Clarendon Press, 1926.

Zemach, Ada, "Alexis de Tocqueville on England," *Review of Politics,* XIII (1951), 320–343.

Index

HARVARD HISTORICAL MONOGRAPHS

Out of print